100 HIKES in

WASHINGTON'S
NORTH CASCADES
NATIONAL PARK REGION

D0957994

100 HIKES in

WASHINGTON'S
NORTH CASCADES
NATIONAL PARK REGION

Mount Baker • Ross Lake NRA • Pasayten Wilderness • Methow–Chelan

THIRD EDITION

**Ira Spring &
Harvey Manning**

THE
MOUNTAINEERS

Published by
The Mountaineers
1001 SW Klickitat Way, Suite 201
Seattle, WA 98134

© 2000 by The Mountaineers

Third edition, 2000

Published simultaneously in Great Britain by Cordee, 3a DeMontfort Street,
Leicester, England, LE1 7HD

Manufactured in the United States of America

Editor: Christine Clifton-Thornton
Maps: Gray Mouse Graphics
All photographs except as noted: Bob and Ira Spring
Cover and book design: Jennifer Shontz
Layout: Gray Mouse Graphics

Cover photograph: *Mount Shuksan from Table Mountain*
Frontispiece: *Mount Baker from a frozen pond on Park Butte (Hike 23)*

Library of Congress Cataloging-in-Publication Data

Spring, Ira.
    100 hikes in Washington's North Cascades National Park Region / Ira
Spring & Harvey Manning.— 3rd ed.
        p. cm.
    Includes bibliographical references and index.
    ISBN 0-89886-694-4
    1. Hiking—Washington (State)—North Cascades National Park
Region—Guidebooks. 2. North Cascades National Park Region
(Wash.)—Guidebooks. I. Title: One hundred hikes in Washington's North
Cascades National Park Region. II. Manning, Harvey. III. Title.
GV199.42.W22 N677 2000
917.97'73—dc21

                                            99-050912

CONTENTS

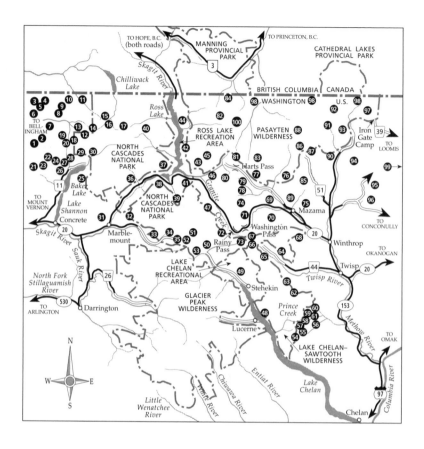

KEY TO MAP SYMBOLS

═══	freeway	⌂	building
++++++++	railroad	⬧	ranger station
▬▬▬	paved road	▲	campground
════	gravel or dirt road	◼	shelter
========	primitive (jeep) road	⌂	backcountry campsite
----------	trail	⛴	ferry
....	cross-country route	♜	lookout
· — · — ·	boundary (park or wilderness area)	⊠	former lookout site
· ▬ · ▬ ·	boundary (state)	✕	mine
(84)	interstate highway	) (	pass
(97)	U.S. highway	—	gate
[3]	Canadian highway	╱	river or stream
(530)	state highway	╫	waterfall
[26]	county highway		lake and dam
3060	National Forest road	ꙮ	marsh
/643/	trail number		glacier

THE MOUSE THAT IS LEARNING TO ROAR

GREEN-BONDING FOR A GREEN FUTURE

Great wilderness has many attributes: spectacular views, flower fields and meadows, lakes and streams, ancient or at least virgin forest, animals and birds, solitude, silence—escape from sounds of motors, a chance to hear birds, wind, and sometimes true silence, and a primitive experience with a physical and mental challenge. Seldom does one find all these on one trail or even in one wilderness. But most of us find a quality wilderness experience with just two or three of these attributes. For a family we met on the Pyramid Lake trail (North Cascades National Park), their hike was an experience of a lifetime, even though the trail has just one of those nine attributes. Again, at Mount Rainier, we were on our way down the Rampart Ridge trail when we were stopped by a couple who just had to tell someone about their wonderful experience, even though they only saw a forest and were experiencing a physical challenge. This is the first step in "green-bonding."

"Bonding" is the term for the ties developed by an offspring to a parent—a newborn baby to its mother, a newborn fawn to its doe. "Green-bonding" describes the emotional ties a person develops to the great out-of-doors while hiking trails, enjoying the fresh air of wild lands and the flowers, trees, wildlife, and surrounding natural beauty.

Green-bonding also results in green supporters—a constituency whose responsibility it is to care for its wildlands, working as advocates by lobbying for its protection and safekeeping. Thousands of such green-bonded people wrote to their Congressmen urging passage of the 1984 Washington Wilderness Act, which was intended to protect Washington wilderness from the devastation of deforestation and development. Their pleas were heard by our Congressional delegates, and 1,000,000 acres were added to our state's wilderness areas. During Forest Management Planning by the U.S. Forest Service, 10,000 green-bonded people wrote the Mount Baker–Snoqualmie National Forest stressing the importance of trails, and the land managers took steps to preserve trails. Often, the only barrier between a wilderness area and its destruction is the thickness of a single sheet of paper—*your letter.*

However, there is bonding other than green—to decent homes, to good schools, to safe streets and highways, to convenient shopping malls, to pleasure domes for athletic contests. As the nation continues a population growth that entails more wooden houses, more factories, more vacation retreats near national parks, more helicopter pads, more space-consumptive toys, the result is a massive de-greening by money-bonded entrepreneurs who efficiently organize and heavily fund a nigh-religious crusade to despoil the public green for private profit. For the last five years Congress has entertained serious proposals to decommission "surplus" park and wilderness land and hand it over to the "private sector." Fortunately, in 1996 there were enough green-bonded people in the nation to halt the giveaway with their letters. But further raids must be expected. Will there be enough green-bonded people in the year 2005 or 2010 to protect public lands?

The money-bonding of commercial-industrial entrepreneurs is the heart of the matter, is the essence of our economy. It cannot be kept in check simply by our taking a hike. However, with lots of green-bonded support it can be redirected. By our feet. That's what this book is for—to mobilize feet.

Pelton Peak from Sahale Arm trail (Hike 35)

Prior to World War II the White Chuck River country had many trails but few hikers—too few to prevent a postwar logging road from climbing the valley nearly to Kennedy Hot Springs, converting a many-day backpack to an afternoon stroll. We had the Golden Horn (Hike 74) all to ourselves, but because there was no trail, few had been there and no constituency existed large enough to obtain it for the North Cascades National Park. The Ragged Ridge, Eagle Rock, and the huge flower fields of the Jackman Creek roadless area had no trails, so therefore no constituency sufficient to obtain 1984 designation as wilderness—and since these areas still have no trails they may lack enough green-bonded support for the next go-around.

There were abundant trails on the motor-infested Dark Divide, Mad River, and Golden Lakes (Hike 61) trails, but hikers too disgusted with the noise and speed of motorcycles that utilized these "multi-use" areas avoided these gems, leaving too few voices to make the case for including the trails in the Washington Wilderness Act.

In the 1950s the trail from Snoqualmie Pass to Snow Lake was hiked by 800 people a year. The annual number now is 25,000! The backcountry was uncrowded back then; that was the good news. The bad news outweighs the good—there wasn't enough green-bonded public support to prevent logging roads from gobbling up thousands of miles of trails or to stop motorcycles from running us off many of our pedestrian favorites.

Pedestrians are the most numerous recreationists, by far, in Washington State. A 1988 survey by the state Interagency for Outdoor Recreation counted in excess of 1,000,000 people, old and young, who walk all sorts of trails, short and long, urban and wildland. They average four day-hikes a year; almost 500,000 backpack at least once a year.

Yet these 1,000,000-plus hikers are led around by 41,300 wheelers, that being the number of off-road vehicle registrations issued by the state Department of Licensing. The Forest Service has set aside 1174 miles of our trails for 41,300 motorcyclists, but only 1622 miles for the 1,000,000 day hikers in this state.

Unfortunately, only a few thousand of those 1,000,000 hikers belong to an organization that will keep them informed of trail use, leaving 997,000 hikers unaware of the overall picture of what may happen to trails without their support. Most new hikers walk the trails with one or two friends, seeing no reason to join a hiking club. But outdoor organizations serve as information gatherers, to direct your letter traffic to the appropriate officials, to save your wildlands.

What good could one letter do? Well, one letter to the Wenatchee National Forest, added to 4999 others, convinced a federal judge to return the North Fork Entiat to non-motorized use. One plus one, plus some more ones—that adds up to green power.

We have been told by Forest Service employees of occasions during meetings where land use was being considered when just one letter has turned a decision. If that letter came from a green-bonded friend, great! If it was from a motorcyclist, yuck! But we have no one but ourselves to blame.

LETTERS

To supervisors of National Forests (for addresses see page 22.) Motorcycles make more noise than feet, but letters can silence the roar, can penetrate the minds and souls of officials.

To government officials—Congresspersons, Senators, Presidents, not to forget, in appropriate cases, state legislators and governors.

To newspapers. Editors welcome letters that have news value, which is to say, really-true information. (But if you don't have fresh information, venting a bit of old-fashioned emotion can't hurt.)

That's what we need. More letters. (Write them!) More well-informed hikers. (Join a group!) More green power. (Flex your muscles!)

FEET

To quote Harvey Manning, "Your feet bones are connected to your leg bones, leg bones to the hip bones, hip bones to the backbones, backbones to the head bones, head bones to the letter-writing finger bones. Your feet know the land better than heads of public officials. Insert into those heads the knowledge your feet have learned by taking one step at a time at a respectful, studious pace." Keep your feet at their studies of the wildlands—*your* land, with *your* obligation to be its steward and advocate. Join a group (or two) dedicated to preserving foot trails. Read the bulletins they publish covering current wildland issues.

When they sound the danger siren, hop to it! Get those letters in the mail! So write. And get cracking!

—Ira Spring

Following are organizations that are strenuously working to preserve trail country. Join one (or more). Read their publications, which alert you to dangers to trails and tell you who needs to get your letters.

ALPS (Alpine Lakes Protection Society)
100 98th Avenue, E-6
Bellevue, WA 98004-5401

Backcountry Llama Packers
Noel McRae, President
2857 Rose Valley
Kelso, WA 98626

Cascade Mountain Backpackers
℅ Thomas Alway
P.O. Box 1024
Stevenson, WA 98648

The Cascadians
P.O. Box 2201
Yakima, WA 98908

Intermountain Alpine Club
P.O. Box 505
Richland, WA 99352-1990

Issaquah Alps Trails Club
P.O. Box 122
Issaquah, WA 98027

Mazamas
909 NW 19th Avenue
Portland, OR 97202

Methow Valley Sports Trail Association
P.O. Box 147
Winthrop, WA 98862

Mid-Forc
P.O. Box 25809
Seattle, WA 98125-1309

Mount Baker Hiking Club
P.O. Box 73
Bellingham, WA 98227

The Mountaineers
300 Third Avenue West
Seattle, WA 98119

The Mountaineers—Bellingham Branch
P.O. Box 3187
Bellingham, WA 98227

The Mountaineers—Everett Branch
P.O. Box 1848
Everett, WA 98206

The Mountaineers—Olympia Branch
P.O. Box 797
Olympia, WA 98507

The Mountaineers—Tacoma Branch
2302 North 30th Street
Tacoma, WA 98403

The Mountaineers—Wenatchee Branch
P.O. Box 4131
Wenatchee, WA 98807

North Cascades Conservation Council
P.O. Box 95980
Seattle, WA 98145-1980

Pacific Northwest Trail Association
P.O. Box 1817
Mount Vernon, WA 98273

Peninsula Trails Coalition
P.O. Box 1836
Port Angeles, WA 98362

Sierra Club, Cascade Chapter
8511 15th Northeast
Room 201
Seattle, WA 98155

Sierra Club, Northern Rockies Chapter
 (for Eastern Washington)
P.O. Box 552
Boise, ID 83701

Skagit Alpine Club
P.O. Box 513
Mount Vernon, WA 98273

Snoqualmie Valley Trails Club
P.O. Box 1741
North Bend, WA 97202

Spokane Mountaineers
P.O. Box 1013
Spokane, WA 99208

Summit Alpine Club
802 North J Street
Tacoma, WA 98403

Thursday Hikers
℅ Jean Worthen
2318 121st Avenue Southeast
Bellevue, WA 98005

Toutle Lake Hiking Club
℅ Casey Wheeler
521 Finkas Road
Toutle Lake, WA 98649

WA Alpine Club
P.O. Box 352
Seattle, WA 98111

WA Trails Association
(publisher of *Signpost* magazine)
1305 Fourth Avenue, Room 512
Seattle, WA 98101

Washington Wilderness Coalition
4649 Sunnyside North
Seattle, WA 98103

Mount Baker from Iceberg Lake (Hike 19)

THE PAST (AND FUTURE?) OF OUR TRAILS

It may correctly be assumed that we do these guidebooks from a desire to share our personal pleasures in wildland walking with other people. It is further correct that we seek to perpetuate these pleasures by warning that our trails are in mortal peril. However, to be nakedly candid, we are not all that enthusiastic about trails, as such. To be brutally frank, neither are we inordinately fond of people, as such. To get down to bone-honesty, saving the trails and pleasuring the people are the means, not the end. Preserving the wildland ecosystems, that's our game. Protecting from too many travelways of the wrong sort, and even from too many trails, especially those that are immoderately elaborate. Protecting from too many people of the wrong sort—meaning those whose bad habits are damaging to the ecosystems.

Since we began publishing trail guides in the 1960s ("to preserve the natural beauty of Northwest America," as a purpose of The Mountaineers was stated in 1906), we have been condemned for contributing to the deterioration of wilderness. We confess our sin, we agree with our critics. It's not nice to air in public the secrets of your love affairs. But in defense we ask, "Which would you prefer? A hundred boots in a virgin forest? Or that many snarling wheels in a clearcut? Or, for that matter, that many silent wheels blitzing down upon you at flank speed, impelled by pedals and gravity?"

Granted, only with the most careful "leave no trace" forbearance can boots be considered to tenderly caress the earth. But whatever violence they may wreak is as nothing compared to the rough handling by wheels, whether eight or six or four or three or only two, whether powered by gasoline engine or muscles. Man can live in the wilderness (in words of the Wilderness Act) as "a visitor who does not remain." But the visitor, the guest, must duly respect and honor the residents, the hosts—the birds and beasts, the plants, the waters—as well as the feelings of other visitors. The ecosystem is the sum of these, including hikers who mind their manners, who accept obedience to the moral imperative, which is (in words of the poet Robinson Jeffers) "not man apart."

THE FUTURE?

Trails within the National Wilderness Preservation System are secure from chainsaws and wheels. But what about outside the statutory Wilderness, where the management is "multiple-use"? The Forest Service has prepared documents describing its "Preferred Management Alternatives."

These plainly mark the trails intended for destruction by new road construction:

- Okanogan National Forest: 381 miles, or 62 percent of its trails not (yet) in dedicated Wilderness
- Wenatchee National Forest: 966 miles, or 78 percent
- Mt. Baker–Snoqualmie National Forest: 484 miles, or 48 percent
- Gifford Pinchot National Forest: 544 miles, or 78 percent
  Total: 2375 miles of trails not (yet) in dedicated Wilderness in jeopardy

THE WILDERNESS VISION

Every attempt to revise the Wilderness Act of 1964 must be repulsed, because to open the door a crack would let in a horde howling that the wilderness be "opened up to the people"—defined as people in helicopters, on bicycles, carrying portable spas and electricity generators and Coke machines.

Every attempt at "reasonable, fair-minded compromise," by amending legislation for proposed new wilderness dedications by letting in wheels, must be shouted down and stomped flat. There is no room here for mugwimps of the "win-win" hypocrisy. Certainly, there are motorcyclists and bicyclists who revere the wilderness—and who have the good sense to park their wheels outside and walk right on in. But those who whine that as American citizens they should be allowed their version of the "wilderness experience"—on wheels, sitting down and traveling at high speed over as many miles of wilderness in a day as a pedestrian can do in a week or two—must be issued dunce caps and made to go stand in the corner. They simply don't understand what we're talking about and should not be permitted to speak in class.The North Cascades Act of 1968 achieved in the purview of this volume the North Cascades National Park, the Lake Chelan and Ross Lake National Recreation Areas, and the Pasayten Wilderness.

In 1984 the 38-member Washington Wilderness Coalition, working at the top and at the bottom and all through the middle all across the state, won the Washington Wilderness Act, which encompassed more than 1,000,000 acres including, in the purview of this volume, three new wildernesses—Lake Chelan–Sawtooth, Mt. Baker, and Noisy-Diobsud; additions to the Pasayten Wilderness; and a Mt. Baker National Recreation Area and a North Cascades Scenic Highway Corridor.

However, the bill drawn up by the member organizations of the coalition encompassed 2,500,000 acres—and that was itself drastically reduced from the want-lists of member groups. Is the glass one-third full? Or two-thirds still empty?

Among the omissions are the Alma-Copper and Hidden Lake areas adjacent to the North Cascades National Park; Beaver Meadows, Tiffany Mountain, and Chopaka Mountain, adjoining or near the Pasayten Wilderness; and the Golden Horn area near the North Cascades Highway.

There also are tragic omissions from the newly created wildernesses: from the Noisy-Diobsud Wilderness, notably the lower reaches of its two

Eldorado Peak massif from Lookout Mountain trail (Hike 32)

namesake creeks, the upper Baker River, and Rocky and Thunder Creeks; from the Mt. Baker Wilderness, Damfino Creek, Church Mountain, Warm Creek, and Shuksan Lake; from the Lake Chelan–Sawtooth Wilderness, Foggy Dew, Safety Harbor, and Eagle Creeks on the south and Cedar Creek on the north.

The existing Pasayten Wilderness still does not enclose the upper Methow River, lower Lost River, South Twentymile Peak, and the Chewuch River at Thirtymile Campground.

The North Cascades Scenic Highway Corridor gives only modest protection; at that, it leaves out upper Canyon Creek, upper East Creek, and Driveway Butte.

As for the Mt. Baker National Recreation Area, its boundaries were drawn specifically to permit snowmobiles to go to the very summit!

That's a very partial list of the remaining tasks. A notorious remaining problem is the management of the Lake Chelan National Recreation Area and its failure, to date, to give the Stehekin valley the care implicit in the 1968 North Cascades Act and still not given by the National Park Service despite continuing vociferous protest by the North Cascades Conservation Council.

SOLITUDE: WILDERNESS DEEPS AND WILDERNESS EDGES

The language of the Wilderness Act might be interpreted as requiring limits on the number of people allowed in any given spot at any given time. Surely, finding the privacy to pick your nose is highly valued in a world of six billions, and will be more so at twelve billions. Yet where a trail presently attracts 100 walkers a day, if the limit is set to preserve solitude for 5, what's to be done about the other 95? If wilderness use shrinks, so will wilderness support—those human letters emanating from those educated foot bones. The wilderness idea cannot well afford the loss of such support when at least 2,000,000 acres of Washington earth subject to multiple-abuse cry out for shelter under the Wilderness Act.

Solitude certainly should be a very high priority in the wilderness cores, the "deep wilderness" demanding a good many miles of hauling a pack, a number of nights of backcountry camping. One method of creating more "deep" is to add those 2,000,000 orphan acres. Another is to put to bed—convert to wheelfree trails—roads that have outlived their usefulness or whose cost of maintenance has become too heavy.

Rationing the "edge wilderness"—that which is accessible on short and easy day hikes and overnights by short legs, gimpy legs, and inexperienced legs—would endanger the popularity of wilderness and, in the long run, its very survival. Many—perhaps nearly all—adult wilderness walkers were introduced to the mysteries beyond reach of the automobile at an early age, were "green-bonded" there in the same way a baby is bonded to a mother. To make such green-bonding difficult for the young is to risk the loss of future adult defenders of wilderness.

When more "edge" is called for by population growth, again the opportunities abound in the 2,000,000 acres. Additionally, outside the dedicated parks and wildernesses there are highlands skinned by "timber miners" at elevations where a second crop of commercial trees will not grow for 500 years or more, far too long for credible tree farming. Within decades, however, the land of "reconstituted roadless areas," of "wilderness-edge backcountry" will green up in scrub and shrubs, streams will restabilize, and wildlife populations will settle into balance. Old logging roads can be allowed to dwindle to footpaths, campsites established where backpackers can look out at night to the lights of farms and cities—and by turning, look inward to starlit wilderness cores.

WHEELS

A defining feature of wilderness is freedom from the wheel—from its speed and, worse than that, its fretful hastiness and, still worse, its inevitable homocentric tendency to arrogantly dominate, to ruthlessly brutalize.

In his novel *Slowness*, Milan Kundera asks, "Why has the pleasure of slowness disappeared? Ah, where have they gone, the amblers of yesteryear? Have they vanished along with footpaths . . . with nature? There is a Czech proverb that describes their easy indolence. 'They are gazing at God's windows.' "

Wheels on vehicles with four apiece and motors attached. Were it not for the automobile, few of us would have much wilderness experience of any kind; if Bellingham were our trailhead, the meadowlands of Mt.

Baker would be next thing to an expedition. Lacking roads, children could not begin their green-bonding so young, and any wilderness newcomer does well to dip toes in the edges before braving the deeps. A review of our guidebooks abundantly testifies to our appreciation of the recreational value of roads. It also can be seen in our pages that there is no shortage of non-wilderness edges.

Incongruously, there are pedestrians—even members of organizations dedicated to wilderness preservation—who so love the "edge" hikes that have been made possible by the logging roads that they want all deeps made into edges and no edges ever restored to pristine deepness. One is torn between pity and contempt.

Wheels on vehicles with two apiece and motors attached. The motorcycle is two-wheels-less and some-tons-less than a car, consumes far less fossil fuel, takes up less space, and what with the wind in your ears and bugs in your teeth is splendid on roads. However, upon leaving a road, it transforms a footpath not to another species of trail but to a totally different genus—a trail becomes a motorway, which is to say, road.

Wheels on vehicles with two apiece and no motors. The bicycle, though probably not, as we are encouraged to believe, second only to wings as the transportation of choice in Heaven, is easy on our ears, our air, and our fossil fuel; it grants freedom from a five-figure, three-ton incubus; in cities it is part of a solution to ossification by gridlock; and in open country it is fun. However, in the brand-new off-road manifestation, the fat-tire ("mountain") bike, it is to trails as the Tatars were to Cathay.

Wheels of bicycles, just as of motorcycles, expel feet. The bicycle transforms a footway not to another species of trail but to a totally different genus—footway becomes bikeway.

There is such a thing as a multi-use, nonmotorized travelway, amicably usable by walkers, joggers, runners, wheelchair users, bikers, and roller-skaters. The way must, of course, segregate them by speed, walkers and wheelchair users in one lane, runners and bikers in another, and whenever space is available for another, a third for horses. Dumping all the cats in the same gunnysack and instructing them to purr does not work.

The Golden Rule of humane civilization is tolerance—don't knock the other guy's national origin, sexual orientation, religion, politics, music, haircut, or sport. Moral relativism has perils, yet surely is superior to intolerant absolutism. Nevertheless, though it certainly was very bad of the Church to burn Joan of Arc at the stake, the only good thing that could be done with a Dracula is drive a stake through his heart.

Though the arrogance of the swift mocks the thoughtfulness of the slow, a material-moral absolutism grounded on the Laws of Thermodynamics judges the wilderness surely and purely good and the destruction of trails by wheels surely and purely bad.

INTRODUCTION

Broad, smooth, well-marked, heavily traveled, ranger-patrolled paths safe and simple for little kids and elderly folks with no mountain training or equipment, or even for monomaniacs scampering from Canada to Mexico. Mean and cruel and mysterious routes through evil brush, over fierce rivers, up shifty screes and moraines to treacherous glaciers and fearsome cliffs where none but the skilled and doughty should dare, or perhaps the deranged. Flower strolls for a song-in-the-heart afternoon, or devil-may-care derring-do for a week.

A storm side (the west), where precipitation is heavy, winter long, snows deep, glaciers large, peaks sharply sculptured, vegetation lush, and high-country hiking doesn't get comfortably underway until late July. A lee side, a rain-shadow side (the east), where clouds are mostly empties, summer is long, vegetation sparse, ridges round and gentle, and meadows melt free of the white by late June.

Places as thronged as a city park on Labor Day, places as lonesome as the South Pole that Amundsen and Scott knew. Scenes that remind of the High Sierra, scenes that remind of Alaska.

In summary, to generalize about the North Cascades: To generalize about the North Cascades is foolish.

LAND MANAGERS

The public lands of the state and nation are managed by various agencies. It is important for hikers to know which agency is managing what so that when the management isn't doing right by the trails the complaints can be properly directed.

The entirety of the northernmost section of the North Cascades is federally administered, except for blocks of state (Department of Natural Resources) land around Chopaka Mountain, scattered enclaves of private lands mostly dating from mining (that is, prospecting and stock-selling) and homestead days, and such miscellaneous bits as the Seattle City Light holdings on the Skagit River. The U.S. Forest Service is the principal trustee, with responsibility shared by Mt. Baker–Snoqualmie and Wenatchee–Okanogan National Forests. Since 1968 the National Park Service has been on the scene in the North Cascades National Park and the accompanying Ross Lake and Lake Chelan National Recreation Areas.

Most of the national forest lands are under "multiple-use" administration, with roads, with mining (that is, prospecting and stock-selling), logging, and other economic exploitation, and with motorcycles and bicycles allowed on (too) many trails. Some areas, however, have statutory protection within the National Wilderness Preservation System, where the Wilderness Act of 1964 guarantees that "the earth and its community of life

Hidden Lake is snowbound most of the year (Hike 33)

are untrammeled by man, where man himself is a visitor who does not remain." The Glacier Peak Wilderness was established in 1960 and the Pasayten Wilderness in 1968. The Washington Wilderness Act of 1984 made additions to these two wildernesses and in the far north of the North Cascades established these new ones: Mt. Baker, Noisy-Diobsud, and Lake Chelan–Sawtooth. Within these, motorized travel is banned, as is any mechanized travel, such as "mountain bikes." Horse travel is carefully regulated, and though wilderness permits are not currently required for hiking, hikers are subject to restrictions on party size and camping, and must acquaint themselves with the travel regulations before setting out.

North Cascades National Park, established in 1968, was set aside, to use the words of the National Park Act of 1916, "to conserve the scenery and the natural and historic objects and the wildlife. Each visitor therefore must enjoy the park in such manner and by such means as will leave it unimpaired for the enjoyment of future generations." (The same umbrella protects the adjunct Ross Lake and Lake Chelan National Recreation Areas.) Most of the park and portions of the national recreation areas are further covered by the Wilderness Act, giving a still higher degree of protection.

MAPS AND ROADS

The sketch maps in this book are intended to give only a general idea of the terrain and trails. Once out of the city and off the highways, the navigation demands precision.

In the 1980s the Forest Service renumbered its roads. A veteran traveler relying on a faithful file of well-worn Forest Service maps had best never leave civilization without a full tank of gas, survival rations, and instructions to family or friends on when to call out the Logging Road Search and Rescue Team. If maps are older than 10 years, a party would do better to obtain the current national forest recreation maps, which are cumbersome for the trail but essential to get about on the renumbered roads.

The new U.S. Forest Service system of road numbers gives main roads two numerals. For example, the Goat Creek road is No. 52 (Hike 75) and is shown on the Forest Service maps and described in this guidebook as road No. 52. The secondary roads have the first two numbers of the main road plus two additional numbers. For example, from road 52 the secondary road toward the Goat Peak trailhead is 5225. Three additional numbers added for a spur road, which becomes 5225200, shown as 200 on Forest Service maps and signs and in this guidebook as road No. (5225)200.

The best maps in the history of the world are the topographic sheets produced by the U.S. Geological Survey (USGS). However, revision is so occasional that information on roads and trails is always largely obsolete. Essential as they are for off-trail, cross-country explorers, in this book we have recommended them only on Mt. Bonaparte, where there is no alternative.

Among the merits of the USGS is that it sells the data "separations" (from which its sheets are published) on a non-profit, cost-only, public-service basis. This has enabled commercial publishers to buy the separations and issue maps designed specifically for hikers. In the Green Trails series, which covers virtually all hiking areas in the Cascades and Olympics, obsolete information (trails that no longer exist, at least not officially) is edited out and surviving maintained trails delineated by a green-ink overlay. Updated versions are issued every two years. Each hike description in this book lists the most useful topographic map, usually the Green Trails modification of the base map produced by the USGS.

The Green Trails and USGS sheets are sold at mountain equipment and map shops, which also carry the quite accurate and up-to-date national forest recreation maps. These also may be obtained for a small fee at ranger stations or by writing the following forest supervisors:

Mt. Baker–Snoqualmie National Forest
21905 64th Avenue West
Mountlake Terrace, WA 98043
Phone: (425) 775-9702

Wenatchee–Okanogan National Forest
215 Melody Lane
Wenatchee, WA 98801-5933
Phone: (509) 662-4335

INFORMATION SUMMARIES

Information summaries for trips generally contain the following information:

"Round trip *xx* miles" and "Elevation gain *xx* feet" tell a person if the trip fits his/her energy and ambition.

"Hiking time *xx* hours" must be used with a personal conversion factor. The figures here are based on doing about 2 miles an hour and an elevation gain of about 1000 feet an hour, about "average" on good trail with a moderate pack. If, instead, the hike is described as "Allow *xx* days," the length is greater than the ordinary person will want for a single day.

"Hikable *month* through *month*" primarily has to do with how much snow falls in winter and how long it mucks up the trail in spring–summer and when it goes at it again in the fall. Estimates are based on experience over the years and total ignorance of what the sky has in mind for the future. By "hikable" is meant, of course, what can be done encumbering the feet no more complexly than with boots.

"One day or backpack," or "One day," or "Backpack" introduces personal judgments. Often the information summary says "One day" and then the details note the possibility of camping, which in the opinion of the authors is not, for the trip in hand, a good idea. No water after June? Meadowlands too fragile for prone bodies en masse? Obviously, camping is always theoretically possible by carrying water, eating cold food, and lying on naked rock. But we say "Backpack" only when the site is desirable or the trip length requires more than a day.

In time of swift transition, a guidebook cannot be revised often enough to keep up-to-date on the condition of roads and trails, rules and regulations governing the backcountry, the need (or not) for permits, the requirement (or not) for fees. Following paragraphs outline the general considerations affecting your behavior. However, the times they are a-changing fast, land managers are engaged in constant experimentation, striving to preserve the natural ecosystems while minimizing restrictions. Nature, too, is ever busy. When in doubt, seek current information by telephone about roads, trails, permits. The Forest Service–Park Service Information Center in Seattle—(206) 470-4060—is worth a try when it's not a toll call. The staffers do their best but they are so few and the roads and trails and ranger districts so many that whatever they say may be out-of-date. Far more reliable are the offices close to the scenes; toll calls though they usually will be, those are the numbers given in our data blocks at the head of trip descriptions. Call well ahead; the offices usually are open only during business hours on weekdays.

FEES AND PERMITS AND RESERVATIONS

A system of parking fees at trailheads has been instituted as a source of funds for trail maintenance, which Congress is loath to supply. Kinks are being worked out. The only sure thing is the wisdom of knowing what the system is before arriving at the trailhead.

Permits for backcountry travel and camping are usual at national parks and some wilderness areas, doubtless at more locations in the future.

The y'all come, camp-anywhere, laissez faire freedom of the past is yielding, at popular sites, to limits on the number of designated sites, beaten-to-death barrens being closed for revegetation. Reservations perhaps must be obtained in advance. Call ahead.

CLOTHING AND EQUIPMENT

No one should set out on a Cascade trail, unless for a brief stroll, lacking warm long pants, wool (or the equivalent) shirt or sweater, and a windproof and rain-repellent parka, coat, or poncho. (All these in the rucksack, if not on the body—as they won't be during the hot hours.) And on the feet, sturdy shoes or boots plus wool socks and an extra pair of socks in the rucksack.

As for that rucksack, it should also contain the Ten Essentials, found to be so by generations of members of The Mountaineers, often from sad experience:

1. Extra clothing—more than needed in good weather.
2. Extra food—enough so something is left over at the end of the trip.
3. Sunglasses—necessary for most alpine travel and on snow.
4. Knife—for first aid and emergency fire building (making kindling).
5. Fire starter—a candle or chemical fuel for starting a fire with wet wood.
6. First-aid kit.
7. Matches—in a waterproof container.
8. Flashlight—with extra bulb and batteries.
9. Map—be sure it's the right one for the trip.
10. Compass—be sure to know the declination, east or west.

CAMPING

Indiscriminate camping blights alpine meadows. A single small party may trample grass, flowers, and heather so badly they don't recover from the shock for years. If the same spot is used several or more times a summer, year after year, the greenery vanishes, replaced by bare dirt. The respectful traveler always aims to camp in the woods or in rocky morainal areas. These alternatives lacking, it is better to use a meadow site already bare—in technical terminology, "hardened"—rather than extend the destruction into virginal places nearby.

Particularly to be avoided are camps on soft meadows on the banks of streams and lakes. Delightful and scenic as waterside meadows are, their use may endanger the water purity as well as the health of delicate plants. Further, no matter how "hard" the site may be, a camp on a viewpoint makes the beauty unavailable to other hikers who simply want to come and look, or eat lunch, and then go camp in the woods.

As the age of laissez-faire camping yields to the era of thoughtful management, different policies are being adopted in different places. For example, high-use spots may be designated "Day Use Only," forbidding camps. In others there is a blanket rule against camps within 100–200 feet of the water. However, in certain areas the rangers have decided it is better to keep existing sites, where the vegetation long since has been gone, than to establish new "barrens" elsewhere. The rule in such places is "use established sites"; wilderness rangers on their rounds disestablish those sites judged unacceptable.

Careful monitoring of backcountry camping has been in progress only a few years. Much remains to be learned. Obviously, meadows can quickly become mudbowls. But though a forest may appear healthy, the trees may be slowly dying from soil compaction. There is, however, general agreement that spreading a sleeping bag on a large granite boulder or on a snowfield doesn't bother anything, except maybe the lichen or ice worms.

A sleeping pad keeps the bag dry and bones comfortable. Tent or tarp must never be ditched if it involves the disturbance of vegetation.

Try always to camp invisibly, well away from the trail, to avoid intruding on the wildland isolation of others. When this isn't feasible, camp quietly. No yelling, no yodeling; learn to whisper and hum. Tell little children how Mohican mothers used to smother their babes lest their squalling be heard by the Iroquois; better a kid or two die rather than the whole tribe. Convey the suspicion that this is Iroquois country.

FEEDING (NOT) THE ANIMALS

Backpackers come from around the nation and world to feed the wild animals on the trail from Tuolume Meadows to Yosemite Valley. Their portable pantries are so gratefully enjoyed that Yosemite National Park estimates about five times more bears inhabit the route than natural food can sustain. The good news, say the rangers, is that this is nature's way of controlling the backpacker population.

Rangers of the North Cascades National Park, where the symbiosis of backpack-carrying visitors and backpack-plundering inhabitants is becoming notorious, have warm feelings for both species. To keep guests and hosts happy and peaceful, they have supplied us with the following information:

"For years North Cascades National Park has encouraged Wilderness users to hang their food to protect it from bears and other animals. Doing this adequately (at least 15 feet above the ground and 5 feet from the nearest tree trunk) can be difficult. At some camps in the park and adjacent national recreation areas, the National Park Service (NPS) has installed wires, poles, or food boxes to make proper food storage easier. More recently the park has acquired wildlife-resistant food canisters, or 'bear cans,' for loan to backpackers.

"The canister is designed to carry food and other fragrant items and to foil the raids of all types of wildlife, from bears to mice. It does not need to be hung. The North Cascades Wilderness Information Center at Marblemount, and NPS and U.S. Forest Service stations at Stehekin, Sedro Woolley, and Glacier have canisters to loan. The cans add a bit more weight to your load but are becoming increasingly popular as an effective and easy way to keep human food from bears and all other wildlife. The North Cascades

National Park Wilderness Steering Committee endorses the use of canisters as an alternative to hanging food, to installing more bear wires and poles, and to dealing with the impacts on vegetation associated with searching for a tree limb to hang food.

"The park also recommends that, where topography allows, you cook and store food at least 100 yards from where you sleep. Bears, mice, and other wildlife will investigate food smells whether they can get at the food or not. Your cooking/food storage area should be in a place you can observe from a distance so that you don't accidentally startle a bear. It's best for food storage and cooking to be done downwind from where you sleep so that curious animals don't follow their noses past you en route. Both kitchen area and sleeping area should be chosen with leaving no trace on either flora or fauna in mind!"

FIRE

Recollecting those long millennia our ancestors huddled in the cave, are we not ungrateful wretches to accuse the campfire of being antisocial? No doubt. But year by year the wood fire is coming down the mountain, already banned absolutely in most meadowlands, elsewhere not allowed above a certain elevation.

Today's novices will not take many backpacks before they learn never to count on a wood fire to keep warm (that's what clothes are for) or to cook meals (that's why you carry a stove). Of course, minimalists (cheapskates) don't encumber themselves with stoves; there is no nutritional value to the warmth in food, as our ancestors knew long before they climbed down out of the trees into caves. "Though the food is cold, the inner man is hot."

The pleasures of a roaring blaze on a cold mountain night are indisputable, but a single party on a single night may use up ingredients of the scenery that were long decades in growing, dying, and silvering, and many parties on many nights convert a green and pleasant swale to a dismal barren of charcoal.

At remote backcountry camps, and in forests, fires perhaps may still be built at some spots with a clear conscience. Again, one should minimize impact by using only established fire pits and using only dead and downed wood. When finished, be certain the fire is absolutely out—drown the coals and stir them with a stick and then drown the ashes until the smoking and steaming have stopped completely and a finger stuck in the slurry feels no heat. Embers can smoulder underground in dry duff for days, spreading gradually and burning out a wide pit or kindling trees and starting a forest fire.

If you decide to build a fire, do not make a new fire ring—use an existing one. In popular areas patrolled by rangers, its existence means this is an approved, "established," or "designated" campsite. If a fire ring has been heaped over with rocks, it means the site has been disestablished.

LITTER AND GARBAGE AND SANITATION

The rule among considerate hikers is: If you can carry it in full, you can carry it out empty. Thanks to a steady improvement in manners over recent decades, American trails are cleaner than they have been since Columbus landed.

Eliminate body wastes at least 200 feet from watercourses: First, dig a shallow hole in the "biological disposer layer"; then, if not using leaves (the likes of maple and thimbleberry are cozy, let the devils club and nettles be), pack out your toilet paper—do not burn it. In heavily used areas, the emerging rule is to double-bag and carry out feces as well. Where privies are provided, use them.

WATER

No reference in this book to "drinking water" is a money-back guarantee of purity by the authors or The Mountaineers.

In the late 1970s a great epidemic of giardiasis began, the villain being a vicious little parasite that spends part of its life cycle swimming free in water, part in the intestinal tract of beavers and other wildlife, dogs, and people. Actually, the "epidemic" was more mental than physical; *Giardia* were first identified in the eighteenth century and have always been present in the public water systems of many cities of the world and many towns in the United States—including some in the foothills of the Cascades. Long before the "outbreak" of "beaver fever" there was the well-known malady, the "Boy Scout trots," and elsewhere in the world, the "Aztec two-step," the "Delhi belly," et cetera. This is not to make light of the disease; though most humans feel no ill effects (but may become carriers), others have severe symptoms, which can include devastating diarrhea; the treatment is nearly as unpleasant. The two reasons giardiasis has become "epidemic" are (1) medical science cures many diseases but invents more; (2) there are more people in the backcountry, more people drinking water that in the olden days only a Tenderfoot Boy Scout would slip past his lips. Us Eagles knew better.

Whenever in doubt, boil the water 20 minutes. Keep in mind that *Giardia* can survive in water at or near freezing for weeks or months—a snow pond is not necessarily safe. Boiling is 100 percent effective against not only *Giardia* but also the myriad other filthy little blighters that may upset your digestion or, as with some forms of hepatitis, destroy your liver. As jet-trekkers knit the global village ever tighter, the little blighters no longer take decades but mere hours to travel from the far side of the planet to your backyard.

If you cannot boil, use one of the several iodine treatments (chlorine compounds have been found untrustworthy in wildland circumstances), such as Potable Aqua or the more complicated method that employs iodine crystals. Rumor to the contrary, iodine treatments pose no threat to the health.

High-tech filters sold in backpacking shops carry certifications and guarantees and hefty price tags and have an impressively tekky, very nifty look, and children enjoy playing with them in camp. As is true of many another advance of technology, a filter is one more thing to go wrong. Murphy's Law applies. *Caveat emptor.* Iodine is cheap and light and never fails.

While protecting against invisible contaminants, also take care to guard the visible purity of the public water supply. Don't wash dishes in streams or lakes, loosing food particles and detergent. Haul buckets of water to the woods or rocks, and wash and rinse there. Don't wash bodies in streams or lakes. Don't swim in waters being taken internally by others.

Carry a collapsible water container to minimize the trips to the water supply that beat down a path through delicate vegetation. A water-carrier has a serendipity. Hikers, especially beginners and fishermen, like to camp near water. Thus, the near-water camps are the mob scenes. By pausing at a stream or lake to fill a container and continuing on the trail a half hour to the top of a dry ridge, a hiker gets away from the madding crowd, finds solitude, and peacefully enjoys the big views.

Party Size

One management technique to minimize impact in popular areas is to limit the number of people in any one group to a dozen or fewer. Hikers with very large families (or outing groups from clubs or wherever) should check the rules when planning a trip.

Pets

Some 12,000 years ago a partnership was struck between humans and canines; there persists among many of us (both people and best friends) the conviction it ain't natural for man to go walking without a dog.

But the handwriting is on the wall. Pets always have been forbidden on national park trails and the ban is spreading to over-peopled national forest wildernesses. Owners who keep their animals under tight control—on a leash—and prevent them from barking at strangers, attacking them, stealing their bacon, and committing nuisances, can help slow expansion of the exclusion policy. Otherwise, try to find trails still empty or leave the best friend home with a dog-sitter.

Theft

Equipment has become so fancy and expensive, so much worth stealing, and hikers so numerous, their valuables so tempting, that theft is a growing problem. The professionals who do most of the stealing mainly hit cars. Authorities have the following recommendations.

Do not make crime profitable. If the pros break into a hundred cars and get nothing but moldy boots and tattered T-shirts, they'll give up. On an extended car trip, store extra equipment at a nearby motel.

Be suspicious of anyone waiting at a trailhead. One of the tricks of the trade is to sit there with a pack as if waiting for a ride, watching new arrivals unpack—and hide their valuables—and maybe even striking up a conversation to determine how long the marks will be away.

The ultimate solution, of course, is for hikers to become as poor as they were in the olden days. No criminal would consider trailheads profitable if the loot consisted solely of shabby khaki war surplus.

Not to be ignored is end-of-the-millennium social restlessness as the rich get egregiously richer and the poor desperately poorer. As common, perhaps, as theft is vandalism for the sake of—well, for the same satisfaction as drive-by shooting. In recent years certain trailheads have become unusable for overnight parking, and some are unsafe even in broad, busy daylight. When visiting a new area, ask for advice from the rangers or the police. Many a fortune-favored hiker keeps his Beamer locked in a garage at home, and at the trailhead parks a beater.

SAFETY CONSIDERATIONS

What makes the Ten Essentials so essential? They will keep your margin of safety from thinning out to nothing. The fact that a trail is included in this book does not mean it will be safe for you. The route may have changed since the description herein was written. Creeks flood. Gravity pulls down trees and rocks. Brush grows up. The weather changes from season to season, day to day, hour to hour. Wind blows, rain soaks, lightning strikes, the sun sets, temperature drops, snow falls, avalanches happen.

A guidebook cannot guarantee you are safe for the trail. Strength and agility vary from person to person. You vary from decade to decade, year to year, day to day, morning to afternoon to dark and stormy night.

You can reduce backcountry risks by being informed, equipped, and alert, and by recognizing hazards and knowing and respecting your limits. However, you cannot eliminate risk, and neither can the authors, or The Mountaineers, or the government, or the attorney hired by your next of kin. An old saying from the Alps is that when a climber is injured, he apologizes to his friends, and when a climber is killed, his friends apologize for him. It's a dangerous world out there. Perhaps you'd be happier as an armchair adventurer. But you may want to strap yourself in as a precaution against earthquakes.

1 HELIOTROPE RIDGE

Round trip: 6½ miles
Hiking time: 5 hours
High point: 5600 feet
Elevation gain: 2000 feet
Trip length: One day or backpack; no fires

Hikable: August through September
Map: Green Trails No. 13 Mt. Baker
Information: Glacier Public Service Center, phone (360) 599-2714. Ask about trail No. 677.

A splendid forest walk leading to a ramble-and-scramble on flowery moraines below (and above) the ice chaos of the rampaging Coleman Glacier. See the mountain climbers—by the hundreds on many summer weekends, because this is the most popular route to the summit of Mt. Baker.

However, hikers be warned! Three streams must be crossed. Ordinarily they are simple-safe in cold mornings or late summer, but on hot afternoons of snowmelt-time hikers may find knee-deep torrents. An even greater danger lies above on broad "snowfields" that actually are snowcovered glaciers, riddled with deep holes—hidden crevasses. In the last four years three hikers have died in these holes. Do not slide down any slope you have not walked up.

Drive Highway 542 beyond the town of Glacier 1 mile and turn right on Glacier Creek road No. 39. At 7.7 miles stay straight ahead 8 more miles to the trailhead, elevation 3650 feet.

Traverse and switchback 2 miles through tree shadows, over cold little creeks, to the site of historic Kulshan Cabin, 4700 feet, just below timberline. The trail climbs on, crossing those streams (beware), passing below

Avalanche lilies pushing through a late-summer snowbank

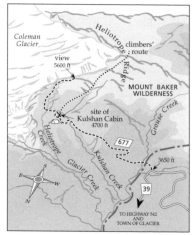

steep flower-covered meadows and through groves of alpine trees, over a rocky moraine whistling with marmots, to another moraine at about 5600 feet with a large glacier-scoured rock on the brink of a gravel precipice. Look down to the blue-white jumble of the Coleman Glacier and up to the ice-gleaming summit of the volcano. Follow the moraine upward, stopping well short of the living (crevassed!) glacier. Good camps below the trail in the timber, at the climbers' camp, and at the old cabin site.

Because of the enormous snowfall on Mt. Baker and its sun-sheltered persistence on this north side of the mountain, hikers who come earlier than August are likely to find the fun country above tree line a great white sea—a dangerous sea. The crevasses are always there, visible or invisible.

Coleman Glacier

2 | SKYLINE DIVIDE

Round trip: To Knoll 6215, 6 miles
Hiking time: 4 hours
High point: 6215 feet
Elevation gain: 2000 feet
Trip length: One day or backpack;
no fires

Hikable: August through September
Map: Green Trails No. 13 Mt. Baker
Information: Glacier Public Service
Center, phone (360) 599-3714.
Ask about trail No. 678.

A large, green meadow. An enormous white volcano—pound for pound, the iciest in the Cascades. Views of forests and glaciers, rivers and mountains, sunsets and sunrises.

Drive Highway 542 to 1 mile beyond the town of Glacier. Turn right on Glacier Creek road No. 39, and in a hundred feet turn sharply left on Deadhorse road No. 37. Follow the south side of the Nooksack River some 5 level and pleasant miles. The road then climbs abruptly. At 7.5 miles pause to view a lovely waterfall splashing down a rock cleft, coming from the country where you're going. At 13 miles is the parking lot and trailhead, elevation 4300 feet. Find the trail at the upper end of the lot.

The trail, moderate to steep, climbs 1500 feet in 2 miles through silver firs and subalpine glades to an immense ridge-top meadow at 5800 feet and the beginning of wide views. South are the sprawling glaciers of the north wall of Mt. Baker. North, beyond forests of the Nooksack valley, are the greenery of Church Mountain and the rock towers of the Border Peaks and, across the border, the Cheam (Lucky Four) Range. On a clear day salt water can be seen, and the Vancouver Island mountains, and the British Columbia Coast Range. Eastward is Mt. Shuksan and a gentler companion, little Table Mountain, above Heather Meadows.

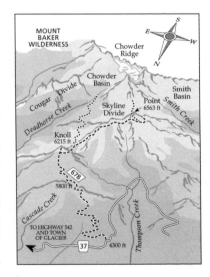

The broadest views are atop the 6215-foot knoll to the south; from the meadow, follow the trail ¾ mile along the ridge and take the sidepath up the knoll, a great turnaround point. Sprawl and enjoy. (Note to photographers: The best pictures of Baker from here generally should be taken before 10:00 A.M. and after 4:00 P.M.)

One must take a look around the

Skyline Divide trail and Mount Baker

next corner. Beyond the knoll the trail follows the ridge another ½ mile to a saddle at 6000 feet. Here, a route to the left contours a scant mile to a dead end in Chowder Basin, headwaters of Deadhorse Creek, and campsites with all-summer water. The trail continues to the right, climbs a step in Skyline Divide to 6500 feet, and proceeds along the tundra crest 2 miles to a 6300-foot saddle (and, perhaps, a snowmelt pool) at the foot of the abrupt upward leap to Chowder Ridge, whose summit is accessible on a track suitable for goats, climbers, and life-weary hikers.

In early summer, water is available for camping all along Skyline Divide, but later a party often must look for springs in Chowder and Smith Basins or snowfield dribbles on the ridge. In benign weather the supreme overnight experience is atop the 6500-foot tundra, watching the Whulge (the name given by the original residents to "the saltwater we know") turn gold in the setting sun and the lights of farms and cities wink on, then awaking at dawn to watch Baker turn shocking pink. However, though the tundra is tough enough to withstand sun and frost and storm, it cannot take human abuse. Do not build fires; if chilly, crawl in your sleeping bag. Do not sack out on soft turf; lay your sleeping pad and bag on a hard rock or bare dirt.

3
CANYON RIDGE—POINT 5658

Round trip: To ridge crest, 6 miles
Hiking time: 3 hours
High point: 5400 feet
Elevation gain: 1200 feet
Trip length: One day

Round trip: To Point 5658, 6 miles
Hiking time: 4 hours
High point: 5658 feet
Elevation gain: 1300 feet
Trip length: One day

Hikable: August through September
Map: Green Trails No. 13 Mt. Baker

Information: Glacier Public Service Center, phone (360) 599-2714. Ask about trails No. 625, 688, and 689.

In an area offering so many spectacular viewpoints, why bother hiking to those that rate no better than merely excellent? For one reason, people. On a day when they're swarming all over the spectacular, a hiker on the Canyon Ridge trail may have the excellent all to himself/herself. Also, scenery isn't everything. (In the fog it's nothing.) The forest here is lovely, the flowers bloom by the million, and the heather-and-huckleberry meadows are large and lonesome. Try these trails in early August for the climax of the flower show, or in September when the frost has turned the mountain ash leaves to the color of gold and the blueberry leaves to the color of wine. The description here is of round trips to two of the more excellent views: south to the snowy summits of Church Mountain and the network of logging roads in Canyon Creek valley, and north to Canadian mountains and the network of Canadian logging roads.

Drive Highway 542 beyond the Glacier Public Service Center 1.8 miles. Turn left on Canyon Creek road No. 31, at 10 miles keep left at a junction and again at 13.8 miles, and 15.3 miles from the highway reach the trailhead, elevation 4277 feet.

Start on Damfino Lakes trail No. 625, climbing gently through forest. In a long ½ mile, turn left on Canyon Ridge trail No. 689. At approximately 1 mile from the road is a junction and a choice. To the right are Boundary Way trail No. 688 and Point 5658—more of that later. For the ridge crest continue on. At approximately 1½ miles traverse a large sidehill meadow, steep and unstable, the tread often slumped

Canyon Ridge

out. At a long 2 miles the trail crosses Canyon Ridge from the south side to the north and emerges from forest to mountain ash, then heather. The way climbs to a shoulder a few feet from the top of a 5400-foot knob less than 1½ miles from Canada. Excellent enough.

Maps show the trail continuing to the western trailhead on road No. 3140, but it is not there and is best described as a bushwhack. Hey, don't complain! Were it not for the unstable hillside on the east end and the bushwhack on the west, the trail would be open to motorcycles.

For Point 5658, back at the junction go right on Boundary Way trail No. 688 through a swampy little cleft, then up in forest to a large meadow. At about 2½ miles from the road, attain a 5050-foot ridge top and look across the broad, deep gulf of Tomyhoi Creek into Canada.

The Boundary Way trail goes right, down along the ridge, 2 miles toward—but not to—the border. Don't go. Climb left on the sidepath to the crest of the summit ridge, to an elevation about 3 feet lower than Point 5658. To gain the tippy-top one would have to creep along a knife-edge catwalk. Dogs will prefer to sit down here and chew their bones while enjoying the view north to Canada, west to flatland farm geometry, south to Church Mountain and Mt. Baker, and east to Mt. Shuksan, Tomyhoi, and the garish red masses of the Border Peaks—American Border, Larrabee, and Canadian Border.

In the beginning no mountains had names, yet the flowers then were as bright in the meadows and the views to far horizons as inspiring. After the map industry took off, almost everything got a name, needed or not. Peak 5658 was missed. So was K2 in the Karakorum. Ponder that as you gaze to panoramas of the North Cascades and whatever, if anything, they call all those mountains in Canada.

4 | EXCELSIOR MOUNTAIN—HIGH DIVIDE

Round trip: From Canyon Creek
 road No. 31, 6½ miles
Hiking time: 4 hours
High point: 5712 feet
Elevation gain: 1500 feet
Trip length: One day or backpack;
 no fires

Hikable: Mid-July through September
Map: Green Trails No. 13 Mt. Baker
Information: Glacier Public Service
 Center, phone (360) 599-2714.
 Ask about trail No. 677.

Views from this meadow summit include Nooksack valley forests and
saltwater lowlands, Mt. Baker and the Border Peaks, the southernmost portion of the British Columbia Coast Range, and more. Flowers in July, ber-
ries and colors in September. Three trails lead to the site of a long-gone
lookout cabin; the easiest and most scenic is recommended here, but take
your pick.

Drive Highway 542 beyond the Glacier Public Service Center 1.8 miles.
Turn left on Canyon Creek road No. 31 and, in 15.3 miles, go left again to
the parking lot in a clearcut at the start of trail No. 625; elevation 4277 feet,
signed "Damfino Lakes, Boundary Trail, Canyon Rim."

Climb gently through forest ½ mile to the junction with Canyon Ridge
trail No. 689. Keep right and go a bit more to 4492-foot Damfino Lakes, two
small ponds surrounded by acres of super-delicious blueberries (in season). Campsites and running water near the smaller lake.

Climb another timbered mile, then go up a narrow draw and shortly enter meadows. Cross a notch, sidehill forest then broad meadows, rising in ½
mile to 5375-foot Excelsior Pass, some 2½ miles from the road. (Pleasant
camps at and near the pass when there is snowfield water—perhaps until

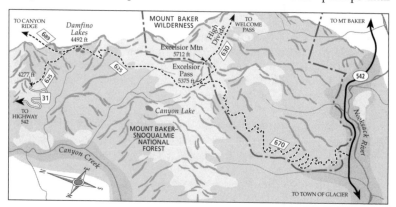

Mount Baker from Excelsior Pass

early August.) Follow the trail another ½ mile, traversing under the peak through meadows and views, then left ¼ mile to the 5712-foot summit.

Sit and look. See the glaciers of Mt. Baker across forests of the Nooksack. See more ice on Mt. Shuksan and other peaks east. See the steep-walled Border Peaks and snowy ranges extending far north into Canada. And see green meadows everywhere. The summit is a magnificent place to stop overnight in good weather, watching a sunset and a dawn; no water, though, except possible snowmelt.

Two alternate trails can be used to vary the descent. (They can also be used to ascend the peak but, for reasons that will be obvious, are not the best choices.)

Alternate No. 1. From Excelsior Pass, descend trail No. 670 4 miles and 3500 feet to Highway 542, reached 8 miles east of Glacier at a small parking area (with a trail sign on the opposite side of the road). The trail switchbacks steeply on south-facing slopes that melt free of snow relatively early in the season; an excellent hike from the highway in May or June, turning back when snowfields halt progress. In summer this route to high country is long and hot and dry.

Alternate No. 2. From the peak, traverse High Divide trail No. 630 along Excelsior Ridge 5 miles to Welcome Pass and descend steeply 2½ miles to the trailhead on an unmaintained logging road (Hike 8, Welcome Pass—Excelsior Ridge). Experienced off-trail roamers can extend their flower wanders west from Excelsior Pass toward Church Mountain and east from Welcome Pass to Yellow Aster Butte.

5 | BEARPAW MOUNTAIN LAKE

Round trip: 3 miles
Hiking time: 3 hours
High point: 4430 feet
Elevation gain: 530 feet
Trip length: One day

Hikable: Mid-July to October
Map: Green Trails No. 13 Mt. Baker
(shows road but not trail)
Information: Glacier Public Service
Center, phone (360) 599-2714

A pretty little subalpine lake ringed by trees, cliffs, and heather and blueberries. No famous views. Some solitude, though. The trail has had no maintenance in a coon's age, except by boots. Logs, rocks, roots, and straight-up scrambles keep the pikers out. (Not fishermen of course.)

Drive Highway 542 beyond the Glacier Public Service Center 1.8 miles. Turn left and go 13.8 miles on Canyon Creek road No. 31 (Hike 4) to a junction. Go straight ahead on road No. 3170. In 1.3 miles from this junction, cross Canyon Creek on a wooden bridge and in 2.8 miles from the junction, find a large parking area on the right side (17.6 miles from Highway 542), elevation 3900 feet. The trail is inventoried on Forest Service books, but not signed, as No. 623.1.

Directly across from the parking area find the tread climbing a cat track. At a junction in 300 feet, go right steeply up an ancient clearcut growing a lush crop of brush. In about ¼ mile the way enters forest and continues the stern upward haul, over or around fallen trees. Eventually the angle eases to a high point celebrated by a sign, "Low Impact Area." A few feet farther is the lake. Camping is allowed at a distance from the shore.

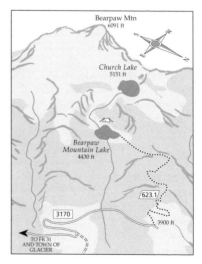

White paintbrush

Fog-covered Bearpaw Mountain Lake

6 | CHURCH MOUNTAIN

Round trip: 8½ miles
Hiking time: 5 hours
High point: 6100 feet
Elevation gain: 3800 feet
Trip length: One day or backpack

Hikable: August through September
Map: Green Trails No. 13 Mt. Baker
Information: Glacier Public Service
Center, phone (360) 599-2714.
Ask about trail No. 671.

The first thrilling view of emerald meadowland while driving east along
Mt. Baker Highway is Church Mountain. The view is straight up, nearly a
vertical mile, yet the green is so vivid and appears so close a person cannot
but wish to go there. A person can readily do so but must be a sturdy person and carry much water because the climb is far longer than it looks and
by midsummer is dry. However, the views back down to the valley and out
to Baker and Shuksan are worth the sweat. (In certain kinds of weather the
problem is not heat.) The viewpoint, on the east peak of Church, is a small
platform atop a rocky pinnacle, just large enough to hold the lookout building that used to be here until it was abandoned because wind kept blowing
the structure off its foundation. Hiking to timberline is a great late-June
flower walk when the upper trails are still snowbound.

Drive Highway 542 beyond the Glacier Public Service Center 5.1 miles.
Turn left on road No. 3040, signed "Church Mountain Road." Drive 2.6
miles to the road-end and trailhead, elevation 2300 feet.

The trail begins on an abandoned logging road, switchbacks up a
brush-choked clearcut to virgin forest, and ascends relentlessly, zigging
and zagging. In a bit more than 3 miles the way opens out in heather and
flowers, and the trail cut can be seen switchbacking up the emerald meadowland to the rocky summit. Shortly below the top is an old storage shed,
now a marmot condominium. From here the path, carved from rock, passes
an odd-shaped outhouse to the lookout site.

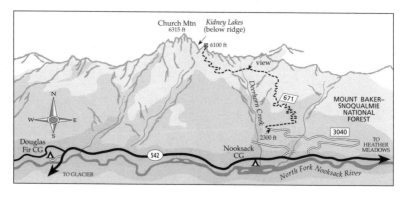

Look down to bugs creeping along the concrete ribbon beside the silver ribbon of river. Look east into the North Cascades, north to Canada, south toward Mt. Rainier. To the west are frightful cliffs of 6315-foot Church Mountain, only 200 feet higher than the lookout peak. Below are the two little Kidney Lakes, snowbound much of the year.

In March and April and May, when the color scheme on high is more white than green, the lower part of the trail offers a fine walk in wildwoods and forest flowers.

Mount Shuksan from Church Mountain trail

7 COUGAR DIVIDE

Round trip: 5½ miles
Hiking time: 5 hours
High point: 5850 feet
Elevation gain: 1300 feet in, 300 feet out
Trip length: One day

Hikable: Mid-July to mid-October
Map: Green Trails No. 13 Mt. Baker (trail not shown)
Information: Glacier Public Service Center, phone (360) 599-2714

Wide-open flower-covered meadows, glowing fields of heather, a bumper crop of blueberries in season, and a cold white view up Bar Creek to the Mazama Glacier tumbling from the summit icecap of Mt. Baker. The trail is on the Forest Service inventory, listed as trail No. 601. It is not, however, on any map and is maintained, as it was built, by boots. As for the road, what with no more logging hereabouts, it gets less maintenance every year and thus gets meaner every year. Nevertheless, there are so many autos at the trailhead, solitude is a sometime thing.

Drive Highway 542 beyond the Glacier Public Service Center 7 miles and turn right on Nooksack Falls–Wells Creek road No. 33 some 12.6 rough miles to its end at 4800 feet.

A jeep track ascends to the high point of the final clearcut, yielding then to a boot-beaten, sometimes steep path into forest. The climb leads to a large meadow and in a scant ¾ mile, 5480 feet, one of the most spectacular views of Baker from any trail. Many hikers are satisfied to sit here and goggle at the ice on Chowder Ridge and the Mazama Glacier emptying into Bold Creek. To the east are Mt. Shuksan and the ice-covered Lasiorcarpa Ridge, which merges with Ptarmigan Ridge; and to the west are the green, green meadows of Skyline Divide.

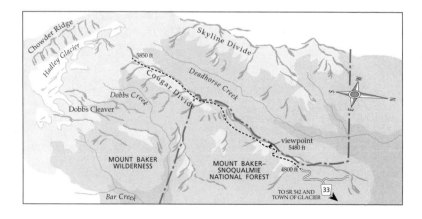

Cougar Divide trail crossing flower-covered meadow, with Chowder Ridge and Mount Baker in distance

In the 2 miles beyond the viewpoint the trail gets rougher with numerous logs to step over, loses 150 feet, gains 100, loses another 150, and climbs into flower fields to a 5850-foot point and more huge white views. A climbers' route goes on.

8 | WELCOME PASS—EXCELSIOR RIDGE

Round trip: To pass, 6 miles
Hiking time: 6 hours
High point: 5200 feet
Elevation gain: 2800 feet

One way: Grand Traverse Excelsior
Ridge from road No. 31, 10 miles
Hiking time: 6 hours
High point: 5699 feet
Elevation gain: 1800 feet

Trip length: One day or backpack
Hikable: July through September
Maps: Green Trails No. 14 Mt.
Shuksan, No. 13 Mt. Baker

Information: Glacier Public Service
Center, phone (360) 599-2714.
Ask about trail No. 698.

The only old-fashioned trail left in the Mt. Baker area—that is to say, that starts low down in the valley and climbs through virgin forest and woodland flowers to brilliant gardens and enormous views. The trail is old-fashioned in another way, too, built as it was by old-fashioned foresters bent on getting from here to there in a long-leggity hurry—the 15–22 percent grade switchbacks 67 times up a super-steep hillside. Logging roads that go so high that they run out of trees worth hauling to the mill have spoiled today's hikers with their sweat-free rides to the scenery; this route therefore is pretty much left to old-fashioned hikers.

By shuttling cars some 30 miles between trailheads for a one-way traverse of Excelsior Ridge, this anachronism can yield a spectacular day or, with sidetrips, a week.

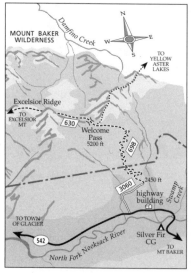

Drive Highway 542 beyond the Glacier Public Service Center 11.4 miles and between mileposts 45 and 46 go left on the unmarked, unmaintained Welcome Pass trailhead road No. 3060. (If you reach the Highway Department maintenance building, you have gone too far.) Drive 0.7 mile on a fright of a road impassible for a low-slung car. Find trail No. 698 a hundred or so feet from the parking spot, elevation 2450 feet.

A long-abandoned logging road is a pleasant forest walk for 1 mile, gaining only 400 feet. Then the fun begins. In the next 2 miles the 67 switchbacks gain 2000 feet, at first steep, then steeper. Grueling! Yes, but brightened by forest flowers, an occasional view out to Mt. Shuksan, and bits and pieces of Mt. Baker gleaming through chinks in the forest wall. At 5200 feet the trail abruptly levels off and bursts into meadows of Welcome Pass, views out to Tomyhoi Peak and numerous unnamed peaks of Excelsior Ridge, and miles of meadows left and right.

What to do? Round-trippers content with a grand panorama go right, up a steep boot-beaten path ½ mile to a 5743-foot high point and views of Baker, Shuksan, and myriad glaciated peaks. If energy is not all spent, in another mile a 5933-foot high point overlooks the lakes below Yellow Aster Butte.

For the grand traverse, go left on High Divide trail No. 630, do the ups and downs of Excelsior Ridge meadows through breathtaking views, heading westward 5 miles (adding another 1000 feet of elevation) to Excelsior Mountain (Hike 4), and from there drop to the Canyon Creek road. However, logic would say to start from the higher trailhead on the Canyon Creek road and end at Welcome Pass, saving almost 2000 feet of elevation gain.

Camping is very fine indeed along the Skyline Divide if there is water from snowbanks or your backpack reservoir.

Mountain dock growing on Welcome Pass, with Mount Shuksan in distance

9 | YELLOW ASTER BUTTE

Round trip: 8 miles
Hiking time: 6 hours
High point: 5800 feet
Elevation gain: 2200 feet
Trip length: One day or backpack
Hikable: mid-July through October

Map: Green Trails No. 14 Mt.
  Shuksan
Information: Glacier Public Service
  Center, phone (360) 599-2714.
  Ask about trail No. 676.1.

If views turn you on, there's plenty to exclaim about here—across the Nooksack valley to Mt. Baker and Mt. Shuksan, over the headwaters of Tomyhoi Creek to gaudy walls of the Border Peaks, and down to mile-long Tomyhoi Lake and out the valley to farms along the Fraser River. However, many a hiker never aspires for the summit, never lifts eyes from the meadows and snowy-cold lakes and ponds set in pockets scooped from the rock by the glacier that appears to have left about a half hour ago. Try the trip in late July for the flower show, in late August for the blueberry feast, and in October for autumn colors and winter frost.

Drive Highway 542 beyond the Glacier Public Service Center 12.8 miles. Just past the highway maintenance building, turn left on Twin Lakes road No. 3065, signed "Tomyhoi Trail 5, Twin Lakes 7." The road becomes narrow, steep, and rough. At 3 miles pass the former Yellow Aster Butte ("Keep Kool") trailhead and at 4.5 miles (the last 1.5 miles very narrow and rugged in spots) at a sharp switchback find the Tomyhoi Lake trailhead, elevation 3600 feet. Very limited parking.

Climb Tomyhoi Lake trail No. 686 (Hike 10) to the first meadow at about 1½ miles, elevation 5000 feet, and go left on Yellow Aster Butte trail No. 686.1. The next 2⅓ miles contour (more ups than downs) a steep sidehill of red and white heather (summer) or brilliant red blueberry leaves (autumn), in views of Baker and Shuksan that may be praised as magnificent, inspiring, breathtaking, supreme, dramatic, grand, splendid, awe-inspiring, superb, or perhaps (if English) "jolly good."

The trail ends at 5800 feet, 4 miles from the road, on the south side of Yellow Aster Butte. Some 200 feet below is the fairyland of ponds and pools—not to omit the

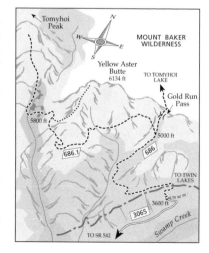

holes and rusty junk left by the prospectors "in search of shining gold." A scramble path leads to the 6145-foot top of the butte. A much longer walk climbs from lush herbaceous meadows to tundra to lichen-black *felsenmeer* very near the summit of 7451-foot Tomyhoi Peak, whose final hundred feet are for climbers only.

Now then: The area having been (largely) given wilderness protection in 1984, the "yellow asters" (actually golden daisies) no longer need the mass support of the boots of citizen-hikers. The crying need is land-lovers who walk softly, cook on stoves or eat cold food, and scatter themselves about on the ridge and in secluded nooks. Particularly tender care is deserved by the most beautiful spot on the entire Nooksack Crest.

Small tarn on the side of Yellow Aster Butte, with Goat Mountain in distance

10 | GOLD RUN PASS—TOMYHOI LAKE

Round trip: To pass, 4 miles
Hiking time: 3 hours
High point: 5400 feet
Elevation gain: 1800 feet

Round trip: To Tomyhoi Lake,
10 miles
Hiking time: 7 hours
High point: 5400 feet
Elevation gain: On return, 1600 feet

Trip length: One day or backpack
Hikable: July through October
Map: Green Trails No. 14 Mt. Shuksan

Information: Glacier Public Service Center, phone (360) 599-2714. Ask about trail No. 686.

Views across the Nooksack valley to Mt. Baker and Mt. Shuksan. Views over the headwaters of Tomyhoi Creek to Tomyhoi Peak and the tall, rough walls of Mt. Larrabee and American Border and Canadian Border Peaks. Views down to a mile-long lake and north into Canada. Mountain meadows along a pretty trail—but a hot and dry trail on sunny days, so start early and carry water.

Drive Twin Lakes road No. 3065 (Hike 9) 4.5 miles to the Tomyhoi Lake trailhead, elevation 3600 feet.

The trail climbs a steep bank then switchbacks steadily up, first in trees,

Clark's nutcracker

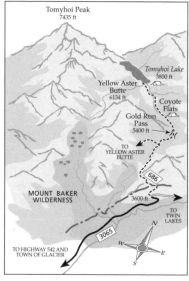

Mount Shuksan from Gold Run Pass

then meadows, then trees, then meadows again. In 1½ miles pass the Yellow Aster Butte trail, leave forest the last time, and enter an open basin, snowcovered until July. The views don't get any better: south are Baker and a shoulder of Shuksan, above are the cliffs of Yellow Aster Butte. The flower show begins with avalanche lily and spring beauty in mid-June, other species carrying on through the summer. At 2 miles is Gold Run Pass, 5400 feet; no camping. Good campsites (no fires) 1 mile farther at Coyote Flats.

Tomyhoi Lake, 3800 feet, is 2 miles and 1600 feet below the pass and 2 miles short of the border where the Canadian logging roads dead-end. Avalanche snow floats in the waters until early summer. Good camps; fires allowed.

11 | TWIN LAKES—WINCHESTER MOUNTAIN

Round trip: To Twin Lakes from
Tomyhoi Lake trailhead, 5 miles
Hiking time: 3 hours
High point: 5200 feet
Elevation gain: 1600 feet

Round trip: To Winchester Mountain from Tomyhoi Lake trailhead,
on road 5 miles, on trail 4 miles;
9 miles total
Hiking time: 6 hours
High point: 6510 feet
Elevation gain: 3000 feet

Trip length: One day or backpack
Hikable: Late July through
September
Map: Green Trails No. 14 Mt. Shuksan

Information: Glacier Public Service
Center, phone (360) 599-2714.
Ask about trail No. 685.

An easy and popular trail through subalpine meadows to two delight-
ful lakes and then to a summit view of Baker, Shuksan, Border Peaks, and
Tomyhoi, plus looks far down to Tomyhoi Lake and forests of Silesia Creek.
Especially beautiful in fall colors.

Drive Twin Lakes road No. 3065 (Hike 9) 4.5 miles to the Tomyhoi Lake
trailhead, elevation 3600 feet. Parking is very limited.

The Twin Lakes road cannot be blamed, for either its condition or its
existence, on the Forest Service. A "mine-to-market" road, funded by the
county and maintained in the upper reaches solely by prospectors, and
then only when they are engaged in
their sporadic rock-knocking and
then only minimally. The 4.5 miles
of the road to the Tomyhoi Lake
trailhead usually can be driven by
the family car, but the 2.5 miles beyond there, ending at Twin Lakes,
are something else. Some years an
agile car may get beyond the Tomyhoi Lake trailhead a short distance,
or even to Twin Lakes, but most
years the attempt should not be
made except in a four-wheel-drive
vehicle, felt by its wealthy owners
to be dispensable. Most hikers prefer to protect cars and nerves from
damage by parking near the Tomyhoi Lake trailhead and walking to

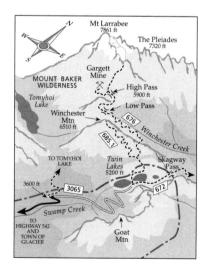

Mount Shuksan from Winchester Mountain trail

the lakes. When the miners finally sell out, the road will be abandoned, returning Twin Lakes to trail country—where they belong.

The two lakes, lovely alpine waters at an elevation of 5200 feet, often are frozen until early August, though surrounding parklands melt free earlier. Between the lakes is an undeveloped campsite with a classic view of Mt. Baker.

Find the Winchester Mountain trailhead at the road-end between the lakes. Within ¼ mile is a junction with High Pass (Gargett Mine) trail No. 626. Take the left fork, trail No. 685.1, and climb a series of switchbacks westerly through heather, alpine trees, and flowers. Near the top a treacherous snowpatch, steep with no runout, often lasts until late August. It may be possible to squirm between the upper edge of the snow and the rocks. Otherwise, drop below the snow and climb to the trail on the far side. Don't try crossing the snow without an ice ax and experience in using it.

In 1½ miles the trail rounds a shoulder and levels off somewhat for the final ½ mile to the summit, a fine place to while away hours surveying horizons from saltwaterways and lowlands to the Pickets and far north into Canada.

Twin Lakes make a superb basecamp for days of roaming high gardens, prowling old mines, and grazing September blueberries. Even if the upper road must be walked, access is easy for backpacking families with short-legged members.

For one of the longer explorations of the many available, take the High Pass trail (see earlier). A steep snowfield near the beginning may stop all but trained climbers; if not, there is no further barrier to Low Pass (about 1½ miles) and 5900-foot High Pass (2½ miles). Follow an old prospectors' trail high on Mt. Larrabee to a close view of the rugged Pleiades. Investigate the junkyard of the Gargett Mine. Wander meadow basins and admire scenery close and distant.

12 | NOOKSACK CIRQUE

Round trip: To end of gravel bars,
  12½ miles
Hiking time: 6 to 8 hours
High point: 3100 feet
Elevation gain: 600 feet
Trip length: One day or backpack

Hikable: August through September
Map: Green Trails No. 14 Mt. Shuksan
Information: Glacier Public Service
  Center, phone (360) 599-2714.
  Ask about trail No. 680.

Park Service backcountry use permit required for camping

A wild, lonesome cirque, a wasteland of glacial violence, one of the most dramatic spots in the North Cascades. Icefalls, waterfalls, rockfalls, moraines, a raging river, the stark pinnacle of Nooksack Tower, and the 5000-foot northeast wall of Mt. Shuksan. But the way is only partly on trail, the rest bushwhacking and cobble-hopping. The trip can only be recommended to rational people for late summer when Ruth Creek is low enough to wade and the Nooksack River is low enough to fully expose gravel bars.

Drive Highway 542 beyond Glacier Public Service Center 13 miles. Just before the Nooksack River bridge, turn left on road No. 32. At 1.3 miles take the right fork, road No. 34, a scant mile to the abandoned bridge over Ruth Creek, elevation 1567 feet.

In high water look for log jams upstream or downstream to avoid having to ford the creek, which may be injurious to your health. Walk the abandoned road 2 miles to the trailhead, elevation about 2550 feet. The way descends from there on a grown-over logging road of the 1950s and then climbs, at about ¾ mile reaching the end of the clearcut. Mount Baker Wilderness is entered and true trail begins at about 2600 feet. Constructed tread goes 1 mile through gorgeous big trees, an old-growth museum, to the end by the river. Cross a large tributary on a log jam or an upstream footlog.

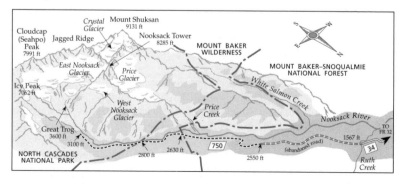

For the next ¾ mile there are two alternates. Depending on how high the river is and where its channel happens to be, scenic gravel bars may be continuous. Icy Peak appears, then the cirque itself, hanging ice cliffs of the East Nooksack Glacier falling from Cloudcap (Seahpo) Peak and Jagged Ridge. If the gravel won't go, the woods will. Find the boot-beaten path across some small sloughs, the start marked by a rock cairn. At several places the woods path and the gravel bars are connected by linking paths, permitting alternation.

At the end of this ¾ mile, at about 2800 feet, the trail enters the national park and goes out on the gravel for good, a large cairn often marking the spot. The next 1 mile is on gravel bars (if not under water) or the riverbank terrace, partly in timber but mostly in fierce brush, particularly nasty on an enormous alluvial fan issuing from a big gulch.

At this fan-maker creek, 2950 feet, are the last of the big trees. The next ¾ mile is easy, walking mossy gravel on brushfree terraces well above high water.

At 3100 feet, about 4¼ miles from the road, the good times are over and the sensible hiker will make this the turnaround. The view of the cirque, "the deepest, darkest hole in the North Cascades," is superb. The camping (no fires allowed; bring a stove) is splendid.

Upstream from here the river gushes from a virtual tunnel through overhanging alder, no gravel bars even in the lowest water. If you insist on persisting, dive into the slide alder, watching for cut branches and blazes and cairns. After about ¾ mile you'll attain the Great Trog (a large rock with an overhang), 3600 feet, formerly the grandest storm camp in the Cascades but now full of boulders. Exploring upward from here is tough going except in spring, when the moraines and cliffs and boulders are buried under fans of avalanche snow, and then it's dangerous.

Icy Peak and North Fork Nooksack River

13 | GOAT MOUNTAIN MEADOWS AND LOOKOUT SITE

Round trip: To lookout site, 5½ miles
Hiking time: 3 hours
High point: 3850 feet
Elevation gain: 1250 feet
Trip length: One day

Round trip: To trail's end, 11½ miles
Hiking time: 6 hours
High point: 5600 feet
Elevation gain: 3100 feet
Trip length: One day or backpack

Hikable: Late June through October
Map: Green Trails No. 14 Mt. Shuksan

Information: Glacier Public Service Center, phone (360) 599-2714. Ask about trail No. 673.

Take your pick. A morning or afternoon hike to great views or a day-long climb to meadows and greater views. The gazing up and down the Nooksack River and ice hanging on the north face of Mt. Shuksan—the West Nooksack Glacier, the Price Glacier, and a lot of little nameless chunks—is stupendous. The way sometimes is hikable in April and May to the site of a fire-lookout cabin removed in the early 1960s. The trail continues 3 more miles to heather fields, blueberry patches, and camps at the 5600-foot level, where the views are at least half again as good.

Drive Highway 542 beyond the Glacier Public Service Center 13 miles. Just before the Nooksack River bridge, turn left on road No. 32. At 1.3 miles stay left and at 2.5 miles find Goat Mountain trail No. 673, elevation 2500 feet. Park either just before or after the trail sign.

Presumably built by hardy prospectors in a hurry to get to the gold and precious jewels, at approximately 2 miles the trail briefly flattens, then switchbacks, and in about ¼ mile more enters the Mount Baker Wilderness and reaches an unsigned junction. The main trail proceeds onward and upward to the flower fields. An unmaintained path, easy to miss and easy to lose, turns off right and contours ½ mile to the rocky knoll where the lookout

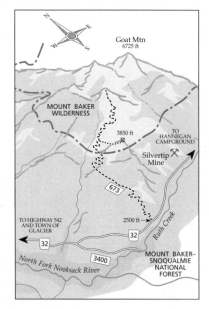

cabin was perched. Valley views and glacier views, plus views to the highway to Baker Lodge, roofs of the recreation area buildings, and all the cars going to and fro, up and down.

Mount Shuksan from Goat Mountain Lookout site

14 | HANNEGAN PASS AND PEAK

Round trip: To Hannegan Pass,
 8 miles
Hiking time: 6 hours
High point: 5066 feet
Elevation gain: 2000 feet

Round trip: To Hannegan Peak,
 10 miles
Hiking time: 8 hours
High point: 6187 feet
Elevation gain: 3100 feet

Trip length: One day or backpack
Hikable: Mid-July through
 September
Map: Green Trails No. 14 Mt.
 Shuksan

Information: Glacier Public Service
 Center, phone (360) 599-2714.
 Ask about trail No. 674.

The classic entry to the Chilliwack and Picket section of the North Cascades National Park begins in a delightful valley dominated by the white serenity of Ruth Mountain and concludes in a relaxed wander to a meadow summit offering a panorama of the north wall of Shuksan, the Pickets, and wildness high and low.

Looking north from the side of Hannegan Peak

Drive Highway 542 beyond Glacier Public Service Center 13 miles. Just before the Nooksack River bridge turn left on road No. 32. At 1.3 miles take the left fork, Ruth Creek road No. 32, and continue 5.4 miles to the road-end at Hannegan Campground, elevation 3100 feet.

The trail enters the Mount Baker Wilderness and for the first mile ascends gently through trees and avalanche-path greenery near Ruth Creek, with looks upward to the waterfall-streaked cliffs and pocket icefields of Mt. Sefrit and Nooksack (Ruth) Ridge. At a bit more than 1 mile the snow dome of Ruth Mountain comes into sight—a spacious expanse of whiteness for so small a peak. Now the path steepens, climbing above the valley floor.

Rest stops grow long, there is so much to see. At 3½ miles, 4600 feet, the trail swings to the forest edge beside a meadow-babbling creek; across the creek is a parkland of heather benches and alpine trees. Just below a switchback is a splendid campsite, the best on the route. No fires here. (*Note:* Due to bear problems, camping is temporarily prohibited within 1 mile of the pass. If this is the case during your visit, proceed 1½ miles into the park to Boundary Camp, where a Park Service camping permit is required.) The final ½ mile switchbacks in forest to Hannegan Pass, 5066 feet.

Views from the pass are so blocked by trees that hikers wishing a climactic vista must take a little sidetrip. Visitors usually are drawn southward and upward on the climbers' track toward Ruth Mountain, a path to lovely meadows and broader views but dwindling to nothing, tempting the unwary onto steep and dangerous snow. Leave Ruth to the climbers. There's a better and safer sidetrip.

From the pass, follow the Hannegan Peak trail a steep mile up open forest, emerging into a steep, lush meadow. Break through a screen of trees to heather and flowers, and wander wide-eyed up the crest of a rounded ridge to the summit plateau of Hannegan Peak, 6187 feet. Roam the meadow flats, looking down into valley forests of Ruth and Silesia Creeks and Chilliwack River, out to glaciers and cliffs of Baker, Shuksan, Ruth, Triumph, Challenger, Redoubt, Slesse, and dozens of other grand peaks.

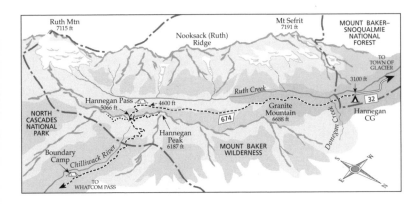

15 | COPPER MOUNTAIN

Round trip: To Copper Mountain
Lookout, 20 miles
Hiking time: Allow 2 to 3 days
High point: 6260 feet
Elevation gain: 4500 feet in, 1100
feet out

Hikable: August through September
Maps: Green Trails No. 14 Mt.
Shuksan, No. 15 Mt. Challenger
Information: Glacier Public Service
Center, phone (360) 599-2714.
Ask about trail No. 674.

Park Service backcountry use permit required for camping

A remote meadow ridge on the west edge of the North Cascades National Park offers a rare combination of easy-walking terrain and panoramas of rough-and-cold wilderness. Views across far-below forests of the Chilliwack River to the Picket Range—and views west to other superb peaks and valleys. However, hikers planning a visit should be aware of restrictions. Due to a water shortage, the Park Service currently permits use of only eleven campsites on the entire 6-mile length of the ridge. Hikers who plan trips for midweek generally have no trouble obtaining a site. No fires allowed anywhere; carry a stove.

Drive to Hannegan Campground and hike 4 miles, gaining 2000 feet, to Hannegan Pass (Hike 14). Descend forest switchbacks into avalanche-swept headwaters of the Chilliwack River, then sidehill along talus and stream outwash patched with grass and flowers. Note chunks of volcanic

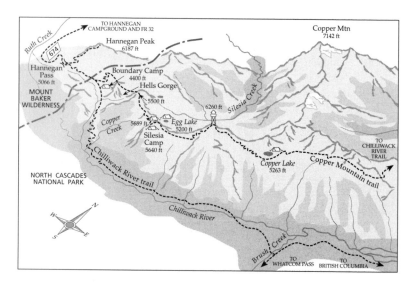

breccia in the debris and look up to their source in colorful cliffs—remnants of ancient volcanoes.

At 1 mile, 650 feet below Hannegan Pass, is a junction and a nice riverside campsite, Boundary Camp, at 4400 feet. The Chilliwack River trail goes right, descending. Take the Copper Mountain trail left and up, entering forest and climbing steadily, switchbacking some, crossing the upper portion of Hells Gorge (sliced in volcanic rocks), and emerging into parkland.

At 7 miles the trail attains the 5500-foot ridge crest between Silesia Creek and the Chilliwack River. A memorable look back to Hannegan Pass, Ruth Mountain, and Shuksan—and the beginning of miles of constant views.

The trail continues along the open crest, up a bit and down a bit, then climbs around a knob to a wide, grassy swale at 8 miles. Some 300 feet and a few minutes below the swale is little Egg Lake, 5200 feet, set in rocks and flowers. Three legal campsites are at the lake; two others are on Knob 5689 and at Silesia Camp.

The way goes up and down another knob to a broad meadow at 9 miles. Now comes the final mile, gaining 1100 feet to the 6260-foot Copper Mountain Lookout, the climax. Beyond the green deeps of Silesia Creek are the Border Peaks and the incredible fang of Slesse—and far-off in haze, ice giants of the British Columbia Coast Range. Look down and down to the white thread of the Chilliwack River and beyond its forest valley to Redoubt and Bear and Indian and the magnificent Pickets. Also see Shuksan and Baker. And more peaks and streams, an infinity of wildland.

Beyond the lookout the trail descends about 1½ miles to the three campsites at 5263-foot Copper Lake (blue waters under steep cliffs), then traverses and descends about 7 more miles. Views much of the way. At 2300 feet is the Chilliwack River trail, 15 miles from Hannegan Pass. A 34-mile loop trip using this return route adds low-valley forests to the high-ridge wander.

For another exploration, leave the trail before the steep descent to Copper Lake and investigate ridges and basins toward the 7142-foot summit of Copper Mountain.

Snowcovered Copper Mountain trail and Mount Shuksan

16 | EASY RIDGE

Round trip: 27 miles
Hiking time: Allow 2 to 3 days
High point: 6100 feet
Elevation gain: 5500 feet in, 2400 feet out
Hikable: Late July through September

Maps: Green Trails No. 14 Mt. Shuksan, No. 15 Mt. Challenger (not on map)
Information: Glacier Public Service Center, phone (360) 599-2714. Ask about trail No. 674.

Park Service backcountry use permit required for camping

A not-so-easy trail to a high green ridge surrounded by rugged and icy peaks. Wander to an old lookout site amid picturesque alpine trees, fields of flowers, and small tarns, admiring the Chilliwack wilderness of the North Cascades National Park. The difficulty of the trip is compensated for by the privacy—and the views. For some unknown reason the Park Service does not admit the existence of this trail.

Drive to Hannegan Campground and hike 4 miles, gaining 2000 feet, to Hannegan Pass (Hike 14). Descend the Chilliwack River trail, dropping 2300 feet in 5½ miles. At 9½ miles, elevation 2800 feet, is the unmarked but easy-to-see Easy Ridge trail junction. Go right a few feet to the Chilliwack River. Except perhaps in late summer, the river is too deep, swift, and cold to ford. Some years a log can be found within ¼ mile, upstream or down. Give preference to searching upstream, since on the far side the trail parallels the river about ¼ mile before heading uphill along Easy Creek. A good plan is to camp the first night a mile back at Copper Creek Camp.

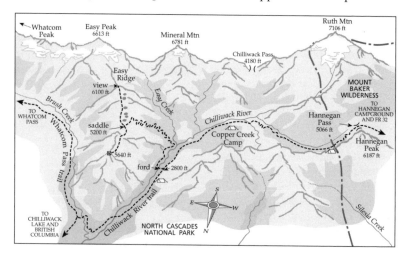

Whatcom Peak and a small tarn on the side of Easy Ridge

The trail was built to a Forest Service fire-lookout cabin, long since demolished. The Park Service maintains the tread for "resource protection," a college-educated term meaning the fallen trees are cut out and water drained off. That's good enough, brush being no problem. The hillside forest is entirely dry so fill canteens at the bottom. Or use the old Boy Scout trick of sucking a prune pit.

The trail switchbacks steeply 2½ miles, gaining 2600 feet, to the first views at a 5200-foot saddle in Easy Ridge. From the saddle the trail continues north ½ mile to the old lookout site on a 5640-foot knoll overlooking the junction of Brush Creek and the Chilliwack River; great looks down into valleys, across to the pleasant ridge of Copper Mountain, and off to rough, white peaks. For the broadest views leave the trail at the saddle and walk the main ridge south, climbing open slopes, past a number of tarns, to a heather-covered knoll at 6100 feet. A tiny pool here, good for cold drinks while looking at Shuksan and Icy Peak west, Canadian peaks north, Redoubt northeast, Whatcom Peak close by to the east, and mountains and valleys beyond number. Wonderful camps near the small tarns. Camp only on bare ground or snow. No fires.

The route to the 6613-foot summit of Easy Peak may be blocked by a steep snow slope—do not try it without an ice ax and knowledge of self-arrest technique. The view from the top isn't much better than from the heather knoll.

17 | WHATCOM PASS

Round trip: 34 miles
Hiking time: Allow 3 to 4 days
High point: 5200 feet
Elevation gain: 5700 feet in, 2600 feet out
Hikable: Late July through September

Maps: Green Trails No. 14 Mt. Shuksan, No. 15 Mt. Challenger
Information: Glacier Public Service Center, phone (360) 599-2714. Ask about trail No. 674.

Park Service backcountry use permit required for camping

A long hike on an old miners' route to the Caribou goldfields in Canada, entering the heart of the most spectacular wilderness remaining in the contiguous forty-eight states. Virgin forests in a U-shaped valley carved by ancient glaciers; rushing rivers; mountain meadows; and a sidetrip to lovely Tapto Lakes, a blend of gentle beauty and rough grandeur. Whatcom Pass is the high point on the walk across North Cascades National Park from the Mt. Baker region to Ross Lake, a classic of North American wildlands.

Drive to Hannegan Campground and hike 4 miles, gaining 2000 feet, to Hannegan Pass (Hike 14). Descend the Chilliwack River trail, which drops rapidly at first and then gentles out in delightful forest, reaching U.S. Cabin Camp at 10 miles.

Mount Challenger from Whatcom Pass

At about 11 miles, elevation 2468 feet (2600 feet down from Hannegan Pass), the trail crosses the Chilliwack River on a cable car and climbs moderately to the crossing of Brush Creek at about 12 miles. Here is a junction.

The Chilliwack trail goes north 9 miles to the Canadian border and about 1 mile beyond to Chilliwack Lake. The forest walk to the border is worthy in its own right; parties visiting the region during early summer when the high country is full of snow may prefer pleasures of the low, green world. (See the note on border crossing in Hike 100, Pacific Crest National Scenic Trail.)

From the 2600-foot junction the Brush Creek trail climbs steadily, gaining 2600 feet in the 5 miles to Whatcom Pass. At 13 miles is Graybeal Camp (hikers and horses), at 16½ miles the two excellent sites of Whatcom Camp (no fires), and at 17 miles 5200-foot Whatcom Pass (no camping).

Views from the meadowy pass are superb but there is vastly more to see. First, ramble the easy ridge south of the pass to a knoll overlooking the boggling gleam of the Challenger Glacier. Tapto Lakes are next. Climb steep slopes north from the pass, following a boot-built path in alpine forest. When the hillside levels off continue left in meadows to rocky ground above the lakes. Enjoy the waters and flowers, the stupendous view of Challenger.

In addition to the on-trail camps, cross-country camping (no fires) is permitted at Tapto Lakes and on Whatcom Arm. The "across the National Park" hike from Hannegan Campground to Big Beaver Landing on Ross Lake covers 38½ up-and-down miles on easy trail beside wild rivers, through gorgeous forests, over three passes. Total elevation gain on the way is 5400 feet. To have time for sidetrips, a party should allow 7 to 9 days. From Whatcom Pass drop abruptly (fifty-six switchbacks!) into headwaters of Little Beaver Creek, an enchanting place where waterfalls tumble from cliffs all around. Camping here at Twin Rocks Camp, 3000 feet. At 6 miles from Whatcom Pass is Stillwell Camp and the 2400-foot junction with the Beaver Pass trail. To conclude the cross-park journey, see Hike 40, Beaver Loop.

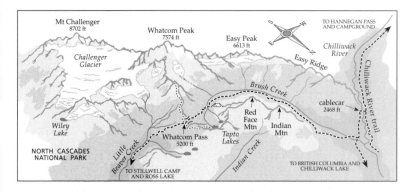

18 | LAKE ANN

Round trip: 8½ miles
Hiking time: 6 to 8 hours
High point: 4800 feet
Elevation gain: 1000 feet in,
1000 feet out
Trip length: One day or backpack;
no fires

Hikable: August through September
Map: Green Trails No. 14 Mt.
Shuksan
Information: Glacier Public Service
Center, phone (360) 599-2714.
Ask about trail No. 600.

When North Cascades climbers and hikers compare memories of favorite sitting-and-looking places, Lake Ann always gets fond mention. The Mt. Shuksan seen from here is quite different from the world-famous roadside view, yet the 4500-foot rise of glaciers and cliffs is at least as grand. And there is plenty to do. However, if taking the trip on a weekend, make it a day hike—you'll be hard-pressed to find an empty campsite.

Drive Highway 542 to the Mt. Baker ski area. Continue on paved road about 1.5 miles upward to the parking lot at Austin Pass, elevation 4700 feet. Until August, snow usually blocks the road somewhere along the way, adding ½ mile or so of walking.

The trail begins by dropping 600 feet into a delightful headwater basin of Swift Creek. Brooks meander in grass and flowers. Marmots whistle from boulder-top perches. Pleasant picnicking.

From the basin the trail descends a bit more and traverses forest, swinging around the upper drainage of Swift Creek. At 2¼ miles, after a loss of 800 feet, reach the lowest elevation (3900 feet) of the trip, an attractive camp in meadows by a rushing stream, and a junction with the abandoned Swift

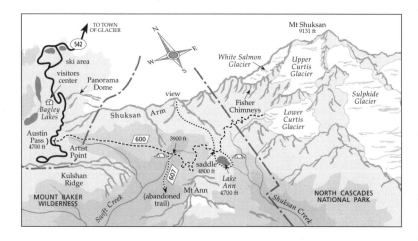

Mount Shuksan from Chain Lakes trail (Hikes 19 and 20)

Above: *Paintbrush and Mount Shuksan from Goat Mountain Lookout site (Hike 13);* below: *Mount Baker from Chain Lakes trail (Hike 19)*

Mount Baker and small tarn on Park Butte (Hike 23)

Pikas (coneys) are often found in rock slides, a safe haven from predators; here one dries grass for winter

Left: *Sunrise over Mount Shuksan;* below: *Blue Lake near Washington Pass*

Clockwise from upper left: *Mount Challenger from Easy Ridge (Hike 16); trail bridge over Thunder Creek (Hike 39); Mount Baker from Shannon Ridge (Hike 29); Thunder Creek trail (Hike 39)*

Above: *Inquisitive mountain goats at Cutthroat Pass (Hike 71);* below: *Sahale Arm above cloud-covered Cascade Pass (Hike 35)*

Lake Ann and the Curtis Glacier on the side of Mount Shuksan

Creek trail. If camping beyond here, carry a stove; the era of building fires at and near the lake is long past.

Continuing left at the junction, now starts a 900-foot ascent in 1½ miles, first in heather and clumps of Christmas trees, then over a granite rockslide into forest under a cliff, to a cold and open little valley. If the way is snow-covered, as it may be until mid-August, plod onward and upward to the obvious 4800-foot saddle and another ½ mile to Lake Ann. When white-ness melts away, the waterfalls and moraines and flowers and ice-plucked buttresses of the little valley demand a slow pace.

What to do next? First off, sit and watch the living wall of Shuksan. Then, perhaps, circumnavigate the lake, noting the contact between gran-ite rocks and complex metamorphics. In September, blueberry upward on the ridge of Mt. Ann. If time allows, go on longer wanders.

Recommended Wander No. 1. Follow the trail from Lake Ann as it dips into the headwater basin of Shuksan Creek, then switchbacks up and up toward Mt. Shuksan. At a rocky gully, a climbers' track branches steeply to the left. Just here the main trail may be nonexistent for a few yards; if so, scramble across gravel to regain the tread. Continue to a promontory a stone's throw from the snout of the Lower Curtis Glacier. Look up to the mountain. Look down forests to Baker Lake. Look beyond Swift Creek to the stupendous whiteness of Mt. Baker.

Recommended Wander No. 2. From the Lake Ann saddle, climb the heathery spur to Shuksan Arm, with spectacular campsites (snowbanks for water) and views of both Baker and Shuksan.

19 | CHAIN LAKES LOOP

Round trip: To Iceberg Lake, 5 miles
Hiking time: 4 hours
High point: 5200 feet
Elevation gain: 100 feet in, 700 feet out
Trip length: One day or backpack; no fires

Loop trip: 9 miles
Hiking time: 5 hours
High point: 5400 feet
Elevation gain: 1600 feet
Trip length: One day or backpack

Hikable: Late July through October
Map: Green Trails No. 14 Mt. Shuksan

Information: Glacier Public Service Center, phone (360) 599-2714. Ask about trail No. 682.

Alpine meadows loaded with blueberries (in season), a half-dozen small lakes, and at every turn of the trail a changing view, dominated by "the magnificent pair," the white volcano of Mt. Baker and the massive architecture of Mt. Shuksan. The area is a wildlife sanctuary, so deer and goat are frequently seen. All this on an easy hike circling the base of a high plateau guarded on every side by impressive lava cliffs.

Drive Highway 542 to closed-in-summer Mt. Baker Lodge (Heather Meadows Recreation Area). If doing the whole loop, drive another mile and park at the Austin Pass Visitors Center and do the climbing first. If a round trip to the lakes is on the agenda, continue 3 miles upward to the 5100-foot road-end at the Artist Point parking area. The winter snowpack here is often 25 feet deep on the level, with much greater depths in drifts, so the road commonly is snowbound until late August. Drive as far as possible and walk the rest of the way.

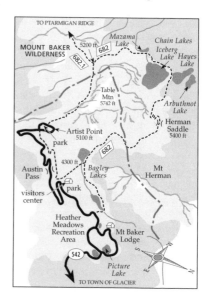

In the Artist Point parking lot find the Table Mountain–Chain Lakes trailhead in the middle of the west side. In a few feet go left. Do not make the mistake of going uphill, toward Table Mountain—unless, of course, that's where you want to go. (The Table Mountain trail climbs 500 feet through lava cliffs to grand views atop the plateau; the walk is

Iceberg on Iceberg Lake

easy this far but steep snowfields make the route so difficult that the summit traverse is not recommended.)

The Chain Lakes trail traverses almost on the level a scant mile around the south side of Table Mountain to a saddle between Table Mountain and Ptarmigan Ridge. At the junction here take the right fork, dropping 700 feet to the first of the four Chain Lakes, tiny Mazama Lake, reached about 1¾ miles from the road. A bit beyond is aptly named Iceberg Lake, which many years never melts out completely. Halfway around the shore on the left, a sidetrail follows the Hayes Lake shore and crosses a low rise to Arbuthnot Lake. Camp at designated sites marked by posts.

The main trail now begins a 600-foot climb to 5400-foot Herman Saddle, attained at about 3 miles. Cliffs of the narrow slot frame Baker west, Shuksan east. Spend some time sitting and looking from one to the other. Then descend amid boulders, heather, and waterfalls, dropping 1100 feet to meadow-surrounded Bagley Lakes. Pause to wander flower fields of the inlet stream. Look for swift little dots on the north side of Table Mountain—diehard skiers or snowboaders who use the permanent snowfields all summer and fall.

Between the Bagley Lakes find a stone bridge and trail climbing to the Austin Pass Visitors Center and the Artist Point parking area, gaining 900 feet in 2 miles. If transportation can be arranged (by use of two cars or a helpful friend), this final ascent from Bagley Lakes can be eliminated.

20 | PTARMIGAN RIDGE

Round trip: To Camp Kiser, about 8 miles

Hiking time: 6 to 8 hours

High point: 6200 feet

Elevation gain: 1400 feet in, 300 feet out

Trip length: One day or backpack; no fires

Hikable: Mid-August through October

Map: Green Trails No. 14 Mt. Shuksan

Information: Glacier Public Service Center, phone (360) 599-2714. Ask about trail No. 682.1.

Begin in meadows, climb a bit to the snowy and rocky crest of a ridge open to the sky, and wander for miles on the high line toward the lofty white mass of Mt. Baker. From a distance this trail appears to traverse a desolate pile of rocks, but when the snow is gone even the first rocky basin holds spectacular pockets of alpine flowers. Hidden from distant view are

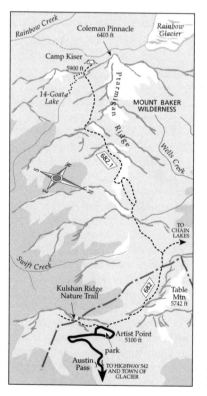

lush meadows, rock piles teeming with conies, and green slopes loud with whistling marmots. End the hike either at the informal area known as Camp Kiser or at an ice-bound, unnamed lake. This hike has no single destination; a party may go a short way until stopped by snow or continue a long way to close-up views of the splendid Rainbow Glacier or accept the invitation of sidetrips. Everything is purely delightful.

But a note of warning: Between hikers slipping on snow and those getting lost in a cloud, this is (as the rangers know all too well) a danger-ous trail! Ptarmigan Ridge is basi-cally "climbers' country." Parts of the trail are snowbound until late August and some years it never melts out at all. Do not attempt—do not even think about—crossing a steep snowpatch. Turn back and try another year. In late summer of light-snowfall years, in good weather, hikers can venture into the wild and

Campsite on Mount Baker's Ptarmigan Ridge

lonesome highland, but even then they must be well equipped and experienced. In fog, even skilled alpine navigators become confused; spur ridges may be mistaken for the main ridge and lead a party far astray.

Drive to the large Artist Point parking area, elevation 5100 feet, and hike the Chain Lakes trail 1 fairly level mile (Hike 19) to the Ptarmigan Ridge trail No. 682.1 junction, elevation 5200 feet.

At the junction go straight ahead on the Ptarmigan Ridge trail, dropping 200 feet into a moonscape of rock and snow. However, in mid-August the basin has bright patches of yellow and pink mimulus (monkeyflower) and bright green mosses. In the middle of the basin the trail splits. Go either way. Climb in volcanic rubble to the ridge line, the beginning of Ptarmigan Ridge. The trail improves, ascending into greenery. Traverse the south side of a very steep hillside; the trail has a neat fence of vegetation that gives a false sense of security, but a misstep could be extremely serious.

The farther one goes the greater the views as the trail traverses flower-covered hillsides and rockslides. At 3½ miles, 5900 feet, on the side of Coleman Pinnacle is a vista of the Rainbow Glacier, flowing from the top of Mt. Baker. A great place to break out the root beer and crackers, contemplate life, and swat flies.

From here the choice is between climbing another 300 feet in ½ mile to a big area known as Camp Kiser, or descending 300 feet in ½ mile to the gray-greenish, cold-looking "14-Goat Lake," only recently emerged from the Ice Age. The name was given by hikers watching a band of fourteen mountain goats feeding there.

21 | ELBOW LAKE

Round trip: From the north,
7½ miles
Hiking time: 5 hours
Elevation gain: 1400 feet

High point: 3450 feet
Trip length: One day or backpack
Hikable: Mid-July through October
Map: Green Trails No. 45 Hamilton

Round trip: From the south, 3 miles
Hiking time: 2 hours
Elevation gain: 300 feet in, 100
feet out

Information: Mount Baker Ranger
Station, phone (360) 856-5700.
Ask about trail No. 697.

Three (well, really two and a half) forest-ringed lakes in a narrow cleft
of Sister Divide. Come alone and you'll find peace and quiet. Take your pick
of the two approaches; the northern is easier on the car and has one great
view; the southern is easier on the hiker but has long miles of dirt road and
just one view and it is from the car, though it is almost worth the drive.

For the northern approach, drive Highway 542 to just short of milepost
17 and the hamlet of Welcome. Turn right and go 5 miles on the Mosquito
Lake road. At Porter Creek, go left on road No. 38 for 4.9 miles and go left
again, staying on road No. 38. At 11.4 miles from the Mosquito Lake road is
trail No. 697, elevation 2100 feet.

Begin by descending to the river. Cross on a horse bridge, skirt a
swampy area, and start a steady ascent along Green Creek. At 2 miles, in a

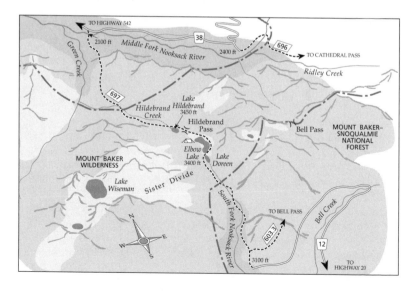

grove of Alaska cedar, a view briefly opens up the valley to the reddish rock of Twin Sisters and Skookum Peak. Back in deep woods, the way parallels Hildebrand Creek, which goes dry in late summer.

At 3 miles, 3450 feet, cross Hildebrand Pass by small, marshy Lake (half a lake) Hildebrand. Continue ½ mile to much larger Elbow Lake, 3400 feet, with several small but comfortable campsites. From the far shore climb a rise to Lake Doreen, boxed in by steep hillsides that cramp the camping.

For the southern approach, drive Highway 20 from Sedro Woolley 16.5 miles and go left on the Baker Lake–Grandy Lake road 12 miles to the national forest boundary. Continue 0.2 mile and go left on road No. 12, signed for the Nooksack River and the Mt. Baker National Recreation Area. Pass road No. 13 at 3.6 miles. At 7 miles keep right and cross the divide between the Baker River and the South Fork Nooksack River. At 8.4 miles pass road No. 1240 and a seasonal wildlife gate; in 14 miles pass Pioneer Camp and the Elbow Lake horse trail. If the road remains drivable, proceed a final 3.6 miles to the upper trailhead, elevation 3100 feet, for an easy 1½-mile walk.

Elbow Lake

22 | CATHEDRAL PASS

Round trip: 19½ miles
Hiking time: 8 hours
High point: 4962 feet
Elevation gain: 2900 feet in, 400 feet out

Loop trip: 25 miles
Hiking time: Allow 2 to 3 days
High point: 4962 feet
Elevation gain: 5400 feet

Trip length: One day or backpack
Hikable: Mid-July through October

Map: Green Trails No. 45 Hamilton
Information: Mount Baker Ranger Station, phone (360) 856-5700. Ask about trails No. 603, 690, 697.

A little-used trail skims ridges and roams meadows to touch the very edge of the mighty glaciers on the south side of Mt. Baker. Why so little use? Because there's a much shorter approach via Schreibers Meadow (Hike 23, Park Butte—Railroad Grade). But why be in such a rush all the time? Half the fun of a hike is the getting there. The longer the trail, the more the fun. However, don't do this one until July 1; before that the entire upper valley of the South Fork Nooksack River is restricted, and the road gated, to let cow elks drop their calves undisturbed.

The loop trip can start at either the north or south approach to Elbow Lake (Hike 21) but is described here from the south, the beginning of the day hike.

Mount Baker from Cathedral Pass trail

Drive the Baker Lake–Grandy Lake road and turn left on Loomis-Nooksack road No. 12 (Hike 21). Drive 17.6 miles to the road-end, elevation 3100 feet.

Hike the Elbow Lake trail a scant ½ mile and turn right on Bell Pass trail No. 603.3. At 2 miles cross the Sister Divide from the south to the north side at Bell Pass, 3964 feet, and enter the Mount Baker Wilderness. Views extend west to the Twin Sisters Range, north over the chainsaw massacre of the Middle Fork Nooksack River, and east to the gigantic dazzlement of Mt. Baker.

At 5 miles overlook Ridley Creek, then drop 400 feet to traverse beneath massive cliffs on the north side of Park Butte and into the meadows of Mazama Park and to the officially designated camping area for the Park Butte vicinity. At about 7 miles is the junction with Ridley Creek trail No. 690, 4400 feet.

For a must-do sidetrip, go right and climb steeply ¾ mile, switchbacking to the narrow slot of Cathedral Pass, 4870 feet. (A hiker-only camp here.) A few feet farther the trail joins the path along the crest of Railroad Grade (Hike 23), as the lateral moraine of Easton Glacier is called, for climax views of a volcano, a crater (perhaps steaming), and a world solely of snow and ice.

Loopers in the mood for a 21-mile day or backpack can round rocky Cathedral Crag and descend Ridley Creek trail No. 690 to a crossing of the Middle Fork Nooksack River—perhaps on a skinny log but probably by fording, best done in early morning when water is reasonable. Another ¼ mile ends in road No. 38, which in 1.7 miles reaches Elbow Lake trail No. 697 (Hike 21). Follow it over the Sister Divide past Elbow Lake and return to road No. 12.

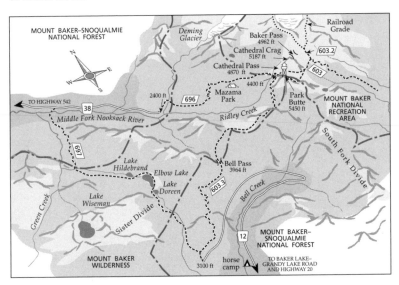

23 | PARK BUTTE—RAILROAD GRADE

Round trip: To Park Butte, 7 miles
Hiking time: 6 hours
High point: 5450 feet
Elevation gain: 2200 feet
Trip length: One day or backpack

Hikable: Mid-July through October
Map: Green Trails No. 45 Hamilton
Information: Mount Baker Ranger
Station, phone (360) 856-5700.
Ask about trail No. 603.

Recommending any one hike in the parklands of Mt. Baker's southwest flank is like praising a single painting in a museum of masterpieces. There are days of wandering here, exploring meadows and moraines, waterfalls and lakes, listening to marmots and watching for mountain goats. The trail to Morovitz Meadow gives a good sampling of the country, with impressive near views of the glaciers of Baker, the towering Black Buttes (core of an ancient volcano much larger than Baker), the Twin Sisters, and far horizons. This is the most popular hike on Baker's southern flanks. On weekends expect to meet hundreds of mountain climbers, hikers in street shoes and dress shirts, little children in sandals, and—curiously enough—horses, incomprehensibly encouraged by the Forest Service on the crowded trail.

Drive Highway 20 east from Sedro Woolley, between mileposts 82 and 83 go left on the Baker Lake–Grandy Lake road. In 12.5 miles, just past the Rocky Creek bridge, turn left on Loomis-Nooksack road No. 12. At 1.8 miles keep straight ahead, at 3.6 miles go right on Sulphur Creek road No.

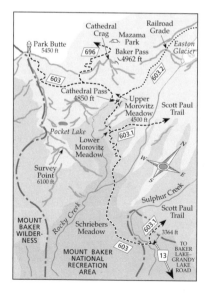

13 for 6 miles to the end. Find the trail west of the road, near the outhouse, elevation 3364 feet.

The trail immediately crosses Sulphur Creek into the heather and blueberries (in season) of Schriebers Meadow, passes frog ponds, and enters forest. In 1 mile is Rocky Creek, an interesting area where meltwater from the Easton Glacier has torn wide avenues through the trees. The drainage pattern changes from time to time; the creek can be crossed on a bouncing cable bridge but some years the bridge spans a dry wash and the creek must be waded.

Beyond the boulder-and-gravel area the trail enters cool forest and switchbacks steeply a long mile to

Lower Morovitz Meadow (watch out for horses). At the last switchback the Scott Paul Trail (Hike 24) goes straight ahead. The main trail goes left, and the grade gentles in heather fields leading to Upper Morovitz Meadow, 4500 feet.

At the trail junction in the upper meadow, go left to Park Butte, climbing to a ridge and in 1 mile reaching the 5450-foot summit. Views of Mt. Baker glaciers (and much more) are magnificent. Parties with spare time and energy may well be tempted to descend to the delightful basin of Pocket Lake or roam the ridge to 6100-foot Survey Point.

There is another direction to go from Upper Morovitz Meadow. Leave the trail near the junction and ramble upward on "the stairway to Heaven," the intriguing crest of Railroad Grade, a moraine deposited by the Easton Glacier in more ambitious days. Look down the unstable wall of gravel and boulders to the naked wasteland below the ice. Walk the tightrope crest higher and yet higher, closer and closer to the gleaming volcano. In late summer hikers can scramble moraine rubble and polished slabs to about 7000 feet before being forced to halt at the edge of the glacier.

From Railroad Grade inventive walkers can pick private ways through waterfall-and-flower country to the edge of a startling chasm. Look down to the chaotic front of the Deming Glacier, across to stark walls of the Black Buttes. All through the wide sprawl of Mazama Park are secluded campsites, beauty spots to explore.

Camping is not allowed at the tarns under Park Butte but there are designated campsites, some among alpine trees, some in open gardens beside snowmelt streams; all are scenic.

Snout of Easton Glacier

24 | SCOTT PAUL TRAIL

Round trip: To Squak Glacier, 7 miles
Hiking time: 6 hours
High point: 5800 feet
Elevation gain: 2400 feet

Loop trip: 8 miles
Hiking time: 5 hours
High point: 5200 feet
Elevation gain: 2300 feet

Trip length: One day; no fires
Hikable: Mid-July through October
Map: Green Trails No. 45 Hamilton

Information: Mount Baker Ranger Station, phone (360) 856-5700. Ask about trail No. 603.1.

A looping route gives a variety of perspectives on Mt. Baker, vistas of the North Cascades, looks down to the snouts of the Easton and Squak Glaciers, and a world of meadows to roam. A one-way trip to the Squak overlook offers a goodly sample of the riches. Scott Paul Trail was named for the young ranger who nursed the trail from conception to completion before he died in 1993 in a forest-related accident.

Drive to the Schriebers Meadow parking area (Hike 23, Park Butte—Railroad Grade), elevation 3364 feet.

For the one-way trip to the Squak Glacier, follow Park Butte trail No. 603 about 100 feet and turn right on Scott Paul Trail No. 603.1, which climbs steadily through forest, gaining 1200 feet in a scant 2½ miles to a 4600-foot saddle and the first views. To the right ¼ mile is a great view of Baker, Blum, and Shuksan. A well-used way trail from the saddle steeply climbs meadows in ever-enlarging views of Shuksan, the Pickets, and south along the Cascade Range to Mt. Rainier.

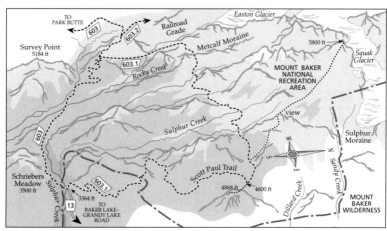

Mount Shuksan from Scott Paul Trail

Directly above is the sharp point of Sherman Peak on the crater rim. The way trail fades out at about 5800 feet and a summit-climbers' route goes onto the Squak Glacier; but this is the end of the line for hikers. Sit! Look! It is enough.

Those who want a loop do it best clockwise, hiking the Park Butte—Railroad Grade trail as described in Hike 23 to the last switchback. Instead of going left, go straight ahead on the Scott Paul Trail as it contours west through meadows, crosses streams to Metcalf Moraine, drops below the snout of the Easton Glacier, crosses Rocky Creek on a suspension bridge, and with ups and downs and in and outs contours a lightly forested hillside to the 4600-foot saddle, closing the loop.

25 | NOISY-DIOBSUD HIKES

Round trip: Anderson Butte, 4 miles
Hiking time: 4 hours
High point: 5420 feet
Elevation gain: 1100 feet
Trip length: One day

Round trip: Watson Lakes, 5 miles
Hiking time: 4 hours
High point: 4900 feet
Elevation gain: 800 feet in, 600 feet out
Trip length: One day or backpack

Round trip: Lower Anderson Lake, 6 miles
Hiking time: 4 hours
High point: 4900 feet
Elevation gain: 600 feet in, 600 feet out
Trip length: One day or backpack

Hikable: Late July through September
Map: Green Trails No. 46 Lake Shannon
Information: Baker River Ranger Station, phone; (360) 856-5700. Ask about trail No. 611.

Take your choices: If it's panoramas, the place for you is Anderson Butte, an old lookout site. Alpine lakes with a view into the Noisy-Diobsud Wilderness, the glaciers on Bacon Peak only a short 4 miles away? Watson Lakes are just right for you. A tarn ringed by meadows? Go for lower Anderson Lake. But don't be fooled by the scantiness of miles. No free rides here. Anderson Butte trail is darn steep, Watson Lakes trail has a 600-foot

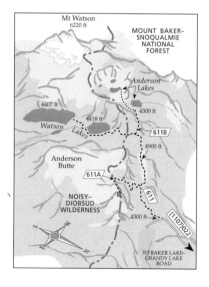

loss, and the final mile to (lower) Anderson Lake is a scratch path beaten out by hikers.

Drive Highway 20 east from Sedro Woolley. Between mileposts 82 and 83 go left on the Baker Lake–Grandy Lake road. Enter Mt. Baker–Snoqualmie National Forest at 12 miles, continue approximately 2 miles more, and turn right on the Baker Dam–Baker Campground road. In 1 mile drive over the Baker Lake Dam and in 2 miles go left on gravel road No. 1107. Follow this scenic road 9-plus miles to a junction and go left on road No.(1107)022 (steep and rough in places) to the trailhead, 10.5 miles from the dam, elevation 4300 feet.

The first mile climbs steadily through a cool forest to the edge of a ⅓-mile-long meadow and the junction of the Anderson Butte trail.

For the butte, go left on the trail built in the 1920s for packhorses. The lookout they supported was removed in 1964 and the tread also is pretty much gone. Lay out your map, line it up with Mt. Baker and Mt. Shuksan, and try to figure out the maze of peaks and glaciers to the north and east.

For the lakes, keep right at the junction, climbing the long meadow of red and white heather and, in the fall, lots of blueberries. At the 4900-foot pass at the top of the meadow, the friendly trail turns mean and drops a very steep 200 feet to the junction of the Watson Lakes and (lower) Anderson Lake trails, 2 miles from the road.

The right fork drops another 400 feet in a scant mile to Lower Anderson Lake, 4300 feet, and a great view of Baker.

The left fork climbs 200 feet to a 4900-foot saddle and drops 400 feet through flower-covered meadows to the first Watson Lake, 4418 feet, 2½ miles from the road. The trail ends in a scant ½ mile more at the second and much larger Watson Lake, 4407 feet.

The upper Watson Lakes

26 | BOULDER RIDGE

Round trip: 8 miles
Hiking time: 7 hours
High point: 4500 feet
Elevation gain: 1800 feet
Trip length: One day or backpack
Hikable: July through October

Map: Green Trails No. 46 Lake Shannon
Information: Mount Baker Ranger Station, phone (360) 856-5700. Ask about trail No. 605.

A rough hike to one of the many alpine ridges radiating octopus-like from the white heap of Mt. Baker. The crest provides a magnificent overlook of the Boulder Glacier. Budget problems have postponed planned reconstruction. The trailhead will be the same, but the trail route will change. The old one is described here.

Drive Highway 20 east from Sedro Woolley. Between mileposts 82 and 83 go left on the Baker Lake–Grandy Lake road. At 12 miles enter the national forest and continue another 5.8 miles; a scant 0.2 mile beyond the Boulder Creek bridge, turn left on Marten Lake road No. 1130. In 1.5 miles go left on road No. 1131 for 4.3 miles to the road-end and trailhead, elevation 2700 feet.

Trail No. 605 goes up and down, through bogs and waist-high huckleberry bushes, gaining only 300 feet in 2 miles. Then, ¼ mile after crossing a little stream, the tread vanishes in a small, marshy meadow; no formal trail ever existed beyond here. At the far right side of the meadow is an obscure blaze and the start of a climbers' path angling leftward toward the ridge crest. The track is steep, alternating among evergreen trees and slide alder. Some 500 feet above the meadow the way bursts from timber onto a moraine grown up in knee-high firs and hemlocks.

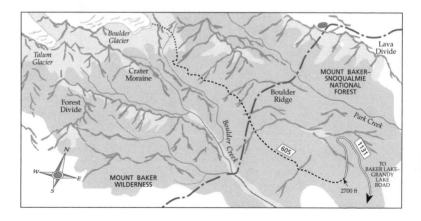

There is now a choice: an easy ¾-mile hike, the route obvious, to the top of the moraine and a close view of Boulder Glacier, or an ascent of 500 feet in 1 mile to Boulder Ridge.

Weather-exposed but scenic camps are possible on the ridge; plan to cook on a stove; water may be supplied by snowfield dribbling.

Baker Lake (reservoir) from Boulder Ridge trailhead

27 | **RAINBOW RIDGE**

Round trip: 4½ miles
Hiking time: 3 hours
High point: 4800 feet
Elevation gain: 1200 feet
Trip length: One day or backpack
Hikable: August through September

Map: Green Trails No. 14 Mt.
Shuksan (trail not shown)
Information: Mount Baker Ranger
Station, phone (360) 856-5700
(trail not officially recognized).

The meadows are simply grand, the looks down to Avalanche Gorge are awesome, and the views of the spectacular south face of Mt. Chalkone across the valley and the crevasses of the Park Glacier close at hand can be a mystical experience. Moreover, the path was built solely by boots, gets limited maintenance, is not shown on maps, and is barely visible on the ground, so the chances of solitude are much better than on the average Mt. Baker trail.

Drive Marten Lake road No. 1130 (Hike 26, Boulder Ridge), passing road No. 1131 at 1.5 miles, road No. 1144 and Rainbow Falls at 4.4 miles. At 9.4 miles is an unmarked trailhead, elevation 3600 feet. The last 4 miles of this road are minimally maintained; some years they are passable, other times they must be walked—all the better for soaking in the splendid views.

The boot-built path, easy to lose, weaves around trees and over logs, across a massive blowdown, through huckleberry thickets. If you lose it, don't play guessing games—backtrack to the last spot the trail was definite and try again. The way gains 800 feet in the first mile to a small meadow with a tantalizing glimpse of Mt. Baker. In the next ¼ mile it gains 250 feet to meadows on the crest of Rainbow Ridge, 4400 feet, and views across the gulf of Swift Creek to the ramparts of Mt. Chalkone.

In fields of heather and alpine blueberries, alternating between views of Mt. Chalkone and Mt. Baker, the trail rides the ups and downs of the ridge crest to a 4800-foot high point. This is a great place to call it quits, to get out

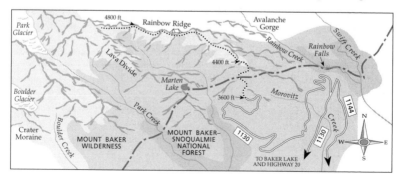

Mount Shuksan from heather-covered Rainbow Ridge

the watermelon and the freeze-dried pizza, to gaze a vertical 2000 feet down into Avalanche Gorge, to admire the snout of the Rainbow Glacier. The trail fades on the way to the next high point, then vanishes; one suspects the construction hereabouts was less by boots than goat feet.

Camps atop the ridge are sensational, with views of the rosy sunset on Chalkone's cliffs and the pink sunrise on Baker's glaciers. However, the only water is from snowbanks, if any. So carry two watermelons. Either that or have supper at the car, hike to the ridge in twilight, and return to the car for breakfast. Camp near the trail so that if a low cloud slips in by night you can find the way down. The vicinity of a 2000-foot cliff is no place to be searching for goat tracks in the fog.

28 | RAINBOW CREEK

Round trip: To Swift Creek, 4 miles
Hiking time: 3 hours
High point: 1600 feet
Elevation gain: 400 feet in, 200 feet out
Trip length: One day or backpack

Hikable: May through October
Map: Green Trails No. 14 Mt. Shuksan

Round trip: To Rainbow Creek, 1 mile
Hiking time: ¾ hour
High point: 1400 feet
Elevation gain: 200 feet out
Trip length: One day

Information: Mount Baker Ranger Station, phone (360) 856-5700. Ask about trail No. 607.

Once upon a time, in days not so olden but that some folks still on the trails don't remember them fondly, the 10-mile trail from Baker Lake to Austin Pass was a major thoroughfare heavily trampled by the Old Rangers, the dirty miners in search of shining gold, and miscellaneous bushwhackers. Nowadays, of course, the parking lot at Austin Pass is generally considered such small satisfaction for walking 10 uphill miles that the old "Swift Creek" trail has been mostly abandoned by the Forest Service and returned to nature ain't it wonderful.

However, the lowermost stretch of the trail is maintained and offers a delightful walk through magnificently virgin forest as far as Rainbow Creek, a glacial torrent whose raging keeps out human feet, thus preserving a wild wilderness as a refuge for wildlife, who badly need some quiet time in a boot-thudding world.

From Highway 20 drive the Baker Lake–Grandy Lake road 20 miles, to just opposite the entrance to Baker Lake Resort. Turn left on road No. 1144 and drive 3 miles to trail No. 607, elevation 1400 feet. Very limited parking.

The trail drops some 200 feet in ½ mile through marvelous old forest to Rainbow Creek. Admire the raging torrent, then take a very slow pace

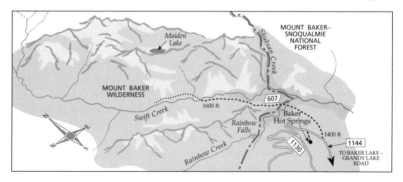

Swift Creek from end of trail

back the ½ mile, the more fully to absorb the good juices from the primeval scene.

This is not to say the wildlife cannot tolerate a few quiet, respectful boots inside their refuge. If you qualify, and if you find a logjam, on the far side the former trail follows within sound of Rainbow Creek, whose mists nourish the moss carpet of the forest floor, and enters Mount Baker Wilderness. After ¼ mile of minor ups and downs, it switchbacks up 300 feet in ½ mile, then levels off and plunges into brush as high as a tall hiker's eye. The tread is as easy to find at night as in day; feet have to do it. At 2 miles, 1600 feet, the way touches the bank of Swift Creek, and is then passable all the way to Austin Pass. It is, that is, if you can first cross Swift "Creek," whose raging on this end combine with the raging on the Rainbow end to preserve a peaceful travel route for animals. When the grizzlies are reintroduced here, they will reinforce the raging.

29 | SHANNON RIDGE

Round trip: 6 miles
Hiking time: 5 hours
High point: 4800 feet
Elevation gain: 2300 feet
Trip length: One day
Hikable: July through September

Map: Green Trails No. 14 Mt.
Shuksan (trail not shown)
Information: Mount Baker Ranger
Station, phone (360) 856-5700.
Ask about trail No. 742.

Park Service backcountry use permit required for camping in the park

Heather-covered Shannon Ridge gives the really big picture of Mt. Baker, lofting high above the canyon depths of Swift and Shuksan Creeks, and the champion views across Baker Lake (reservoir, that is) to glaciers on Hagan Mountain and Mt. Blum. Getting there demands much blood in fly time, a lot of sweat on hot days, and occasionally a fair number of tears.

Drive from Highway 20 on the Baker Lake–Grandy Lake road 23 miles (10.2 miles beyond the national forest boundary) to just opposite Shannon Creek Campground. Turn left on road No. 1152 and drive 4.5 miles. Go right on road No. (1152)014 (unsigned in 1998) another 1.4 miles, to where it becomes impassable, elevation 2500 feet. Very limited parking.

Begin on an abandoned logging road overgrown with willows. At about 1 mile this road/trail enters a steep basin (see the meadows high above, keep the faith) and switchbacks twice. At 1½ miles the road ends and trail No. 742 (unsigned) begins, elevation 3200 feet. The trail climbs a steep, brush-covered clearcut of 1980 or so and still not reforested, a heritage of the era when the high priests of the College of Forestry taught that trees could be farmed to timberline.

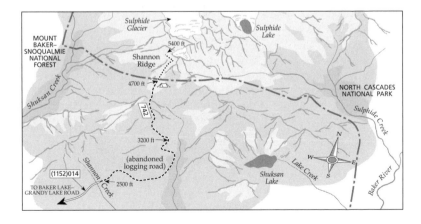

Then, virgin forest (ain't Nature wonderful?). Alternating between steep and very steep, at about 2½ miles the trail gains the ridge top and with a little down and a lot of ups leaves forest for heather meadows. The recommended turnaround is some 3 miles from the car, at the boundary of the North Cascades National Park, 4700 feet. The views climax here and camping is possible on both sides of the boundary; sites on the inside have the best water and sleeping-bag spreads, but do require some paperwork.

A rude climbers' path leads to a 5400-foot pass directly above. The views there are nothing special and when snow-covered the route is slippery.

Mount Baker from Shannon Ridge

30 | BAKER RIVER

Round trip: 6 miles
Hiking time: 3 to 4 hours
High point: 900 feet
Elevation gain: 200 feet
Trip length: One day or backpack
Hikable: March through November

Map: Green Trails No. 14 Mt.
Shuksan (trail not shown)
Information: Mount Baker Ranger
Station, phone (360) 856-5700.
Ask about trail No. 606.

Park Service backcountry use permit required for camping

Luxuriant rain forest, a lovely milky-green river, and tantalizing glimpses of glacier-covered peaks. Because of the very low elevation (and such low-altitude virgin valleys are now rare indeed in the Cascades), the trail is open except in midwinter and offers a delightful wildland walk when higher elevations are buried in snow. Even bad weather is no barrier to enjoyment, not with all the big trees, understory plants, and streams. For true lonesomeness, try the trip on a rainy day in early spring. It's also a good place to escape guns during hunting season, since the no-shooting North Cascades National Park is entered partway along.

Drive from Highway 20 on the Baker Lake–Grandy Lake road to the national forest boundary and 18 miles more to the road-end; go left on road No. 1168 another 0.5 mile to the start of Upper Baker trail No. 606, elevation 760 feet.

The first ¼ mile lies on and near old logging roads, then civilization is left behind. In ½ mile is a junction with the Baker Lake trail, whose 240-foot bridge over the Baker River gives gasper views up to glaciers of 7683-foot Mt. Blum.

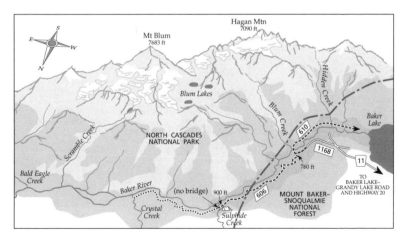

At 1 mile the trail climbs a few feet above the river, a beauty, and drops again to go by large beaver ponds. In 2 miles, about where the national park is entered, see Easy Ridge at the valley head and, a little farther on, the sharp outline of 7574-foot Whatcom Peak, northern outpost of the Pickets. In a scant 3 miles the way reaches raging Sulphide Creek, dominated by Jagged Ridge and its small glaciers. Partly hidden by trees is the huge expanse of the Sulphide Glacier on the south side of Mt. Shuksan.

If Sulphide Creek is high and a bridge is lacking, this is far enough for most hikers. The camp has four sites, elevation 900 feet.

The trail continues, sort of, 2 miles to Crystal Creek and once went 3 more miles to Bald Eagle Creek, 1100 feet. The upper section is now lost in brush and the best route beyond Crystal Creek is on gravel bars.

Baker River

31 | Cow Heaven

Round trip: 11 miles
Hiking time: 8 hours
High point: 4400 feet
Elevation gain: 4000 feet
Trip length: One day
Hikable: July through October

Map: Green Trails No. 47 Marblemount
Information: Marblemount Ranger Station, phone (360) 873-4500. Ask about trail No. 763.

Years ago, Skagit ranchers chased cows way up here to chew the alpine salads. Now only the occasional horse gobbles the flowers, so it's a heaven for hikers, with views from the Skagit Valley to the Pickets, Eldorado, Whitehorse, and countless peaks between. But the route to heaven lies through purgatory—gaining 4000 feet in 5½ miles. Moreover, from August onward a water shortage just about forces the trip to be done in a single grueling day. ("A pint's a pound, the world around," and a gallon on your back—a warm day's ration—is 8 pounds.) In early summer snowmelt may permit thirstless camping.

Drive Highway 20 to Marblemount. At the town's western edge turn north and drive 0.8 mile on the road signed "North Cascades National Park Wilderness Information Center." Drive past the center another 0.2 mile to the well-signed "New Cow Heaven trail," elevation a meager, low-down 400 feet.

Trail No. 763 is listed as 4 miles. Don't believe it—the best views are at least 5½ miles. Eager to get the job done, the path wastes no time flirting but starts steep and stays steep. The initial 2 miles are in fine shape, the tread wide and edged by soft moss, cooled by deep shadows of virgin forest. A

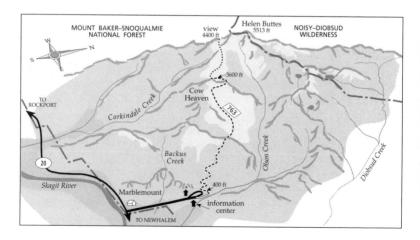

creek is crossed at 1 mile and recrossed at 1½ miles, the last for-sure water. At about 2½ miles the tread dips into a shallow ravine and for the next ½ mile often is gullied to naught. Just beyond 3 miles the way passes above an all-summer (usually) stream. Tall trees yield to short ones and at 4 miles to a dense tangle of mountain ash, white rhododendron, and huckleberry. At 4¼ miles, about 3600 feet, a brief flat with bits of heather invites camping but provides no lake, pond, river, creek, dribble, or spring, only a snow-field that may last into July.

Maintained trail ends here, but a sketchy path, beaten out mainly by hunters, heads over the knoll on the skyline, climbing to the 4400-foot viewpoint. If aggrieved leg muscles and swollen tongue permit, continue up the alpine ridge to steadily broader views.

Skagit Valley from Cow Heaven, with Whitehorse Mountain in distance

32 | LOOKOUT MOUNTAIN— MONOGRAM LAKE

Round trip: To Lookout Mountain, 8½ miles
Hiking time: 9 hours
High point: 5699 feet
Elevation gain: 4500 feet

Round trip: To Monogram Lake, 7½ miles
Hiking time: 9 hours
High point: 5400 feet
Elevation gain: 4200 feet in, 550 feet out

Trip length: One day or backpack
Hikable: July through October
Map: Green Trails No. 47 Marblemount

Information: Marblemount Ranger Station, phone (360) 873-4500. Ask about trail 743.

Park Service backcountry use permit required for camping at Monogram Lake

What's your pleasure? A fire lookout with a commanding view of North Cascades peaks and valleys? Or a cirque lake, a fine basecamp for roaming, nestled in the side of a heather-covered ridge? Or both?

Drive Highway 20 to Marblemount and continue east 7.3 miles on the Cascade River road to the trailhead between Lookout and Monogram Creeks, elevation 1255 feet.

The trail climbs steeply in a series of short switchbacks along the spine of the forested ridge between the two creeks, gaining 2400 feet in the 2½ miles to a campsite at the first dependable water, a branch of Lookout Creek at 3600 feet. At 2¾ miles is a junction, elevation 4100 feet.

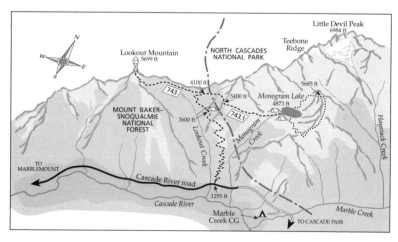

Lookout Mountain and Eldorado Peak

Lookout Mountain. Go left from the junction, shortly emerging into meadow and switchbacking relentlessly upward. The tread here may be hard to find and difficult to walk. In 1½ miles from the junction, gaining 1500 feet, the 5699-foot summit is attained.

Flowers all around—and views. Look north and west to the Skagit River valley, southeast and below to the Cascade River. Mountains everywhere, dominated by giant Eldorado Peak. About ¼ mile below the summit, in a small flat, is a spring that runs most of the summer. Magnificent camps here for enjoyment of the scenery in sunset and dawn—but disaster camps in a storm.

Monogram Lake. Traverse right from the junction on a steep, lightly timbered hillside. The trail leaves trees for meadow and in a mile crosses a creek, climbs to a 5400-foot crest with broad views, and descends to 4873-foot Monogram Lake, usually snowbound through July. Designated no-fire campsites around the meadow shores.

The lake is a superb base for wanderings. For one, climb open slopes to the southeast and then follow the ridge northerly to a 5685-foot knoll looking down into Marble Creek and across to the splendor of 8868-foot Eldorado—a closer and even better view of the peak than that from Lookout Mountain. Continue on the ridge for more flowers, then drop through gardens to the lake. For a more ambitious tour, ascend meadows on the southern extension of Teebone Ridge and ramble to the 6984-foot south summit of Little Devil Peak, with looks down to small glaciers. Climbers can continue on and on along the rocky-and-snowy ridge, but hikers must stop when the terrain gets too rough for party experience.

Mostly unprotected area, partly in North Cascades National Park

33 | HIDDEN LAKE PEAKS

Round trip: To Sibley Creek Pass, 6 miles

Hiking time: 5 hours

High point: 6050 feet

Elevation gain: 2700 feet

Trip length: One day

Hikable: July through October

Map: Green Trails No. 47 Marblemount

Round trip: To Hidden Lake Lookout, 8 miles

Hiking time: 8 hours

High point: 6890 feet

Elevation gain: 3500 feet

Trip length: One day or backpack

Hikable: August through October

Information: Marblemount Ranger Station, phone (360) 873-4500. Ask about trail 745.

Park Service backcountry use permit required for camping at Hidden Lake

Flower fields, heather meadows, ice-carved rocks, and snow-fed waterfalls on an alpine ridge jutting into an angle of the Cascade River valley, an easy-to-reach viewpoint of North Cascades wilderness from Eldorado through the Ptarmigan Traverse to Dome Peak.

Drive Highway 20 to Marblemount and continue east on the Cascade River road 10 miles (2 miles past the Marble Creek bridge) to road No. 1540, signed "Hidden Lake Peak." Turn left and drive 4.7 miles to the road-end (the way rough but passable to suitably small and spry cars) in a 1950s clearcut, elevation 3600 feet.

Trail No. 745 begins in "second growth" brush that decades after the logging still doesn't look much like a "renewable resource," entering virgin forest in ¼ mile and switchbacking upward 1 mile. The way then emerges from trees into lush avalanche brush and crosses East Fork Sibley Creek. (Some years avalanche snow may linger in the creek bottom all summer, in which case look for the obvious trail cut through very steep sidehill greenery.) The trail switchbacks up alder clumps and deep grass and flowers to a recrossing of Sibley Creek at 2½ miles, 5200 feet. Note, here, the abrupt transition from metamor-

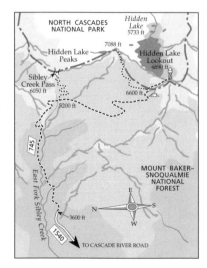

Mostly unprotected area, partly in North Cascades National Park

phic to granitic rocks, the first supporting richly green herbaceous flora, the other dominated by heather. Just past the crossing is a minimal little campsite.

From the second crossing the trail traverses wide-open heather-and-waterfall slopes, then rounds a corner and climbs. One snow-filled gully may be too treacherous for hikers lacking ice axes. If so, don't attempt to cross, but instead go straight uphill to find a safe detour, or turn back and visit Sibley Creek Pass. The trail may be snow-covered at other points but by proceeding straight ahead the tread can be picked up. At 3½ miles is a tiny basin, a lovely non-storm campsite. The abandoned lookout cabin can now be seen atop cliffs. Continue a short way, usually on a gentle snowfield, to the 6600-foot saddle and look down to Hidden Lake and out to a world of wild peaks.

Though it's only ½ mile and 300 feet from the saddle to the broader views of the 6890-foot lookout (maintained by volunteers), parts of the trail may be lost in extremely dangerous snow, suited only for trained climbers. Even without snow the final section of trail is airy.

From the saddle an easy off-trail walk over loose boulders leads to the 7088-foot highest summit of Hidden Lake Peak. Or descend rough talus to the 5733-foot lake, ordinarily snowbound through most of the summer. Designated no-fire campsites above the lake.

Hidden Lake Peak Lookout

34 | BOSTON BASIN

Round trip: To first high moraine,
7 miles
Hiking time: 8 hours
High point: 6200 feet
Elevation gain: 3000 feet
Trip length: One day or backpack;
no fires

Hikable: July through October
Maps: Green Trails No. 48 Diablo
Lake, No. 80 Cascade Pass
(trail not shown)
Information: Marblemount Ranger
Station, phone (360) 873-4500

Park Service backcountry use permit required for camping

When Forbidden Peak was included in a book as one of the "50 classic climbs in North America," the meadowlands of Boston Basin were infested by climbers from all over North America lusting for the 50 Peak Pin. Since a normal hiker, finding him-/herself amid a throng of sixty or seventy peak baggers clicking carabiners, is liable to start screaming, and since the trail is unmaintained and poor, and since the camping is lousy, why go? Well, on a Tuesday or Thursday in late October, when the classicists are back in school, a person might just sneak up to the basin for a day and find the solitude proper for savoring the contrast of yellowing meadows and gray moraines and white glaciers.

Drive Highway 20 to Marblemount and continue east on the Cascade River road 22.5 miles to the junction with the former Value Mines sideroad,

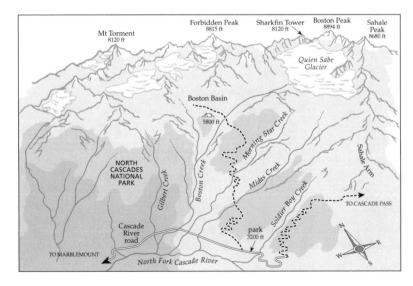

ransomed from privateers with public money. Parking for six to eight cars, elevation 3200 feet.

Walk 1 steep mile on the abandoned "mining" road. Just past the fourth switchback the views open up and the old road levels off. Watch carefully now: A few feet farther, near some boulders, is a switchback; for a short bit the way is true trail, then road again. At the end of the road the trail turns steeply up and deteriorates into a very difficult climbers' scramble-path (no wonder it is not on a map) that intersects an ancient prospectors' trail. Prospectors of old did neater trail work than modern climbers, so things improve. Vintage tread leads through a short bit of woods and then across a ½-mile-wide swath of avalanche greenery, down which tumble Midas Creek and Morning Star Creek. Next come switchbacks in deep forest to a broken-down cabin of a long-ago prospector.

Mount Johannesburg from Boston Basin

About ½ mile from the cabin ruins the trail emerges from timber and swings around the foot of an open moraine to a raging torrent; boulder-hop across (the best crossing is upstream from where the trail meets the creek) and climb to a viewpoint atop the moraine. Look up to the fearsome cliffs and spires of Forbidden Peak and Mt. Torment, and to the glacier falling from Boston and Sahale Peaks, and across the valley to the mile-high wall of Johannesburg and its fingerlike hanging glaciers.

For one exploration of Boston Basin, traverse and climb westward over moraines and creeks to rich-green, marmot-whistling flower fields and beyond the waterfalls pouring down ice-polished buttresses under Mt. Torment. For another exploration, look for intermittent tread of an old prospectors' trail that ascends a moraine crest to tunnels and artifacts close under Sharkfin Tower, right next to the glacier falling from Boston Peak.

To conclude, there's a world of wandering in Boston Basin, if you can get there when the place isn't up to the scuppers in ropes and hard hats. However, absolutely no camping is allowed in the meadows. You must stay at the 5800-foot "climbers' camp," three sites, bouldery and wretched, just above timberline between the forks of Boston Creek, or up high on the snow or rock; if in doubt, go with the latter.

35 | CASCADE PASS—SAHALE ARM

Round trip: To Cascade Pass,
　7 miles
Hiking time: 5 hours
High point: 5400 feet
Elevation gain: 1800 feet
Trip length: One day

Round trip: To Sahale Arm, 11 miles
Hiking time: 10 hours
High point: 6600 feet
Elevation gain: 3000 feet
Trip length: One day or backpack

Hikable: Mid-July through October
Map: Green Trails No. 80 Cascade
　Pass

Information: Marblemount Ranger
　Station, phone (360) 873-4500

Park Service backcountry use permit required for camping

A historic pass, crossed by Native Americans from time immemorial, by explorers and prospectors since early in the nineteenth century, and recently become famous as one of the most rewarding easy hikes in the North Cascades. But the beauty of the pass is only the beginning. An idyllic ridge climbs toward the sky amid flowers and creeklets of sparkling water and views that expand with every step.

Drive Highway 20 to Marblemount and continue east 23.2 miles on the Cascade River road to the road-end parking lot and trailhead, elevation 3600 feet.

In some thirty-three switchbacks, the 10 percent–grade "highway"

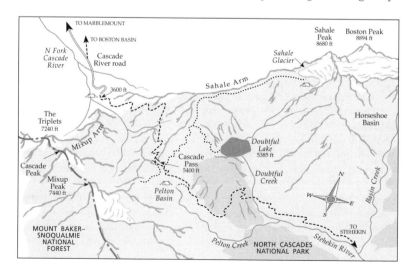

Eldorado Peak from Cascade Pass

climbs forest for about 2 miles, then makes a long, gently ascending traverse through parkland and meadows to Cascade Pass, 3½ miles, 5400 feet. Spectacular as the scenery is from the road-end, the hiker runs out of superlatives before reaching the pass. The 8200-foot mass of Johannesburg dominates: Hardly an hour goes by that a large or small avalanche doesn't break loose from its hanging glacier; several times a summer a huge section of ice roars all the way to the valley floor.

Cascade Pass retains its famous vistas, but during years of overuse the meadows were loved nearly to death. Camping and fires are now forbidden at the pass, and the Park Service has succeeded in rehabilitating the subalpine vegetation. A few campsites are available below the pass to the east, in Pelton Basin, enabling a longer stay for extended sidetrips. (There also are several cozy pack-in sites close by the road-end—as scenic camps as one could want.)

One short ¼-mile sidetrip from the pass, easy and quick, is the wandering way south up the meadow crest of Mixup Arm to a tiny tarn.

To explore the sky, climb north on a steep and narrow trail through meadows; find the start a few feet over the east side of the pass below a rock outcrop. In 1 mile and 800 feet the trail reaches the ridge crest and a junction. The right fork descends heather 800 feet in 1 mile to 5385-foot Doubtful Lake, a great hike in its own right, the shore cliffs riddled with old prospectors' holes.

However, Sahale Arm calls. Walk the old prospectors' trail up and along the gentle ridge of flowers, and up some more. Look down to the waterfall-loud cirque of Doubtful Lake and east into the Stehekin River valley. Look west to Forbidden Peak and the huge Inspiration Glacier on Eldorado. Look south to nine small glaciers on the first line of peaks beyond Cascade Pass. Walking higher, see range upon range of ice and spires, finally including the volcano of Glacier Peak. To see it all in sunset and starlight and dawn, continue on and camp in the rocks at the toe of the Sahale Glacier. This is permitted.

36 | THORNTON LAKES—TRAPPERS PEAK

Round trip: To Lower Thornton Lake, 9½ miles
Hiking time: 6 to 8 hours
High point: 5050 feet
Elevation gain: 2600 feet in, 400 feet out

Trip length: One day or backpack
Hikable: Mid-July through October
Map: Green Trails No. 47 Marblemount
Information: Marblemount Ranger Station, phone (360) 873-4500

Park Service backcountry use permit required for camping

Three deep lakes in rock basins gouged by a long-gone glacier. Close by are living glaciers, still gouging. All around are icy peaks on the west edge of the North Cascades National Park. From a summit above the lakes, a splendid view of Triumph and Despair and the Picket Range. Not realizing they are in a national park, many hikers come here with dogs and guns and without a permit, and go away with tickets. The camping is unpleasant to miserable and not recommended unless you're there for the fishing (which also is poor). Make it a day hike.

Drive Highway 20 east of Marblemount 11 miles to the Thornton Creek road, signed "Thornton Lakes"; spot it between mileposts 117 and 118. Turn left and drive 5 very steep and often rough miles to a parking area, elevation 2500 feet.

The first 2 miles are on an abandoned logging road. Then begins the trail, which was never really "built" but just grew; it's very steep in places and mucky in others. Except for where the abandoned road crosses clearcuts, most of the way lies in forest. At a bit more than 1 mile from the abandoned road is an opening and a small creek. The trail then switchbacks up a forested slope to the ridge crest.

Recuperate atop the 5050-foot ridge crest. Look down to the lake basin and out to Mt. Triumph. A miserable trail drops 500 difficult feet to the lowest and largest Thornton Lake. Across the outlet stream are poor campsites designated by posts; no fires allowed.

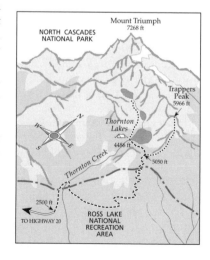

To reach the middle and upper lakes, traverse slopes west of the lower lake. The middle lake usually has some ice until the end of July; the upper lake, at 5000 feet in a steep-walled cirque, ordinarily is frozen until mid-August.

If views are the goal, don't drop to the lakes. Leave the trail at the 5050-foot crest and follow a faint climbers' track up the ridge to the 5966-foot summit of Trappers Peak. See the fantastic Pickets. And see, too, the little village of Newhalem far below in the Skagit Valley. The route is steep in places and requires use of the hands but is not really tough. Early in the season there may be dangerous snowpatches; go above or below them. Turn around content when the way gets too scary for plain-and-simple hikers.

Lower Thornton Lake and Mount Triumph

37 | SOURDOUGH MOUNTAIN

Round trip: To viewpoint, 7 miles
Hiking time: 6 hours
High point: 4800 feet
Elevation gain: 3900 feet
Trip length: One day
Hikable: May through October

Maps: Green Trails No. 48 Diablo
Dam, No. 16 Ross Dam

Round trip: To summit, 12½ miles
Hiking time: 12 hours
High point: 5985 feet
Elevation gain: 5100 feet
Trip length: One day or backpack
Hikable: July through October

Information: Marblemount Ranger
Station, phone (360) 873-4500

Park Service backcountry use permit required for camping

Want an incomparable view of the rocks and ice and forests of the North Cascades National Park? Lo! Look down to Diablo and Ross Lakes (reservoirs) of the drowned Skagit River and to forests of Thunder Creek. Look south to Colonial and Snowfield and southeast to Buckner and the sprawling Boston Glacier. Look east to the "King of the Skagit," Jack Mountain, and north to Canada, and northwest and west to the Pickets.

But you gotta really want it. No free lunch here. Even the "little" hike to the window view has so many switchbacks the hiker hardly can keep track of where he's headed, and doing the summit in a day is good training for the Olympic Games.

Drive Highway 20 east past Newhalem 5.3 miles to milepost 126. Turn left through the Seattle City Light hamlet of Diablo, past the houses to the trailhead beside the garages that are next to the covered swimming pool.

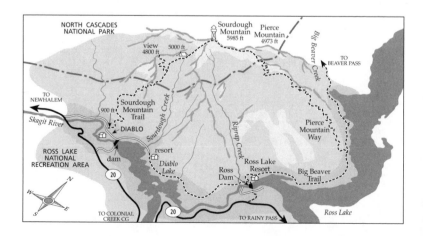

Diablo Lake (reservoir) from Sourdough Mountain trail

For a day hike park here; for an overnight proceed 0.3 mile to the main lot at the base of Diablo Dam, elevation 900 feet.

The dizzy-making switchbacks gain 3000 feet in the first 2 miles before the trail relents enough to go up a mere 2000 feet more, taking 4 miles to do it. That's a lot of huffing. Most day-hikers are more than content with the forest window view at 3½ miles, 4800 feet. For a look into the Pickets, follow the sidetrail to the former reflector site. Thanks to the southerly exposure, the way to here is often snowfree in May, and a spectacular springtime hike it is to the edge of winter.

Though dribbles can be found at several spots, the designated campsite at Sourdough Creek, 4½ miles, 5000 feet, has the only water supply sufficient to satisfy the mightiness of thirst and to rehydrate the freeze-dried hoosh. The final 2⅔ miles to the summit fire lookout are hardly enough to work out the leg cramps from the climb to the creek.

In fact, it's a darn shame to spend all that energy hauling your too too solid flesh (and pack) so high up in such scenery and the very next day taking on the descent, which has been known to decommission every knee in a Boy Scout troop. The summit itself demands a full day of just plain eyeball excursions. The legs can use the vacation. Exploring the tundras of Sourdough Ridge part or all the way to the startling upthrust of the Southern Pickets easily can fill a couple more days. Cross-country, no-fire camping is permitted and numerous nooks cry out for your sleeping bag.

Using the old horse trail on the northeast side of the mountain, experienced hikers can make a loop. However, the trail becomes so sketchy the loop is not recommended.

38 | PYRAMID LAKE

Round trip: 4½ miles
Hiking time: 3 hours
High point: 2630 feet
Elevation gain: 1550 feet
Trip length: One day

Hikable: May through October
Map: Green Trails No. 48 Diablo
Dam
Information: Marblemount Ranger
Station, phone (360) 873-4500

A trail in mostly spindly forest to a nondescript lakelet beneath the tower of 7182-foot Pyramid (actually, more cone-shaped) Peak. But popular! Climbers pass by on their way to and from ascents of Pyramid, Colonial, Paul Bunyan's Stump, and Snowfield—usually they do so before dawn and after dark, in a hurry, never so much as a glance at the little hole full of water. Fishermen don't come at all—no fish. No camping, either. So why the popularity? Because it is the first signed trail on the North Cascades Highway beyond Newhalem. Feet get itchy.

Drive Highway 20 east from Newhalem some 5 miles to the Diablo (town) junction. Keep right on the highway another 0.8 mile, crossing Gorge Lake (reservoir), and between mileposts 126 and 127 spot the signed trailhead, elevation 1100 feet. Park across the highway.

The trail climbs a short cliff and settles into a steady ascent of very young forest (from a not-long-ago fire) and a dense understory of salal. At about ¾ mile the vegetation becomes more exciting as the way enters a narrow valley of ancient giants, crosses a delightful creek, and continues uphill in a mixture of the young and the old, of the fir and the hemlock. At 2 miles note a monster of a Douglas fir leaning at such an impossible angle it surely can't last another day—as has obviously been true for a century or two.

At 2¼ miles is Pyramid Lake, 2630 feet. On two sides cliffs plunge to the water and continue on down; look deep into blue-green depths and see—not the bottom—but pale faces with staring eyes.

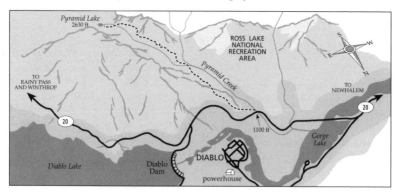

Pyramid Lake and Pyramid Mountain

39 | THUNDER CREEK

Round trip: To McAllister Creek, 12 miles
Hiking time: 5 to 7 hours
High point: 1800 feet
Elevation gain: 600 feet
Trip length: One day or backpack
Hikable: April through November

Round trip: To Park Creek Pass, 36 miles
Hiking time: Allow 3 to 5 days
High point: 6040 feet
Elevation gain: 5600 feet
Hikable: Late July through October

Maps: Green Trails No. 48 Diablo Dam, No. 49 Mt. Logan, No. 81 McGregor Mtn.

Information: Marblemount Ranger Station, phone (360) 873-4500

Park Service backcountry use permit required for camping

One of the master streams of the North Cascades, draining meltwater from an empire of glaciers. The first portion of the trail, easy walking, is nearly flat for miles, passing through groves of big firs, cedars, and hem-locks, in views of giant peaks. The route continues to a high pass amid these peaks; for experienced wilderness travelers, the crossing of the range from Thunder Creek over Park Creek Pass to the Stehekin River is a classic. Designated camps are scattered along the way, permitting easy stages.

Thunder Creek trail

From the west, drive Highway 20 beyond Newhalem 9.7 miles. Between mileposts 130 and 131 turn right and pass through Colonial Creek Campground 0.5 mile to the trailhead, elevation 1200 feet.

The trail follows Thunder Arm of Diablo Lake about 1 mile, crosses Thunder Creek on a bridge, and in another 1 mile comes to a junction. The left fork climbs to Fourth of July Pass and Panther Creek (Hike 41). The Thunder Creek trail continues straight ahead on the sidehill, going up and down a little, mainly in big trees except in a burn meadow from a 1971 lightning fire at 4¼ miles, and another from a 1970 fire at 5 miles; the openings give neck-stretching looks to the summits of Snowfield and Colonial. At about 2 and 2½ miles, respectively, are Thunder and Neve Camps.

At 5½ miles is the site of long-gone Middle Cabin, and ½ mile farther is the bridge to McAllister Creek Camp, a good turnaround for a day or weekend trip. The trail to here offers one of the best forest hikes in the North Cascades and is open to travel early in the season and late.

At 6 miles the way goes from national recreation area to national park; dogs must stop. At 7½ miles the trail crosses Fisher Creek to Tricouni Camp and in ½ mile more begins a 1000-foot climb above the valley floor, which upstream from here becomes a vastness of swamp and marsh forbidden (by Nature) to human entry. Following Fisher Creek all the way, at 9 miles the trail levels out at Junction Camp, 3000 feet, and a junction with the Fisher Creek trail (Hike 47).

Off the trail a bit are grand views down to the valley and across to glaciers of Tricouni and Primus Peaks. Beyond the junction ¼ mile an obscure spur trail descends 1000 feet in 1 mile to the two decrepit Meadow Cabins, at the edge of the "Great Dismal Swamp," largest in the North Cascades and as wild as any scene this side of Mars.

The main trail passes stunning viewpoints of the enormous Boston Glacier, Buckner and Boston and Forbidden thrusting above, drops steeply to the valley bottom at 2200 feet, and climbs to Skagit Queen Camp, 13 miles, 3000 feet, near where Skagit Queen Creek joins Thunder Creek. The way climbs, then gentles out somewhat in a hanging valley; at 15½ miles, 4300 feet, is the last designated campsite, Thunder Basin Camp. No fires. From here the trail ascends steadily up and around the meadow flanks of Mt. Logan to 6040-foot Park Creek Pass, 18 miles, a narrow rock cleft usually full of snow. To continue down to the Stehekin River, see Hike 51, Park Creek Pass.

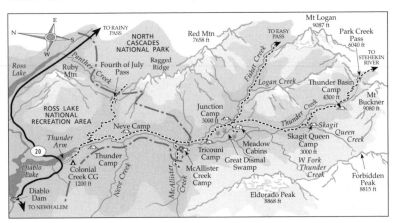

40 | BEAVER LOOP

Loop trip: 26½ miles
Hiking time: Allow 3 to 5 days
High point: 3620 feet
Elevation gain: 3500 feet
Hikable: June through October

Round trip: To Beaver Pass, 27 miles
Hiking time: Allow 2 to 3 days
High point: 3620 feet
Elevation gain: 2000 feet
Hikable: Late July through October

Maps: Green Trails No. 15 Mt.
Challenger, No. 16 Ross Lake

Information: Marblemount Ranger
Station, phone (360) 873-4500

Park Service backcountry use permit required for camping

This loop hike from Ross Lake to close views of the Picket Range and back to Ross Lake offers perhaps the supreme days-long forest experience in the North Cascades. The 27-mile trip up the Little Beaver Valley and down the Big Beaver Valley passes through groves of enormous cedars, old and huge Douglas firs and hemlocks, glimmery-ghostly silver fir, lush alder, young fir recently established after a fire (in 1926, enormous

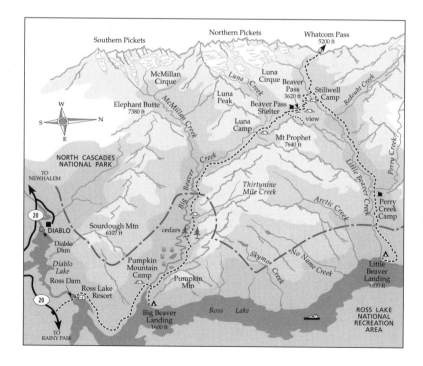

Big Beaver valley

acreages of the Skagit country burned), and many more species and ages of trees as well. And there are brawling rivers, marshes teeming with wildlife, and awesome looks at Picket glaciers and walls. While the hike is recommended as a loop, the Big Beaver trail to Beaver Pass makes a great round trip, though the Park Service has a severely limited budget and some years is unable to brush the trail.

Drive Highway 20 east from Marblemount to Colonial Creek Campground (see Hike 39). Go another 3.9 miles and between mileposts 134 and 135 park at the Ross Lake (reservoir) trailhead. Walk the trail to Ross Lake Resort (Hike 44, Desolation Peak) and arrange for water-taxi service up the reservoir and a pickup at trip's end. The loop (or day or weekend hikes) can begin at either end; the Little Beaver start is described here.

After a scenic ride up Ross Lake (reservoir), debark at Little Beaver

Landing; a campground here, elevation 1600 feet. The trail starts by switchbacking 300 feet to get above a canyon, then loses most of the hard-won elevation. At 4½ miles is Perry Creek Camp, an easy ford-or-footlog crossing of several branches of the creek, and a passage along the edge of a lovely marsh. At 9 miles is Redoubt Creek; scout around for a footlog. At 11½ miles, 2450 feet, is a junction.

The Little Beaver trail goes upstream 6 miles and 2800 feet to Whatcom Pass (Hike 17). Take the Big Beaver trail and cross Little Beaver Creek (a bridge is in place but the creek may not be under it; beware if you must wade—the creek isn't so little in early summer). Pass a sidetrail to Stillwell Camp, and climb a steep mile to Beaver Pass, 3620 feet. The trail goes nearly on the level a mile to designated campsites at Beaver Pass Shelter (emergency use only), the midpoint of the loop, 13½ miles from Little Beaver Landing and 13 miles from Big Beaver Landing.

An hour or three should be allowed here for an off-trail sidetrip. Pick a way easterly and upward from the shelter, gaining 500 to 1000 feet through forest and brush to any of several open slopes that give a staggering look into rough-and-icy Luna Cirque; the higher the climb the better the view.

Descend steeply from Beaver Pass into the head of Big Beaver Creek; two spots on the trail offer impressive glimpses of Luna Cirque. Pass Luna Camp and ford a tributary creek, difficult at high water. At 6 miles from Beaver Pass Shelter (7 miles from Big Beaver Landing on Ross Lake), the Big Beaver tumbles down a 200-foot-deep gorge; a good view here of Elephant Butte and up McMillan Creek toward McMillan Cirque. The moderately up-and-down trail crosses avalanches that have torn avenues through forest, passes enormous boulders fallen from cliffs above, and goes by a marsh.

At 8 miles from Beaver Pass (5½ from Ross Lake), cross Thirtynine Mile Creek; campsite. The way now enters the world-famous lower reaches of Big Beaver Creek, a broad valley of marshes and ancient trees, including the largest stand of western red cedar (some an estimated 1000 years old) remaining in the United States. Seattle City Light planned to flood the lower 6 miles of the valley by raising Ross Dam, but after an epic fifteen-year battle, in 1983 the plans were permanently dropped.

Passing one superb marsh after another, one grove of giant cedars after another, at 3 miles from Ross Lake (reservoir) the trail for the first time touches the banks of Big Beaver Creek, milky-green water running over golden pebbles. Finally the trail reaches Big Beaver Landing, from which a ¼-mile trail leads left to Big Beaver Camp. (This is a boaters' camp. Hikers should use Pumpkin Mountain Camp, 100 yards south of the bridge over Big Beaver Creek on the Ross Lake trail.)

There are two ways to return to Ross Dam. One is by hiking the 6-mile Ross Lake trail, which branches right from the Big Beaver trail at a junction ¼ mile before the landing. The second is to arrange in advance with Ross Lake Resort to be picked up at Big Beaver Landing.

Ross Lake National Recreation Area–North Cascades National Park

41 | PANTHER CREEK—FOURTH OF JULY PASS

Round trip: To Fourth of July Pass, 11½ miles
Hiking time: 6 hours
High point: 3500 feet
Elevation gain: 2000 feet
Trip length: One day or backpack

Hikable: July through mid-October
Maps: Green Trails No. 48 Diablo Dam, No. 49 Mt. Logan
Information: Marblemount Ranger Station, phone (360) 873-4500. Ask about trail No. 758.

Park Service backcountry use permit required for camping

Rolling, bubbling, cascading, whirling, jumping, foaming, roaring, gurgling, singing—a whole thesaurus couldn't adequately summarize the lifestyle of this wondrous creek, deep in a verdant canyon between the glacial barrens of Ruby Mountain and Beebe Mountain. Follow the course for a single day of exploration or backpack to scenic camps just beyond Fourth of July Pass. If transportation can be arranged, plan a one-way trip ending at Colonial Creek Campground.

Drive Highway 20 east 8.2 miles from Colonial Creek Campground and between mileposts 138 and 139, just before the Panther Creek bridge, park at the East Bank trailhead, elevation 1850 feet. (There is no room to park at the Panther Creek trailhead.) Cross the bridge on foot and walk the highway shoulder ⅓ mile to the Panther Creek trail and set out upward, switchbacking through open forest of lodgepole pine. In ¾ mile, at around 2200 feet, the trail levels and then, to duck under a cliff, goes stark, staring insane—turning back downvalley, losing several hundred feet of the hard-won elevation. The trail comes to the creek and turns back upvalley. The

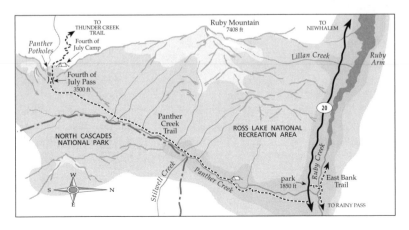

ferns are lush, the red cedars ancient. Pause often to watch the creek thrashing and splashing along its narrow course. At 3 miles the way crosses the creek on a sturdy bridge to a designated campsite, a good turnaround for day-hikers.

Proceeding onward, the trail soon crosses the first of several avalanche slopes and several small streams. At 4¾ miles, 2700 feet, the route abruptly leaves the creek and in a forest mile climbs to Fourth of July Pass, 5¾ miles, 3500 feet.

The pass is fairly flat and wide for ⅓ mile, reflecting its past history as a glacier's trough. The forest is broken by small swamps. At the far end of the pass flat is an overlook of the inviting Panther Potholes. The trail then descends northward ¼ mile to Fourth of July Camp, which has a front-row seat for the big show of Colonial Peak, Neve Glacier, and Snowfield Peak.

One-way hikers are now not far from their pickup, via a quick 2½-mile drop to the Thunder Creek trail and an easy 1½ miles to Colonial Creek Campground, 1240 feet, 10¼ miles from the Panther Creek trailhead.

Panther Creek trail

Ross Lake National Recreation Area–North Cascades National Park

42 | EAST BANK TRAIL

One-way trip: From North Cacades Highway trailhead to Hozomeen Camp, 31 miles

Hiking time: Allow 3 to 5 days

High point: 2853 feet

Elevation gain: About 5000 feet

Hikable: Mid-June through October

Trip length: One day or backpack

Maps: Green Trails No. 48 Diablo Dam, No. 16 Ross Lake, No. 17 Jack Mtn.

Round trip: From North Cascades Highway trailhead to Rainbow Camp, 15 miles

Hiking time: 8 hours

High point: 2600 feet

Elevation gain: 900 feet in, 1250 feet out

Hikable: May through October

Information: Marblemount Ranger Station, phone (360) 873-4500

Park Service backcountry use permit required for camping

When full, Ross Reservoir (known erroneously as Ross "Lake") indeed simulates a veritable inland fjord. The dark side of this picture is the drowning of many square miles of uncut virgin forest and irreplaceable wildlife habitat. Further, the beauty when full vanishes as drawdowns of water for power production expose dreary wastelands of mud and stumps. Because of the low elevation, the hike is especially suitable in spring, when most mountain trails are deep in snow; sorry to say, that's when the "lake" is at its ugliest. Generally the reservoir is full from late June to October and at a lower level other months, the maximum draw-down of as much as 150 feet usually coming in March or April.

At the worst, however, there still are grand views above the stumps to high peaks across the water. To learn the valley in all its moods, to enjoy the panoramas from end to end, hike the East Bank Trail, mostly through forest, a little along the shore, and finally detouring inland to reach Hozomeen Campground. The complete trip can be done in several days or any portion selected for a shorter walk.

If only a portion of the trail is to be hiked, travel to Ross Dam and

Grouse

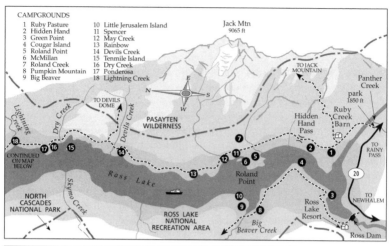

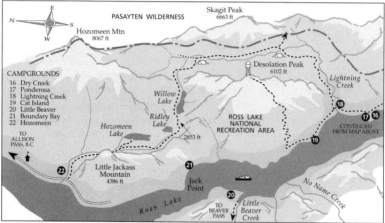

arrange with Ross Lake Resort for water-taxi service to the chosen beginning point and a pickup at trip's end (Hike 44, Desolation Peak).

To do the entire route, drive Highway 20 east 8.2 miles from Colonial Creek Campground and between mileposts 138 and 139, just before the Panther Creek bridge, find the trailhead in the large parking area, elevation 1850 feet.

The trail drops 200 feet to the crossing of Ruby Creek and a junction. Go left to Ruby Creek Barn, a scant 3 miles from the highway. The way leaves the water's edge to climb 900 feet over Hidden Hand Pass, returning to the reservoir near Roland Point Camp, 7½ miles.

The next 7½ miles to Lightning Creek are always near and in sight of the water. Some stretches are blasted in cliffs; when the reservoir is full the

Ross Lake National Recreation Area–North Cascades National Park

tread is only a few feet above the waves, but when the level is down the walking is very airy. There are frequent boat-oriented camps, including the one at Lightning Creek, 16 miles from the highway.

Here the trail forks. The left continues 2 more miles up the reservoir, ending at the Desolation Peak trailhead (Hike 44).

For Hozomeen, take the right fork, switchback up 1000 feet to a glorious view of the reservoir, then lose all that elevation descending to a camp at Deer Lick Cabin (locked), 4 miles from the reservoir. The trail bridges Lightning Creek to a junction with the Elbow Basin Trail (Hike 82). Go left 7 miles to the junction with the abandoned Freezeout trail; go left on a bridge over Lightning Creek to Nightmare Camp, in a spooky cedar grove. The way leaves Lightning Creek and climbs to Willow Lake Pass at 10 miles, 2853 feet. Another 2 miles of some ups but mostly downs lead past a sidetrail to Hozomeen Lake and at last to the road-end at Ross Lake (reservoir), 31 miles from the trailhead at Panther Creek.

East Bank Trail bridge across Lightning Creek

43 | LITTLE JACK MOUNTAIN

Round trip: To view knoll, 19 miles
Hiking time: 9 hours
High point: 6745 feet
Elevation gain: 5097 feet
Trip length: One day or backpack

Hikable: July through September
Map: Green Trails No. 49 Mount Logan
Information: Marblemount Ranger Station, phone (360) 873-4500

Park Service backcountry use permit required for camping

Few hiker-accessible vantages in the Ross Lake area offer gazing the likes of this: up and down the fjordlike sinuosity of reservoir that drowned Skagit Valley, across to Elephant Butte and up the saved-from-drowning Big Beaver Valley to the heart of the Picket Range, west to Mt. Baker and Mt. Shuksan, and if that's not enough, south to such stars of the North Cascades show as Eldorado and Snowfield. So much for the good news. The trail is a bear—long, steep, and dry. No camping along the trail, but hikers are welcome to find private places off trail. For water carry a super canteen. Liquid may be found in a small pond at the trail's end but should not be taken internally until every purification procedure known to modern science has been used—twice.

Drive to the East Bank trailhead near the Panther Creek bridge (Hike 41), elevation 1850 feet. Descend 200 feet to Ruby Creek and a junction. Go left 2½ nearly flat miles along Ruby Creek to a major junction, 1920 feet, where the trail branches into three. Take the far right, heading back upvalley and uphill in forest toward Little Jack.

The next 6 miles have more than sixty switchbacks, all up, though not steeply. At about 4 miles from the road views begin from the frequent

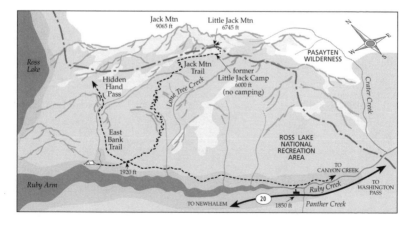

Meadow on the side of Little Jack Mountain

openings. Progress can be measured by the dwindling size of cars streaming to and fro on Highway 20. At about 7½ miles from that thoroughfare, the path enters sweetly green meadows and turns east 1 more mile to the viewpoint at the former Little Jack Camp, 6000 feet, and its scummy little pond.

Just before the pond a vague sidetrail goes through a clump of trees and climbs to the ridge crest for a full panorama of Crater and Jack Mountains, as great a view as the trip has to offer. The path disappears in heather and rich blueberry meadows. Take your choice of knoll summits. The views aren't any better here than before, they just feel better. Trail tread reappears, aiming toward Jack Mountain. Forget it. Once the route leaves the meadow it's for climbers only, and not many of those because the ascent is not so much interesting as nasty, and the "King of the Skagit" is mostly allowed to reign in lonesome splendor.

44 | DESOLATION PEAK

Round trip: From Desolation Landing, 9 miles
Hiking time: 7 hours
High point: 6085 feet
Elevation gain: 4400 feet landing

Trip length: One day from the
Hikable: Mid-June through October
Map: Green Trails No. 16 Ross Lake
Information: Marblemount Ranger Station, phone (360) 873-4500

Park Service backcountry use permit required for camping

A forest fire swept the slopes bare in 1926, giving the peak its name. In the late 1930s the lookout cabin on the summit was manned by the photographer's brother-in-law. But in literary circles its fame came after a summer's residence by the late Jack Kerouac, "beat generation" novelist and occasional Forest Service employee. Some of his best writing describes the day-and-night, sunshine-and-storm panorama from the Methow to Mt. Baker to Canada, and especially the dramatic close-up of Hozomeen Mountain, often seen from a distance but rarely from so near. Before and since Kerouac, the lookout frequently has been the summer home of poets and is a shrine that draws a pilgrimage stream (dwindling) of beatniks. The steep trail is a scorcher in sunny weather; carry a lot of water.

The start of the Desolation Peak trail can be reached by walking 18 miles on the East Bank Trail (Hike 42) or by riding the water taxi. For the taxi, from home or while driving up the Skagit Valley, telephone Ross Lake Resort at (206) 386-4437 to learn the current price and make arrangements. To catch the taxi, drive Highway 20 eastward from Colonial Creek Campground 3.8 miles and between mileposts 134 and 135 find the parking lot of the Ross Lake (reservoir) trailhead, elevation 2200 feet. Drop 450 feet

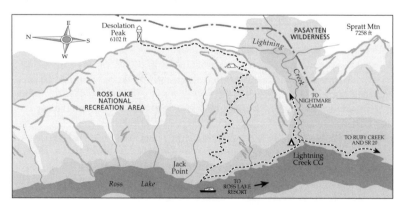

Ross Lake (reservoir) from Desolation Peak trail

from the trailhead to the dam and boat dock opposite the resort; here the resort boat will ferry you to your destination and return to pick you up at a prearranged time.

The trail starts steep and stays steep, climbing 1000 feet a mile. For such a desolate-appearing hillside there is a surprising amount of shade, the way often tunneling through dense thickets of young trees. This is fortunate because the sun can be unmerciful on the occasional barren bluffs.

Views come with every rocky knoll. In ½ mile see a small grove of birch trees. In 2 miles there may be a spring. At 3 miles the trail enters steep, open meadows, and at 4 miles is the ridge crest. A high bump remains to be climbed over before the lookout is sighted. The flower fields include species that properly "belong" on the east slopes of the Cascades.

The horizons are broad and rich. Only Mt. Baker stands out distinctly among the distant peaks, though those who know them can identify Shuksan, the Pickets, Colonial, Snowfield, Eldorado, and scores of other great mountains. Closer, the spectacular glacier of 8928-foot Jack Mountain dominates the south. To the north rise the vertical walls of Hozomeen. West is the fjordlike Ross Lake (reservoir), dotted by tiny boats of fishermen; beyond are the deep valleys of No Name Creek, Arctic Creek, and Little Beaver Creek. East are the high meadow ridges of the Cascade Crest and the Pasayten Wilderness.

A designated campsite (no fires) is in the trees just below the high meadows; water is from snowfields only, usually gone by late July. If you do the longer hike instead of taking the boat, the best plan for a weekend trip is to travel the first day to Lightning Creek Camp, stay there overnight, and do the climb the second day.

45 | CRATER LAKE—JACKITA RIDGE— DEVILS LOOP

One-way trip: To Devils Dome
Landing, 27 miles; complete loop,
43 miles
Hiking time: Allow 5 to 9 days
High point: 6982 feet
Elevation gain: About 7300 feet in,
600 feet out
Hikable: Mid-July through October

Maps: Green Trails No. 16 Ross
Lake, No. 17 Jack Mtn., No. 49
Mt. Logan
Information: Forest Service Visitors
Center, open mid-May to end of
September, phone (509) 996-4000,
or Methow Valley Ranger Station,
phone (509) 997-2131. Ask about
trails No. 738 and 752.

Park Service backcountry use permit required for camping in the recreation area

Hoist packs and wander meadow ridges east of Ross Lake (reservoir), encircling the far-below forests of Devils Creek and the cliffs and glaciers of 8928-foot Jack Mountain, "King of the Skagit," looking to peaks and valleys from Canada to Cascade Pass, the Pickets to the Pasayten. The trip is recommended as a loop, but for shorter hikes the climaxes can be reached from either end.

Drive Highway 20 eastward from Colonial Creek Campground 11 miles. Between mileposts 141 and 142 find the large Jackita Ridge–Canyon Creek trailhead, elevation 1900 feet.

The way begins by crossing Granite Creek on a substantial bridge, then going downstream a bit and crossing Canyon Creek on a commodious footlog. Once across Canyon Creek the work begins—trail No. 738 gains 3400 feet in 4 miles. Fortunately, the labor is mostly shaded by big trees, water is found at several well-spaced points, and ultimately there are glimpses of peaks. At 4 miles, 5280 feet, is a junction.

For a compulsory sidetrip, go left ¾ mile to the impressive cirque and shallow waters of 5800-foot Crater Lake. Just before the meadow-and-cliff-surrounded lake, a 2-mile trail climbs eastward to a lookout site on the broad, 7054-foot easternmost summit of Crater Mountain. From the lake a 2½-mile trail climbs westward to another lookout site on the 8128-foot main summit of Crater; the final ½ mile is for trained climbers only, but the panoramas are glorious long before difficulties begin. When this higher lookout was staffed, the uppermost cliff was scaled with the help of wooden ladders and fixed ropes. Maintenance proved too difficult and summit clouds too persistent, causing installation of the lower lookout. Now both cabins are long gone.

From the 4-mile junction, go straight ahead on trail No. 738, descending the gently sloping table of McMillan Park to Nickol Creek, 4900 feet, then climb an old burn, loaded with blueberries in season, to Devils Park Shelter, 7 miles, 5800 feet. One can roam for hours in this plateau of meadows, clumps of alpine trees, and bleached snags.

The climb continues northward along Jackita Ridge into a larch-dotted basin at 8¾ miles, 6200 feet. Now commences a roller coaster—up to a shoulder, down to a basin, up and down again, and again, at 13¼ miles coming to North Fork Devils Creek at 5500 feet.

The trail traverses sweeping gardens of Jackita Ridge, up some and down more, to Devils Pass, 15¼ miles, 5800 feet. The best camping is at Devils Pass Shelter, several hundred feet and ½ mile below the pass in a pretty meadow with a year-round spring, reached via the Deception Pass trail and then a sidetrail.

From Devils Pass head west on Devils Ridge trail No. 752, going through open woods near and on the ridge top, then climbing a lush basin to Skyline Camp, 18 miles, 6300 feet—a lovely spot for a star-bright sleep but waterless after the snows are gone. (In fact, there is no dependable water

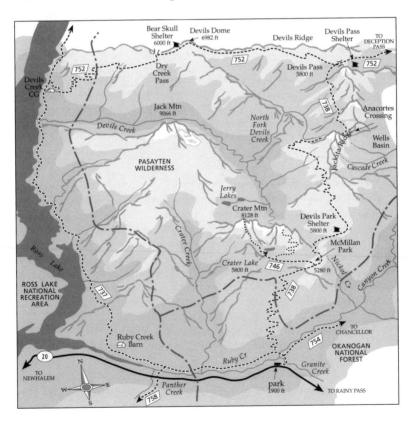

Crater Mountain from Devils Peak trail

anywhere near the trail between Devils Pass shelter and Bear Skull shelter.)

A flower-and-blueberry traverse and a short ridge-crest ascent lead, at 20 miles, to the 6982-foot site of the demolished Devils Dome Lookout, the trip's highest elevation. A descent into a basin of waterfalls and boulders and blossoms and a contour around the flowery slopes of Devils Dome leads at 21½ miles to a ¼-mile sidetrail to 6000-foot Bear Skull Shelter, the first possible camp if the loop is being done in the reverse direction and a long day—5½ miles and 4500 feet—above Ross Lake (reservoir).

At last the highlands must be left. The trail goes down the crest a short bit to Dry Creek Pass, descends forests and burn meadows to the only dependable creek, at 23 miles, enters young trees of an old burn, crosses the East Bank Trail, and ¼ mile later, at 27 miles, ends at the lakeside camp at Devils Dome Landing.

To return to the start, either hike the East Bank Trail (Hike 42) or, by prearranged pickup, ride back in a boat to Ross Lake Resort (Hike 44, Desolation Peak).

46 | CANYON CREEK—CHANCELLOR TRAIL

Round trip: To Boulder Creek, 7 miles
Hiking time: 4 hours
High point: 2400 feet
Elevation gain: 500 feet

Round trip: To Mill Creek, 14 miles
Hiking time: 8 hours
High point: 2600 feet
Elevation gain: 700 feet

Trip length: One day or backpack
Hikable: June through October
Map: Green Trails No. 49 Mt. Logan

Information: Forest Service Visitors Center, open mid-May to end of September, phone (509) 996-4000, or Methow Valley Ranger Station, phone (509) 997-2131. Ask about trail No. 754.

Walk a canyon-narrow valley through groves of giant trees, partly on the remnant of an ancient road (a person who didn't know there was such a thing as a narrow-gauge truck would wonder what vehicle ever traveled it). Once a main route from the Skagit Valley to shining gold of the Harts Pass area (the gold actually was—and still is—located in distant cities, the lodes worked by stock salesmen), lined by an almost continuous string of mining claims, many with cabins, the trail eventually reaches Chancellor, a thriving community in 1880, now a ghost town at the end of the road down from Harts Pass. If transportation can be arranged (and if the trail is known in advance to be passable the whole way), start at Chancellor and hike downstream. Otherwise, start at the lower end and hike upstream. The 3½ miles to Boulder Creek are a fine day hike. If backpacking, continue to Mill Creek, 7 miles, for campsites. But if the trail has slid out at the several spots where it is wont to do so, turn back.

For the lower start, drive Highway 20 to Chancellor trail No. 754

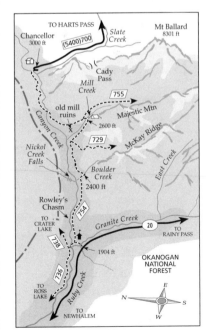

(Hike 45, Crater Lake-Jackita Ridge-Devils Loop). From the east side of the parking lot, follow Granite Creek upstream 100 feet to a bridge. Cross to a trail junction and take the right.

The big trees and the creek provide entertainment. So does keeping an eye out for collapsed cabins and rusty tools, though the generations of wet rot and green-jungling have left precious little evidence of the "mining" (prospecting, stock-selling) excitement. Conjure up a vision of Owen Wister and his bride riding down the trail on their honeymoon journey from the Methow Valley, real-life setting of his novel *The Virginian*, to Western Washington.

In a scant 2 miles look through trees to a good view of Crater Mountain and at 3 miles to the white splash of Nickol Creek Falls. At 3½ miles, 2400 feet, Boulder Creek may have to be forded, which at high water may be too neat a trick.

At 6 miles, 2600 feet, trail ends and narrow-gauge road begins at Mill Creek (the bridge may be missing). Campers will want to poke about such scant remains as may be found of the sawmill that supplied mine timbers.

At 9 miles from Highway 20, at 3000 feet, is Chancellor and the end of the road from Harts Pass (Hike 80, Grasshopper Pass).

A glimpse of Snowfield Peak from Canyon Creek trail

47 | EASY PASS—FISHER CREEK

Round trip: To Easy Pass, 7 miles
Hiking time: 7 hours
High point: 6500 feet
Elevation gain: 2800 feet
Trip length: One day or backpack

One-way trip: From Easy Pass to Colonial Creek Campground, 19 miles
Hiking time: Allow 3 to 4 days
High point: 6500 feet
Elevation gain: 5300 feet

Hikable: Mid-July through September
Maps: Green Trails No. 16 Ross Lake, No. 48 Diablo Dam, No. 49 Mt. Logan

Information: Forest Service Visitors Center, open mid-May to end of September, phone (509) 996-4000, or Methow Valley Ranger Station, phone (509) 997-2131. Ask about trail No. 741.

Park Service backcountry use permit required for camping in the park

Dramatic the views are, but the trail definitely is not easy, though early prospectors found no better way across Ragged Ridge, and thus the name. However, the tread is rough, at times very steep, and in spots muddy. Finally, the pass area is very small and extremely fragile, and camping is not allowed.

Drive Highway 20 east 20.6 miles from Colonial Creek Campground or 6.2 miles west from Rainy Pass to a spur road between mileposts 151 and 152 leading to the parking area, elevation 3700 feet.

In a scant ¼ mile the trail crosses Granite Creek. Eventually there will be a (replacement) bridge but for now fording is advised. A thin footlog may be found downstream. Fall off and you will get more than your belly wet. The photographer–co-author, faint of heart, sat down and scooted across. The other co-author enjoys getting his belly wet and did so, and part of his chest, too. From across the creek the trail climbs 2 miles in woods to the edge of a huge avalanche fan, 5200 feet,

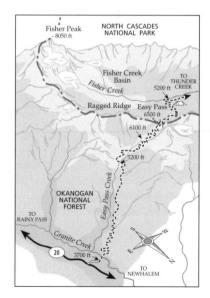

Fisher Creek valley and Mount Logan from Easy Pass

under the rugged peaks of Ragged Ridge. The trail beyond may be elusive, buried in snow or greenery. (Make very sure not to lose the path altogether; cross-country exploration here is agonizing.) The way goes over the avalanche fan and Easy Pass Creek and begins a long, steep ascent along the south side of the valley to the pass. Flower gardens. Small groves of trees. Watercourses. Boulder fields. Up, always up. The route crosses Easy Pass Creek again and at about 6100 feet comes within a few feet of a gushing spring, the source of the creek. Tread shoveled from a steep talus slope leads to the 6500-foot pass, a narrow, larch-covered saddle.

For the best views wander meadows up the ridge above the pass and look down 1300 feet into Fisher Creek Basin and out to glaciers and walls of 9080-foot Mt. Logan.

To continue to Diablo Lake, descend 1½ miles to a designated no-fire camp in Fisher Basin, 5200 feet. At 5½ miles is Cosho Camp and, just beyond, a footlog crossing of Fisher Creek. At 10½ miles is Junction Camp, where is met the Thunder Creek trail (Hike 39), which leads to Colonial Creek Campground at 19 miles from the pass.

48 | CHELAN LAKESHORE TRAIL

One-way trip: From Prince Creek, 17½ miles

Hiking time: Allow 3 to 4 days

High point: 1700 feet

Elevation gain: Perhaps 2000 feet

Hikable: Late March through early June

Maps: Green Trails No. 82 Stehekin, No. 114 Lucerne, No. 115 Prince Creek

One-way trip: From Moore Point, 6½ miles

Hiking time: Allow 2 days

High point: 1600 feet

Elevation gain: About 900 feet

Information: Marblemount Ranger Station, phone (360) 873-4500, or Chelan Ranger Station, phone (509) 682-2549. Ask about trail No. 1247.

The way to know Lake Chelan is to walk beside it, sometimes near waves slapping the shore, sometimes on high bluffs in sweeping views. There are green lawns atop rock buttresses, groves of old ponderosa pine and Douglas fir, glades of mystic aspen, slot gorges of frothing waterfalls. The views and trees and many of the creeks are grand in any season but spring is the prime time, when the sun is dependable but not too weighty, cool breezes blow, and the flowers are in rich bloom. Early on, the trail is lined by trillium, chocolate lily, glacier lily, spring beauty, yellowbells, Johnny-jump-up, red currant, and more. Later, the show features spring gold, prairie star, blue-eyed Mary, naked broomrape, primrose monkeyflower, death camas, balsamroot, miners lettuce, calypso, and more.

Note: By summer the country gets so dry that wood fires within 1 mile of the shore are banned except where metal rings are provided—namely, at Prince Creek, Moore Point, and Fish Creek Shelter. Carry a stove. You should've come earlier anyhow.

Drive to the town of Chelan or up the lake to Field Point and board the

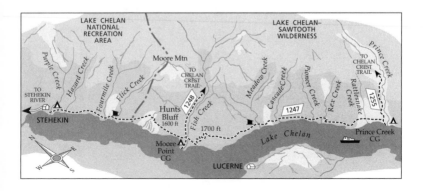

passenger boat, *Lady of the Lake*. Call the National Park Service–Forest Service Information Center in Seattle, (206) 420-4060, to learn the current schedule. The past pattern has been a single trip daily from mid-May to mid-September, uplake in early morning, downlake in early afternoon, and Sunday, Monday, Wednesday, and Friday trips the rest of the year (no Sunday boat in midwinter).

For a 2-day trip, hikers can start at Moore Point with day packs and have their overnight gear dumped on the dock at Stehekin to await them; this gives an afternoon on the trail and a morning poking around Stehekin.

To do the full 17½ miles from Prince Creek to Stehekin, the nice allowance is 4 days (including the going-home day), though 3 is tolerable. The map fails to say that though the trail never climbs higher than 1700 feet and generally is some several hundred feet above the shore (1098 feet above sea level), it magically manages to go uphill virtually the whole way.

At Prince Creek, hikers have the choice of being put off downlake from the creek, perhaps to stay the first night at the campground there, or—if the captain is agreeable—uplake (a campsite here, too) to save ½ mile of trail.

Since the debarkation at Prince Creek is at about 11:00 A.M., most hikers camp the first night in the vicinity of Meadow Creek, 7 miles, after crossing Rattlesnake, Rex, Pioneer, and Cascade Creeks. The shelter cabin in the viewless forest at Meadow Creek is unattractive except in a storm; other spots nearby in the open are a happier choice.

By the nice plan, a relaxed second day attains the trail's high point at 1700 feet on a long, wide shelf, descends to Fish Creek, 10½ miles from

Lakeshore trail

Left: *Paintbrush;* below: *Skyline Divide trail and Mount Baker (Hike 2)*

Left: *Mount Hardy from Pacific Crest Trail near Snowy Lakes (Hike 74);* below: *North Fork Nooksack River (Hike 12);* opposite: *Liberty Bell and Washington Pass (Hike 89)*

Trail over Cascade Pass (Hike 35)

Phlox

Right: *Chelan Lakeshore trail (Hike 49);* below: *Middle Hidden Lake in Pasayten Wilderness (Hike 86)*

Clockwise from upper left:
*Buckwheat; Boundary Trail
(Hike 98); white-winged
crossbill; ptarmigan in summer
plumage*

Overleaf: *Larch trees at Upper Eagle Lake (Hike 58)*

Lake Chelan

Prince Creek, then takes the sidetrail ½ mile down the creek to Moore Point, once a famous resort and now a spacious Forest Service campground. Spend the afternoon exploring the ancient orchard and the New England–like stone walls fencing a deer pasture.

The 6½ miles from Fish Creek to Stehekin are an easy morning for a 3-day trip. (Since the boat doesn't go downlake until afternoon, a party can finish the trip the morning of "boat day.") The way starts by climbing to 1600 feet on Hunts Bluff and its climactic views of lake and mountains. The trail then drops to the lake, crossing more creeks, and comes to Lakeshore (Flick Creek) Shelter, a choice camp on a jut of forest and rock out into the waves. It never again climbs high, wandering the base of cliffs and through woods to Flick Creek, Fourmile Creek, Hazard Creek, and finally Stehekin, 17½ miles. (To be technical, the sign here says "Fish Creek 6.6, Prince Creek 17.2.")

Overnight camping is permitted where the trail enters the Stehekin complex (this campground is designated "overflow") and ¼ mile up the road at Purple Point Campground.

49 | RAINBOW LOOP

Loop trip: 6 miles (with shuttlebus) or 9 miles (without)

Hikable: March through November
Map: Green Trails No. 82 Stehekin

Hiking time: 5 hours (or 7 hours)
High point: 2600 feet
Elevation gain: 1500 feet
Trip length: One day or backpack

Information: Marblemount Ranger Station, phone (360) 873-4500, or Chelan Ranger Station, phone (509) 682-2549

Park Service backcountry use permit required for camping

The high country of Stehekin is a long way up and for much of the year is up to a hiker's eyebrows in snow. The low country, on the other hand, offers relaxed walking almost year-round.

A favorite plan, especially among families with small children, is to take the boat to Stehekin (Hike 48, Chelan Lakeshore Trail), then the Park Service shuttlebus 5 miles up the Stehekin River road and establish camp on the banks of the Stehekin River at Harlequin (formerly Company Creek) Campground, elevation 1195 feet. By walking the short bit out from the campground and across the Harlequin Bridge, a party can be whisked by shuttlebus up the Stehekin River road to any number of trailheads that provide nice day hikes: Agnes Gorge, Coon Lake, and others. The party then can be whisked back to Harlequin for supper.

Lake Chelan from Rainbow Lake trail (Harvey Manning photo)

Contact the National Park Service Information Center in Seattle, phone (206) 470-4060, before the trip to learn the current bus schedule. The past pattern has been several round trips daily from spring to fall.

The bus isn't needed for the Stehekin River Trail, which takes off from the campground and in 4 flat and easy downstream miles of forest flowers and river vistas emerges at Weaver Point Camp, on the shore of Lake Chelan; the swimming is invigorating.

The bus also isn't needed, though it can be used, for the classic Rainbow Loop. The upper and lower trailheads are a scant 3 miles apart on the Stehekin River road; the walk between them can be enlivened by a cooling sidetrip to Rainbow Falls and a tour of the historic Stehekin School.

Note: Rainbow has a reputation as the snakiest trail in the valley, but on none of his trips has the surveyor ever seen a rattler. However, standard precautions are in order while admiring the penstemon, cinquefoil, monkeyflower, naked broomrape, linear phacelia, broadleaf montia, death camas, willow herb, balsamroot, stonecrop, paintbrush, lava alumroot, tiger lily, larkspur, suksdorfia, lupine, buckwheat, sandwort, luina, arnica, pinedrops, prairie star, snowbrush, and friends.

The recommended start is the upper trailhead, elevation 1240 feet, a long ½ mile up the valley road from Harlequin Bridge. Views through the forest grow steadily on the 2½-mile ascent to a junction, 2150 feet. The views here are very big, but don't be satisfied.

Sidetrip up the left fork, the Rainbow Lake trail, a long ½ mile to where it zigs right at 2600 feet. Zag left, out onto a bald slope of rock slabs and green grass. Find a piece of soft granite to sit on, break out the pickle sandwiches and the jug of orange juice, and gaze: across the valley to massive Si Si Ridge, crags of Devore Peak, the tower of Tupshin, but, especially, out to Lake Chelan, rippled by wind, sparkling in sun, and down the long fjord to Moore Point, Domke Mountain, and the big peaks of Milham Pass.

Having returned from the sidetrip to the junction, descend 2½ miles to the lower trailhead, passing on the way: a few feet from the junction, Rainbow Creek, with a nice little woods camp; the Boulder Creek trail, branching left; a series of switchbacks on the naked valley wall, with more views of the lake and others straight down to the river, one meander picturesquely enwrapping Buckner's Orchard; Boulder Creek. The road is reached at 1160 feet, 2½ miles from Stehekin Landing.

If the trip schedule is meshed with the bus schedule, a party can ride back to Harlequin. However, it's only 2½ miles up the road. Halfway along are the Stehekin School and the short sideroad and path to Rainbow Falls, where sunburnt hikers have been known to sit in forest shadows and let the billows of spray wash over them until their pink skin turns a nice shade of blue.

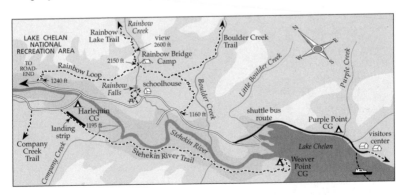

50 | NORTH FORK BRIDGE CREEK

Round trip: To cirque, 21 miles
Hiking time: Allow 2 to 3 days
High point: 4200 feet
Elevation gain: 2000 feet
Hikable: Early July through October

Map: Green Trails No. 81 McGregor Mountain
Information: Marblemount Ranger Station, phone (360) 873-4500, or Chelan Ranger Station, phone (509) 682-2549.

Park Service backcountry use permit required for camping

The North Cascades are notable for tall peaks—and also for deep holes. Among the most magnificent holes in the range is the huge cirque at the head of North Fork Bridge Creek, where breezes ripple meadow grasses beneath the ice-hung precipices of 9160-foot Goode Mountain, 8515-foot Storm King Peak, and 9087-foot Mt. Logan.

Travel by shuttlebus to Bridge Creek, 16 miles from Stehekin (Hikes 48, Chelan Lakeshore Trail, and 49, Rainbow Loop). Just before the creek is the trailhead, elevation 2200 feet.

The trail starts with a short, stiff climb of 400 feet, then goes up and down in woods, emerging to a view of Memaloose Ridge and reaching the bridge over Bridge Creek at 2½ miles, 2600 feet. Across the bridge and ¼ mile beyond is a junction; go left on the North Fork trail.

The way ascends steeply a bit and gentles out. From brushy openings in the forest are views of rugged cliffs, a promise of what is to come. To achieve fulfillment of the promise, it is necessary to camp somewhere in the North Fork. There are three choices: Walker Park Camp, 5½ miles, 3120 feet, a miserable, fly-ridden pit; Grizzly Creek Camp, about 6 miles, 3200 feet, in open woods near the stream; and Grizzly Creek Horse Camp, 6⅓ miles, 3180 feet. None of these is the least scenic. Pity.

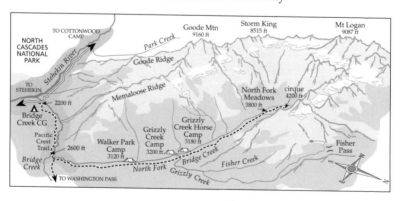

Mount Goode (Dick Brooks photo)

The ford of Grizzly Creek is not life-threatening except in snowmelt season, yet neither are its wide, cold, rushing waters a novice's joy. Beyond the creek the way leaves woods and wanders along the valley bottom in cottonwood groves, avalanche brush, and patches of grass. Immense views begin, up and up the 6000-foot north wall of Goode to icefalls of the Goode Glacier and towers of the summit.

At 7¼ miles, about 1⅔ miles past Grizzly Creek, the maintained trail ends in North Fork Meadows. The old path continues, a bit less gentle. At about 9½ miles, 3800 feet, is the site of once-beloved Many Waterfalls Camp, where the scenery is glorious but camping is now banned. Fields of hip-high grass whip in the wind, many waterfalls from hanging glaciers roar. Gazing up the walls of Goode and Storm King stretches the neck.

Paths here are confusing; climb the brushy knoll above to a resumption of tread amid small and sparse trees. In a stand of alpine timber that has grown old by dodging avalanches is a heather-surrounded, rotted-out prospector's cabin. The trail emerges into grass and flowers of the cirque, 10½ miles, 4200 feet, and fades away. The views of Goode are better than ever and Logan's walls are close above.

51 | PARK CREEK PASS

Round trip: To pass, 16 miles
Hiking time: Allow 3 to 4 days
High point: 6100 feet
Elevation gain: 3900 feet
Hikable: Mid-July through
September

Map: Green Trails No. 81 McGregor
Mountain
Information: Marblemount Ranger
Station, phone (360) 873-4500,
or Chelan Ranger Station, phone
(509) 682-2549

Park Service backcountry use permit required for camping

A wild and alpine pass on the Cascade Crest between the 9000-foot summits of Mt. Buckner and Mt. Logan, dividing snow waters flowing east to the Stehekin River and Lake Chelan and snow waters flowing west to the Skagit River and the Whulge (the name by which the original residents knew "the saltwater"). The pass and its surroundings rank among the scenic climaxes of the North Cascades National Park. A base can be established at Buckner Camp for roaming, or a one-way trip made over the mountains from lowlands east to lowlands west. Keep in mind that there is no camping in the alpine areas around the pass. From the last permitted camp in Park Creek it is 5 miles, with a 2000-foot climb, over and down to Thunder Basin Camp.

Travel by shuttlebus (or walk) 18.5 miles from Stehekin (Hikes 48, Chelan Lakeshore Trail, and 49, Rainbow Loop) to Park Creek Campground and trailhead, elevation 2300 feet.

The trail switchbacks steeply from the Stehekin River road into the hanging valley of Park Creek, then goes along near the stream through forest and occasional open patches with views up to Goode Ridge. At 2 miles, 3200 feet, is a two-site designated camp and a footlog crossing of the creek. Beyond here the grade gentles, continuing mostly in trees but with openings that give looks to Park Creek Ridge. At 3 miles is an obscure

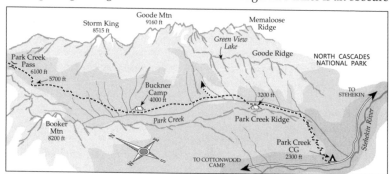

Air view of Park Creek Pass, with Mount Buckner (left) and Mount Logan (right)

junction with a rough-and-sketchy climbers' route to 7680-foot Goode Ridge and broad views; the scramble is for experienced hikers only, but well worth the effort.

Crossing numerous creeks in green avalanche tracks, views growing of high peaks, the trail ascends gradually to 4000 feet, 4½ miles. Now the way leaves the main valley of Park Creek, which falls from the glaciers of Mt. Buckner, and traverses and switchbacks steeply into a hanging side-valley, gradually emerging into parkland. At 7 miles, 5700 feet, the trail flattens out in a magnificent meadow laced by streams and dotted by clumps of alpine trees, the view dominated by the north wall of 8200-foot Booker Mountain.

A final wander in heather and blossoms leads to the rocky, snowy defile of 6100-foot Park Creek Pass, 8 miles from the Stehekin River road.

In order to preserve the fragile meadows, camping is not permitted in the area near the pass; however, fair basecamps for exploration are located in the forest at 5 miles (Buckner Camp) and 2 miles west of the pass in Thunder Basin.

For one wandering, with grand views of Buckner, Booker, Storm King, and Goode (tallest of all at 9160 feet, and third-highest nonvolcanic peak in the Cascades), find an easy, flowery route to the ridge southeast of the pass, overlooking the head of Park Creek. For another, descend west from the pass about ½ mile, leave the trail, and contour meadows and moraines to a jaw-dropping vista of the giant Boston Glacier and great peaks standing far above the valley of Thunder Creek.

If transportation can be arranged, a one-way trip can be made on down Thunder Creek to Diablo Lake (Hike 35, Cascade Pass—Sahale Arm).

52 | HORSESHOE BASIN (STEHEKIN)

Round trip: From the Cascade River road, 18 miles
Hiking time: Allow 3 to 4 days
High point: 5400 feet
Elevation gain: 3000 feet in, 1800 feet out

Hikable: Mid-July through September
Map: Green Trails No. 80 Cascade Pass

Round trip: (As of 1999) from the Stehekin River road-end, 17 miles
Hiking time: 7 hours
High point: 4800 feet
Elevation gain: 2300 feet
Trip length: One day or backpack

Information: Marblemount Ranger Station, phone (360) 873-4500, or Chelan Ranger Station, phone (509) 682-2549

Nine or more waterfalls tumble to the meadow floor of this cliff-ringed cirque. Above are glaciers on Sahale and Boston Peaks, both nearly 9000 feet, and the spires of Ripsaw Ridge. Wander the flowers and rocks and bubbling streams. The basin is well worth a visit in its own right and makes a splendid sidetrip on the cross-mountain journey described in Hike 53, Lake Chelan to Cascade River.

The Horseshoe Basin trail can be reached either from the west side of

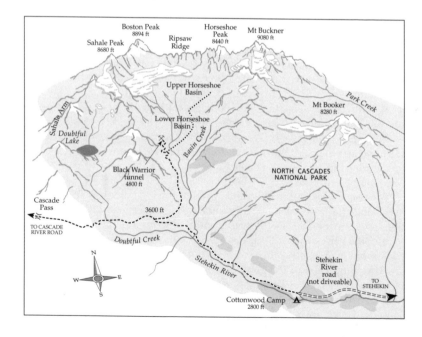

the Cascades or the east. For the west approach to the junction, ascend to Cascade Pass (Hike 35) and descend 3 miles into the Stehekin valley. For the east approach to the junction (see "Boy Scout 50-Mile Hike," Hike 53), walk or ride the shuttlebus to the end (as of 1999) of the Stehekin River road, elevation 2500 feet, and walk upvalley on traces of the truck road, built by prospectors in the late 1940s and abandoned in the early 1950s, 2 miles to Basin Creek Camp and another 2 miles to a junction.

At an elevation of 3600 feet, the Cascade Pass trail goes left. The washed-out, bouldery, "mining" road switchbacks sharply in a rockslide, climbing around and up the mountainside to enter the hanging valley of Basin Creek. At 1½ miles the way emerges from brush and flattens out amid boulder-strewn meadows, 4200 feet. Impressive looks upward from flowery knolls to ice and crags, and a magical view and sound of white water on the glacier-plucked walls.

The road remnants continue ½ mile upward across the sloping floor of the basin to the Black Warrior tunnel at 4800 feet, close under the froth and splash of the falls. The Park Service has tidied up the "mine" to make explorations safe; bring a flashlight. Hours can be spent roaming the basin.

Experienced off-trail hikers can go higher. Cross the creek a short way below the tunnel and, to the right of the vertical walls, scramble brushy slopes, amid small cliffs, to the upper cirque of Horseshoe Basin. The ascent is not easy but doesn't require the ropes and other gear of mountain climbers; traces of an old prospectors' trail may be found, simplifying progress. Once on the high shelf under Mt. Buckner and Ripsaw Ridge, the way is open for extended explorations, always looking down waterfalls to the lower basin and out to peaks beyond the Stehekin.

Glory Mountain (left) and Trapper Mountain from Black Warrior Mine tunnel

53 | LAKE CHELAN TO CASCADE RIVER

One-way trip: "Boy Scout 50-Mile Hike" from Prince Creek, 50 miles
Hiking time: Allow at least 6 days
High point: 5400 feet
Elevation gain: 5900 feet; elevation loss: 2600 feet
Hikable: July through October
Maps: Green Trails No. 80 Cascade Pass, No. 81 McGregor Mtn.

Information: For Cascade River, Marblemount Ranger Station, phone (360) 873-4500; for Lake Chelan, Chelan Ranger Station, phone (509) 682-2576. Ask about trail No. 1258; ask also about the Stehekin River road and current shuttlebus schedule. In Seattle, ask about the shuttlebus schedule at the Forest Service–Park Service Information Center, phone (206) 470-4060.

"Stehekin" translates as "the way through," and for millennia the Stehekin River–Cascade River corridor was a major trade route through the mountains from sagebrush to tidewater. To this day the Stehekin River in its full length and the Cascade River in its upper reaches remain only just less than purely wild. Pristine forests ascend the valleys either side to Cascade Pass, the meadow cleft between precipices and glaciers.

Hike the Chelan Lakeshore Trail (Hike 48) 17½ miles from Prince Creek to Stehekin Landing, elevation 1098 feet.

Hike the Stehekin River to Cottonwood Camp, 2800 feet, 23 miles from Stehekin Landing. For some years after its post–World War II extension beyond High Bridge by mine promoters, this was the end of the road. However, as of the new millennium, who knows where the end will be when you arrive? Phone ahead before leaving home. Whether shared with wheels or not, the Stehekin River road is a delightful footpath, wide enough for hikers to be chummy yet narrow enough to feel like a veritable trail; not being connected to the state highway system, it is virtually carfree.

Between Stehekin Landing and what was, until the 1940s, the road-end at High Bridge, 11 miles, are pleasant campgrounds at Purple Point, by the Landing; Harlequin, 5 miles; Bullion, 10 miles; and High Bridge, 11 miles. These provide non-backpack (shuttlebus-served) camping for a family week of day hikes to Rainbow Falls, Buckner's Orchard, Weaver Point, the Rainbow Loop, Coon Lake, and Agnes Gorge.

At High Bridge is the junction of two streams, the Stehekin River and river-size Agnes Creek. Above here the "upper valley" of the Stehekin is markedly different from its "lower valley," narrower and steeper, the road rougher and the river more rambunctious and winter longer. The road is gated for snow-melting and washout reconstruction until late June or early July (or maybe "next year"!), and during the winter-spring-whenever closure is magnificent for solitudinous day-hiking or backpacking; even in high summer the intrusions by automobiles are few, and their speed slow, as required by the rough and skinny road. Each step the walker takes increases his inner distance from the rattles and jangles and howls and moans of "The Outside," and the progression is not merely arithmetic or even geometric but exponential. The trees grow greener, the birdsongs sweeter, the bears friendlier. More sidetrips for that family week can be staged from campgrounds along the road at Tumwater, 12 miles; Dolly Varden, 14 miles; Shady, 15 miles; Bridge Creek, 16 miles; and Park Creek, 18½ miles.

A joyous alternative to the road is the ancient way of the Original Inhabitants and olden-day prospectors, predating the road and now used by the Pacific Crest Trail. This path takes off from the road at Bullion Camp and High Bridge, climbs to Coon Lake, sidehills high above the river, and rejoins the road at Bridge Creek. Beyond Bridge Creek the route commences an opening-out from forest and closely follows the river, which flows through groves of cottonwood and aspen, in views up mountainsides of vine maple and talus to cliffs and waterfalls, to snowfields and crags.

When the road-end was at Cottonwood Camp, 2800 feet, 23 miles from the Landing, the trail distance to Cascade Pass was 6 miles. However, in November 1995 the river reclaimed from the intrusive road most of its primeval bed above Park Creek. Further reclamations in years ahead are as certain as falling rain and melting snow. In a recent year two bridges over the Stehekin River collapsed in a single winter and the trail began, as in days of yore, at High Bridge, 18 miles from Cascade Pass. This posed no problem for the Boy Scout 50-Miler, indeed was a major improvement, but did rule out day-hiking to the pass from the road. Phone ahead. As of 1999 the Park Service has reopened (temporarily, of course) a sufficient semblance of a road to make the hiking distance to the pass perhaps 8 miles or so, possible but not comfortable for a day's round trip of 16 miles or so.

Beyond Cottonwood, the camp at Basin Creek, 24½ miles, 3100 feet, can

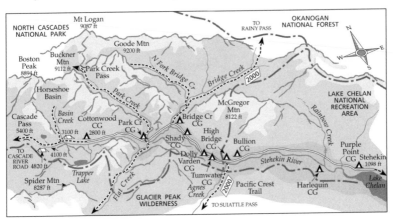

Stehekin valley and McGregor Mountain from trail to Cascade Pass

be the base for day hikes to the pass, as well as into Horseshoe Basin on the trail taking off at 25¼ miles, 3600 feet (Hike 52).

An enormous talus is climbed to Doubtful Creek, 26 miles, 4100 feet. The ford can be difficult and in high water insane. Switchbacks ascend in forest above Pelton Basin, where, 28 miles from the Landing, at 4820 feet, wooden tent platforms allow camping in the meadows without destroying them.

A scant mile more culminates in Cascade Pass, 5400 feet, 29 miles from the Landing. A 3¾-mile supertrail descends to Johannesburg Camp at the end of the Cascade River road, 3600 feet (Hike 35).

The Once and Future Way Through

Before World War II, the round-trip hiking distance to Cascade Pass from Mineral Park, on the Cascade River, was 16 miles; from High Bridge, on the Stehekin River, 36 miles. Deep wilderness. Semi-expeditional stuff. But when you did get there, perhaps once in several years—or a lifetime—you knew you'd been somewhere.

The road extensions after World War II were not the work of public officials serving the public convenience and necessity, but of flim-flam men exploiting the federal Mining Laws of 1872 and the state "mine-to-market road" pork barrel of the 1930s. In so doing, they shortened the Cascade River trail to Cascade Pass from 8 miles to 4 and the Stehekin River trail from 18 miles to 6. No ore worth hauling to a smelter ever was extracted, but the crude roads incidentally put Cascade Pass in easy-quick reach.

The environmentalist coalition that fought for and won the North Cascades National Park in 1968 sought to have the stock-promotion Cascade River and Stehekin River roads shortened in order to return Cascade Pass to relatively deep wilderness. Led by the North Cascades Conservation Council, the coalition continues to insist on that goal. Make no mistake, it will be achieved, one way or another.

Both roads, from west and east, fail to meet federal standards for safety, and the Park Service never will be allowed by federal environmental restriction to widen and smooth the road. Even if geography and climate would permit the formidable task (and they could not), the staggering cost would forbid it. Both roads are hideously expensive to maintain even in their present dangerous condition, and are a continuing financial anguish to the impoverished Park Service.

Finally, Nature takes offense at the existence of the roads, as demonstrated by the Stehekin River's latest fit of pique. Rather than pouring millions of taxpayer dollars into a war against Nature, it would be much more sensible to make peace, to permanently close the upper portion of the Stehekin River road and return the last 4½ to 6 miles to trail.

An argument is heard that this shortening would deny the splendors of the upper valley to old people. However, even when the road is at its best, old people frequently are observed being helped off the shuttlebus groaning, bones aching from the buffeting. The scenery? Old or young, who has time to look out the windows while hanging on for dear life? Creeping from chuckhole to boulder, grinding gears, the bus forbids listening to waterfalls and watching dippers in the river; excludes scents of forest and flowers, songs of birds.

Indeed, it is specifically the road that denies people the splendors of the

Stehekin River road was never more than a wagon track and has been washed out most winters since the 1890s

upper valley. Pilgrims from across America are commanded by the laws of tourism to do a bus ride, add it to their bag of vacation trophies. No ride, no battered bones and addled brains, and you haven't been there. They are not permitted to experience afoot the most transcendent scene in the North Cascades National Park—made so by its freedom from the tyranny of wheels, a sanctuary from the freeway, a shrine of the peaceful slow. Permanent abandonment of the upper road would let visitors walk through the glory. Even if they were to do no more than step off the bus, breath the air in which the flowers bloom and the river roars and the birds warble, they would return to homes across America knowing the wilderness peace that surpasseth understanding.

As for the west approach via the Cascade River road, the last 2 miles of road up the gut-wrenching and car-busting switchbacks of rough track gouged in avalanche slopes, never wide enough that meeting an oncoming car is less than a major trauma, are more agony than joy. By contrast, on foot one bathes in glacial spray from the torrents of Gilbert, Boston, Morning Star, and Soldier Boy Creeks, stretches neck to look up up up the mile-high walls of Johannesburg Mountain to hanging glaciers, listens in awe to ice chunks tumbling to the valley floor.

The existing parking area could be converted to a picnic area and an expansion of Johannesburg Camp, an ideal base for overnights (or longer) and easy day-trips the 3¾ miles to Cascade Pass and beyond to Sahale Arm and Mixup Arm. The increased distance from the road would help curb degradation of the fragile pass ecosystem by overuse, as well as enhance the "somewhere" feeling.

Not to belittle the pass, the final 2 miles of tortuous road, a comfortable afternoon stroll, offer the same close-up alpine drama—for a pedestrian from Iowa (or, for that matter, Tukwila) an experience of a lifetime. Definitely somewhere.

54 | CHELAN SUMMIT TRAIL

One-way trip: 38 miles
Hiking time: Allow 5 to 9 days
High point: 7400 feet
Elevation gain: About 8500 feet
Hikable: Early July through
September

Maps: Green Trails No. 115 Prince
Creek, No. 83 Buttermilk Butte,
No. 82 Stehekin
Information: Chelan Ranger
Station, phone (509) 682-2576.
Ask about trail No. 1261.

A miles-and-miles and days-and-days paradise of easy-roaming ridges and flower gardens and spectacular views westward across the deep trench of Lake Chelan to the main range of the Cascades. Snowfree hiking starts earlier and the weather is better than in the main range, which traps many winter snows and summer drizzles. Only twice before the final plunge does the trail dip as low as 5500 feet, in forest; eight times it climbs over passes or shoulders, the highest 7400 feet; mainly it goes up and down (a lot) through meadows and parkland on the slopes of peaks that run as high as 8795-foot Oval Peak, in the Sawtooth Group. Good-to-magnificent camps are spaced at intervals of 2 to 3 miles or less. Sidetrips (on and off trails) to lakes, passes, and peaks are so many that one is constantly tempted; for that reason a party should allow extra days for wandering.

The trail can be sampled by short trips from either end or via feeder trails from Lake Chelan on one side or the Methow and Twisp Rivers on the other. (For examples of the latter, see Hikes 56, Foggy Dew Creek, and 58, Eagle Lakes—Boiling Lake.) The perfect dream trip is hiking the whole length to Stehekin, but this requires either a two-car switcharound or a very helpful friend to do drop-off and pickup duty. Further, the road accesses to the south-end trailheads range from rude to disgusting. Some years cars simply can't get there. Most parties thus settle for a nearly perfect dream trip that starts on a feeder trail from the lake and uses the *Lady of the Lake* (Hike 48, Chelan Lakeshore Trail) to handle the drop-off and pickup.

Thanks (no thanks) to the maddening motorcycles still permitted on the south end of the Summit Trail, experienced hikers will opt to bypass part of it on the rough and steep Summer Blossom Trail (Hike 55). Beginners, however, had best take earplugs and dust masks and sedatives and set out where the wheels do—notebooks in hand to compose the letters of complaint that will be sent to Congresspersons after the trip, with copies to the Forest Service.

The Summit Trail has two trailheads other than the Summer Blossom alternate—from South Navarre Campground and Safety Harbor Creek. Because some years the final 2 miles of road to the former generally are too rough for a family car (check at the Chelan Ranger Station), the Safety Harbor Creek trail is described here.

Drive the North Shore Road from Chelan past Manson and turn right on the Grade Creek road, signed "Antilon Lake," at this point becoming road No. 8200. At 36 miles from Chelan go left on road No. (8200)150, signed "Safety Harbor Trailhead," and continue 2 miles to the end and trailhead, elevation 4400 feet.

Safety Harbor trail No. 1261 follows an abandoned pipeline a scant 2 miles and then turns uphill. At 4 miles, 5700 feet, it intersects Chelan Summit Trail No. 1259, which has just descended 600 feet in 3 miles from the

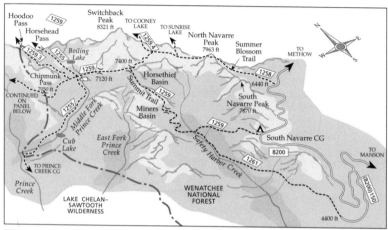

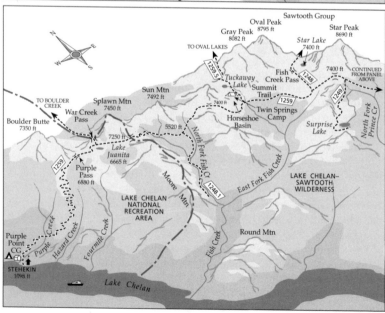

Headwaters of East Fork Prince Creek

South Navarre Campground. The Summit Trail now climbs to meadows of Miners Basin (5 miles) and a ridge crest. A traverse above headwater meanders of Safety Harbor Creek in Horsethief Basin leads to a 7400-foot pass (6½ miles) to East Fork Prince Creek. At the pass is a junction with the Summer Blossom Trail, which has come here in 6 miles from the road.

The way drops 700 feet to the broad meadow basin of the East Fork and makes a big swing around it, under the foot of 8321-foot Switchback Peak to a 7120-foot pass (8 miles) to Middle Fork Prince Creek. Down and around another wide parkland at 10 miles are the junction with the Middle Fork Prince Creek trail and a basecamp for sidetrips to Boiling Lake and Hoodoo Pass and all.

Note: The Middle Fork Prince Creek trail is the best feeder for a tidy loop. Have the *Lady of the Lake* drop you at Prince Creek, preferably on the uplake side where the trailhead is (Hike 48, Chelan Lakeshore Trail), and gain 5500 feet in 12 miles. Camps at 4, 6, and 8 miles from the lake.

The trail climbs to Chipmunk Pass, the 7050-foot saddle (11½ miles) to North Fork Prince Creek, and here enters the Lake Chelan–Sawtooth Wilderness, the end of motorcycles. It descends to a 5560-foot low point in forest (14 miles) and climbs to flowers again and the 7400-foot pass (18½ miles) to East Fork Fish Creek. In odd-numbered years, sheep that have been driven up Buttermilk Creek graze northward, devouring the flowers and fouling the water. (That's another letter for you to write your Congressperson, with a copy to the Forest Service.)

A short, steep drop leads to a 6800-foot junction with the trail to Fish Creek Pass (the sheep route). From a camp here, sidetrips include a stroll to larch-ringed Star Lake beneath the great wall of Star Peak and scrambles to the summits of 8690-foot Star Peak and 8392-foot Courtney Peak. On the other hand, if camp is made after a meadow traverse to Twin Springs Camp in Horseshoe Basin, there are sidetrips to Tuckaway Lake, Gray Peak, and Oval Lakes.

The way ascends to the 7400-foot pass (22 miles) to North Fork Fish Creek, descends to 5520-foot woods (24½ miles), and climbs through gardens (camps off the trail, near Deephole Spring) to a 7250-foot pass (27½ miles) to Fourmile Creek. A descent and an upsy-downsy traverse lead to Lake Juanita, 6665 feet, 30 miles. The quick and terrific sidetrip here is to Boulder Butte, 7350 feet, one-time lookout site.

At 30½ miles is 6880-foot Purple Pass, famous for the gasps elicited by the sudden sight—5800 feet below—of wind-rippled, sun-sparkled waters of Lake Chelan, seeming close enough for a swandive, and, except for one brief glimpse earlier, the first view. Hundreds of switchbacks take your poor old knees down Hazard and Purple Creeks to Stehekin, 38 miles, and the ice cream.

Chelan Crest from South Navarre Peak

55 | SUMMER BLOSSOM TRAIL

One-way trip: To Chelan Summit Trail, 6 miles
Hiking time: 4 hours
High point: 7850 feet
Elevation gain: 1800 feet in, 600 feet out
Trip length: One day or backpack

Round trip: To North Navarre viewpoint, 5 miles
Hiking time: 4 hours
High point: 7850 feet
Elevation gain: 1400 feet
Trip length: One day

Hikable: Mid-July through September
Map: Green Trails No. 115 Prince Creek

Information: Chelan Ranger Station, phone (509) 682-2576. Ask about trail No. 1258.

You say horse manure ruins your lunch? Motorcycles make you see the bright side to Earth's getting smacked by a runaway asteroid? The south end of the Chelan Summit Trail weakens your belief in a Benign Creation? Is that what's bothering you, Bunky? Cheer up! Take the Summer Blossom Trail! Sniff the blossoms in peace on a "hikers-only" trail! Enjoy the horizons unobstructed by the blue haze of exploding hydrocarbons! But note that this Utopia is for experienced backpackers, not beginners.

The ancient sheepherders' driveway, recently resurrected and lovingly renamed, parallels the Summit Trail for 6 miles, traversing gardens in sky-high views. There are two problems. The first is driving to the trailhead. The second is that the path is steep, in part rough, and in part hardly there at all. However, if the trailhead can be reached, the route provides a magnificent day hike to the top of North Navarre Peak, or a gorgeous 2- or 3-day round trip, or the start of a week-long journey along the Sawtooth Ridge and on down to Stehekin.

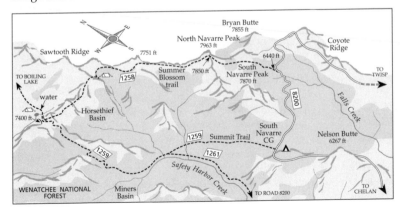

Shoulder of South Navarre Peak from Summer Blossom trail

The road (if such a cliffhanger deserves the name) often is impassable to ordinary passenger cars; before setting out, phone the Chelan Ranger Station. One approach is via Grade Creek road (Hike 54, Chelan Summit Trail); however, the 2 miles beyond the Safety Harbor trailhead to South Navarre Campground are sporty for jeeps but a misery for the Family Circus Wagon, though the 2 final miles from the campground to the Summer Blossom trailhead are quite decent.

In 1999 the least bad approach was from the Methow Valley. From Pateros on the Columbia River, drive the Methow Valley Highway 17 miles toward Twisp. Just before crossing the Methow River the seventh time, turn left on Gold Creek Road. In 1 mile turn left on road No. 4340, and in 1 mile more left again on road No. 4330. At about 5.5 miles from this junction is another; go right, following the sign "Cooper Mountain Road 7." These 7 miles grow steeper. The junction with Cooper Mountain Road is in a scenic parkland saddle on the divide between the Methow River and Lake Chelan. Turn right and go 9 miles on road No. 82, sliced just far enough into the flowery sidehill for two hikers to walk side by side comfortably (or to barely accommodate the wheels on both sides of the car). At 23.5 miles from the Methow Valley Highway is Summer Blossom trail No. 1258, elevation 6440 feet.

Daisies

The wheelfree, horsefree, narrow, sometimes meager trail ascends "Narvie" Basin, as the locals pronounce "Navarre," then the ridge of North Navarre Peak. At about 1½ miles it rounds a knob, crosses fields of boulders and blossoms of arid-land flowers, and at about 2½ miles tops out on a 7850-foot shoulder that is a quick stroll from the summit of North Navarre, 7963 feet. On shoulder as on summit, the views are from snow giants of the Cascade Crest to open steppe of the Columbia Plateau. For a day hike, this is a most spectacular turnaround.

The trail continues to be steadily and wildly scenic as it loses about 450 feet in tight switchbacks and a scary use-your-hands balcony traverse under a cliff, then roams open meadows on the very crest of Sawtooth Ridge and swings around the slopes of a 7751-foot peaklet. At 4½ miles it drops to a tiny basin with water and luscious camps in early summer, then ascends a bit and contours to a junction with Chelan Summit Trail No. 1259 at the 7400-foot pass between Horsethief Basin and East Fork Prince Creek headwaters, attained at 6 miles from the Summer Blossom trailhead.

For a campsite with guaranteed water (providing the sheep haven't been there first) go another ½ mile down into the lush basin at the headwaters of the East Fork.

56 | FOGGY DEW CREEK

Round trip: To Sunrise Lake, 13 miles
Hiking time: Allow 2 days
High point: 7228 feet
Elevation gain: 3700 feet
Station,
Hikable: July through early October
Map: Green Trails No. 115 Prince Creek

Information: Forest Service Visitors
Center, open mid-May to end of
September, phone (509) 996-4000,
or Methow Valley Ranger
phone (509) 997-2131. Ask
about trail No. 417.

The name has magic for those who love the folk song, and the scene has
more. Maybe the stiff climb of 3700 feet doesn't usually stir the poetry in a
hiker's soul, but the loud waters of Foggy Dew Creek do, as do the lake in
a horseshoe cirque amid meadows, cliffs, and parklike larch and alpine firs.
Try it in late September when the larch has turned to gold. However, since
hunters are here then, maybe you'd prefer the midsummer solitude, caused
in no small measure by the fishless condition of the shallow lake. A party
could spend many days happily here, exploring old sheep trails on both
sides of the divide and, as well, the Chelan Summit Trail (Hike 54), to which
this trail leads.

From Pateros on the Columbia River, drive the Methow Valley Highway (Highway 153) 17 miles toward Twisp. Between mileposts 16 and 17,
just before crossing the Methow River for the seventh time, turn left on the
narrow county road signed "Gold Creek Loop." At 1 mile turn left on road
No. 4340, signed "Foggy Dew Campground." If coming from Twisp, drive
15 miles toward Pateros and between mileposts 18 and 17 turn right on the
Gold Creek Loop, and in 1.5 miles turn right on the above-mentioned road
No. 4340. Whichever way you reach it, from this point drive North Fork
Gold Creek road No. 4340 for 5 miles and turn left on road No. (4340)200

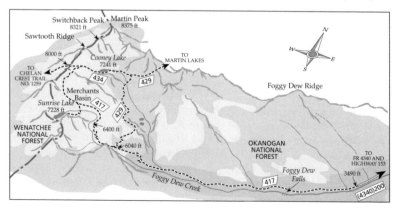

Sunrise Lake

for another 3.7 miles. At 9.1 miles are the road-end and trailhead, elevation 3490 feet, 8.8 miles from the county road.

Foggy Dew trail No. 417 starts in selectively logged (all the big pines selected) forest, climbs steadily, and at 2½ miles passes Foggy Dew Falls, something to sing about. At 3½ miles the valley and trail turn sharply right. At 4 miles cross a small tributary and at 5 miles come to a junction with motorcycle-open Martin Peak trail No. 429 and the end of the motorcyclists on this trail.

At 5½ miles, 6400 feet, steepness lessens and the path ascends moderately in ever-expanding meadows. At 6 miles reach Merchants Basin and a junction with a way trail to Sunrise Lake. From here the Foggy Dew trail to the Chelan Summit is little traveled.

The Sunrise Lake trail climbs ½ mile to the shores at 7228 feet, 6½ miles from the road. Explorations abound but campsites are limited; Merchants Basin is a nice base.

For a different way back, adding to the round trip an extra 2 miles and 1200 feet of more elevation gain, more meadows, and another lake, at the trail junction in Merchants Basin take the path climbing toward an unnamed 8000-foot pass to the north. From the pass the trail switchbacks above a rockslide 1½ miles to Cooney Lake; return to the Foggy Dew trail by trail No. 429.

57 | COONEY LAKE

Round trip: 16 miles
Hiking time: 10 hours
High point: 7241 feet
Elevation gain: 3750 feet
Trip length: One day or backpack
Hikable: Mid-July through September

Map: Green Trails No. 115 Prince Creek
Information: Forest Service Visitors Center, open mid-May to end of September, phone (509) 996-4000, or Methow Valley Ranger Station, phone (509) 997-2131. Ask about trails No. 417 and 429.

The jewel of the Sawtooths—that's what many hikers call Cooney Lake, located just at timberline, the shores sprinkled with lovely larches, the waters mirroring cliffs of the cirque.

You might very well call it a crime that the Forest Service has let a hundred-odd ORV drivers drive away thousands of hikers from the Cooney vicinity while nearby Oval Lakes (Hike 63) are in wilderness and thus are being trampled by those thousands of feet and hooves. Beauty is in the eye of the beholder, but Cooney Lake, Sunrise Lake, Martin Lakes, Boiling Lake, Eagle Lakes, both Crater Lakes, and their surrounding meadows are—in the eye of these here surveyors—lovelier than the three Oval Lakes. But because of the possible encounters with motorcycles, most hikers shun these beauties like the plague.

Now, contrarily, this is a blessing of sorts. To the dismay of the Forest Service, which fondly pampers motorcyclists, few actually use "their" Gold Creek trails. After all, put them all together and you've got a grand total of a 2-hour ride, not worth unloading machines. Even fewer bother to get off their machines to walk the short distance to the lakeshores. Hikers who brave the trails may have a degree of solitude unknown elsewhere.

Drive to the start of Foggy Dew trail No. 417 (Hike 56), elevation 3490 feet. Ascend the Foggy Dew trail 5 miles to a junction, 6040 feet, and go right on Martin Creek trail No. 429. The way switchbacks upward 3 miles, gaining 1200 more

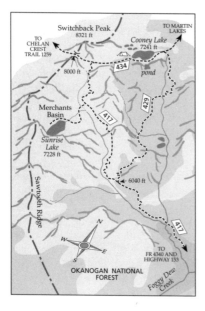

feet, crossing two forks of Foggy Dew Creek. At 8 miles from the road the Martin Creek Motorcycle Expressway on which you have been jaywalking goes right and a hiker/horse path crosses the creek, enters a meadow, and reaches the shore of Cooney Lake, 7241 feet.

To help the Forest Service revegetate the shore, don't camp here, but continue on the trail above the left side of the lake to areas less brutalized.

For extra stimulation, add a loop trip to the basic trip, and a sidetrip from the loop to Sunrise Lake (Hike 56, Foggy Dew Creek). Stay on the trail from Cooney Lake as it climbs over a low cliff on the south side, past a shallow (maybe dry) pond, and steeply switchbacks to an 8000-foot pass. Descend to Merchants Basin and proceed down the Foggy Dew trail, past the sidetrail to Sunrise Lake, to the starting point. The loop adds 2 miles and 1000 feet of elevation gain, plus the numbers for the sidetrip.

Cooney Lake

58 | EAGLE LAKES—BOILING LAKE

Round trip: 17 miles
Hiking time: Allow 2 days
High point: 7950 feet
Elevation gain: 2900 feet in, 600
 feet out
Hikable: July through September
Map: Green Trails No. 115 Prince
 Creek

Information: Forest Service Visitors
 Center, open mid-May to end of
 September, phone (509) 996-
 4000, or Methow Valley Ranger
 Station, phone (509) 997-2131
 Ask about trail No. 431.

Pretty Eagle Lakes under beetling crags. A 7590-foot pass across the
Chelan Summit to Boiling Lake. A bushel of byways to meadow nooks.
Easy-roaming routes to peaks with views over forests and sagebrush to
ranches in the Methow Valley, over the Lake Chelan trench to ice giants of
the North Cascades.

The "National Recreation Trail" (whatever that is) has been rebuilt
smooth and wide, with banked corners. For the benefit of racing hikers?
Galloping horses? Not at all. For the motorcyclists who burrowed into the
state gas-tax money and—making sure to keep the plot from hikers—
turned the former foot trail into a machine speedway. To avoid dust and
danger and aggravation, it is recommended you do this trip in late June or
early July when snowpatches still stop wheels but not feet.

Take note of the mint of money the Forest Service spent to "improve"
the trail for motorcycles and the obviously costly maintenance. Note, too,
that for the benefit of horse-riders, who in the beginning were the earliest
to do battle against the invasion by wheels, the Forest Service has installed
at the trailhead a water system for horses, several corrals, and picnic tables.
This is called "multiple use," or "something for everybody." For hikers it
means dodging hot wheels and finding a safe place to pass horses. (Have

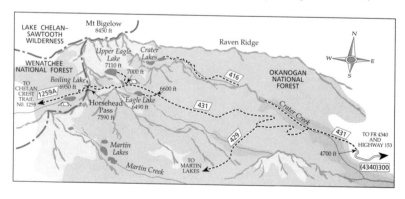

Boiling Lake

you written your letter to your Congressperson, with a copy to the Forest Service?)

Drive North Fork Gold Creek road No. 4340 (Hike 56, Foggy Dew Creek). At 5 miles pass the Foggy Dew road. At 6.7 miles is a junction. Turn left on road No. (4340)300, signed "Crater Creek" (sign missing in 1998), and go another 4.6 miles to Eagle Lake trail No. 431, elevation 4700 feet, 11.3 miles from the county road.

The first mile is fairly level, then a steady ascent begins. Pass the Crater Lakes trail (Hike 59) and the Martin Creek trail (Hike 60). At 4½ miles, 6600 feet, a hiker-only sidetrail goes off left, dropping 120 feet in ½ mile to lower Eagle Lake, elevation 6490 feet; good camping. The main trail proceeds to campsites near a small tarn and then, at 7000 feet, a short sidetrail to Upper Eagle Lake, 7 miles, 7110 feet.

At 7½ miles the main motorcycle raceway slices through the Sawtooth Ridge at Horsehead Pass, 7590 feet, between two 8000-foot peaks of the crest. The wheel-easy switchbacks descend 1 mile to 6950-foot Boiling Lake, not (as the name implies) a hot puddle in a sunbaked desert, but a cool pool in green meadows, ringed by widely scattered and pleasant campsites. (The "boiling" is bubbles of air rising from bottom mud.) The trail continues down a bit more to join the Chelan Summit Trail (Hike 54). Via that thoroughfare and its offshoots, or the old sheep trails from the lake, restless souls may wander to any number of flower gardens (early July is most colorful) and summit views.

59 | CRATER LAKES

Round trip: 8 miles
Hiking time: 5 hours
High point: 6814 feet
Elevation gain: 2100 feet
Trip length: One day or backpack
Hikable: Mid-June through September

Map: Green Trails No. 115 Prince Creek
Information: Forest Service Visitors Center, open mid-May to end of September, phone (509) 996-4000, or Methow Valley Ranger Station, phone (509) 997-2131. Ask about trails No. 416 and 431.

Oh yes, the Gold Creek scenery is terrific and the greenery is luscious, but the wheels wheels wheels razzing this way and that! The cavalry regiments beating the trails to dust! Who can handle it? Cheer up, hiker, because in the middle of the uproar lies an oasis of clean peace, a trail to two alpine lakes ringed by rugged peaks, surrounded by groves of neat trees and patches of pretty meadow. Motorcycles are prohibited—the trail is too steep for them. Horses are not—but the trail is too short and mean to please the heavy cavalry. So don't complain about the steepness. If the trail were improved it would become just another half-hour sidetrip for the wheel-spinners.

Drive to Eagle Lake trail No. 431 (Hike 58), elevation 4700 feet.

Hike the dusty Eagle Lakes razzerway No. 431 a long ½ mile to a junction at about 4900 feet, just past Crater Creek. Go right on Crater Lakes trail No. 416, signed "No Motorcycles." The hiker is immediately struck by the fact the tread is covered not by inches of dust, as on ORV trails (roads), but needles. Ah, wilderness! In a long ½ mile (1 mile from the road), the path bridges Crater Creek. Several very steep stretches have been badly

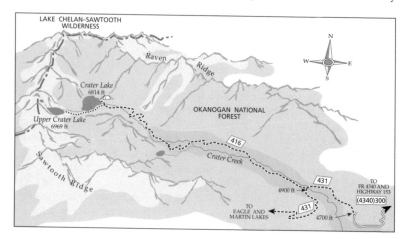

Upper Crater Lake

chewed up by the few horses that venture here. Otherwise the tread is in fair shape considering the gain of 2000 feet in 3 miles. The hiker will want to take the excuse of two viewpoints to pause, inhale deeply, and gaze across rolling hills to Methow ranches.

At 3¼ miles from the Eagle Lakes trail (4 miles from the road), 6814 feet, is the first of the two Crater Lakes. The horse camp is ¼ mile below the lake, but horse manure and hoof pits in campsites at the little meadow at the lakehead show that horses don't care.

The upper Crater Lake has no formal trail. At the lower lake go right, around the shore, cross an inlet stream in the lakehead meadow, and continue to the second stream rushing down the mountainside. Cross it and follow the course up. A person who stays close to the tumbling water can't get lost but will have numerous windfalls to dodge. In ½ mile, at 6969 feet, is the shallow upper lake. The ragged ridge to the south is a nameless spur of Mt. Bigelow. To the north is an extension of Raven Ridge. The surveyor found no horse souvenirs in the camps.

60 | MARTIN LAKES

Round trip: 14 miles
Hiking time: 8 hours
High point: 6729 feet
Elevation gain: 2400 feet in, 400 feet out
Trip length: One day or backpack
Hikable: July through September

Map: Green Trails No. 115 Prince Creek
Information: Forest Service Visitors Center, open mid-May to end of September, phone (509) 996-4000, or Methow Valley Ranger Station, phone (509) 997-2131. Ask about trails No. 429 and 431.

Beneath the cliffs of 8375-foot Martin Peak nestle two small lakes, the shores lined with larch trees; late September, when the needles turn golden before falling, is an especially fine time for a visit. But the flowers of early July are nothing to sneeze at either, unless you're allergic.

Drive to Eagle Lake trail No. 431 (Hike 58), elevation 4700 feet.

Hike the Eagle Lakes Obstacle Course (you being one of the obstacles), pass the Crater Lakes trail at ½ mile, and continue to another junction at 2 miles, 5700 feet. Turn left onto Martin Creek Expressway No. 429, dropping 400 feet in a bit less than 1 mile to a crossing of Eagle Creek. Watch Grand Prix motorcycles doing 20 miles per hour.

In long switchbacks suitably banked for the Indianapolis Speedway, ascend Martin Creek valley, never near the creek; thanks to a wonderful old-growth forest, views are few to the outside world. At about 6½ miles from the road is a junction, 6400 feet. Go right on Martin Lake trail No. 429A. See the sign "No Motorcycles," and make a happy face. Then make a different face on stretches of steep tread torn up by motorcycles (don't blame the machines—they can't read). At 7 miles, 6729 feet, is the first Martin Lake. Settle in to enjoy the peace under the larches. However, before your

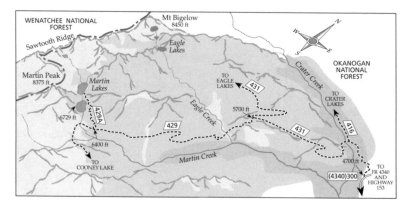

Lower Martin Lake

trip check with the State Wildlife Department on the bag limit for illegal motorcycles.

A way trail along the shore leads in a scant ¼ mile to the second lake.

61 | GOLDEN LAKES LOOP

Loop trip: 23 miles
Hiking time: Allow 3 days
High point: 8000 feet
Elevation gain: 4200 feet
Hikable: Mid-July through
September
Map: Green Trails No. 115 Prince
Creek

Information: Forest Service Visitors
Center, open mid-May to end of
September, phone (509) 996-
4000, or Methow Valley Ranger
Station, phone (509) 997-2131.
Ask about trails No. 431, 434,
and 429.

The Enchantment Lakes have gained wide and well-deserved fame, so much that the Forest Service has been forced to adopt restrictions to preserve the quality of the land and the recreational experience. Trembling on the brink of comparable fame is the Golden Lakes Loop, a route that goes through miles of meadows, passes five lakes and looks down to three others, and tops ridges with views from the Columbia Plateau to the Cascade Crest. The trip is a glory in summer, the grass lushly green and the flowers many-colored. In fall it's absolutely mystical, the larch trees turned to gold, giving the name by which this tour will become famous.

The hiker who takes the 3-day introduction will want to return for a week—for many weeks over many years. The first trip also will stimulate strong letters to Congresspersons (copies to the Forest Service), asking why the Enchantments are treated so tenderly as to exclude horses and dogs and limit the number of hikers, yet in this companion piece of wonderland the motorcycles are permitted—more accurately say, officially encouraged.

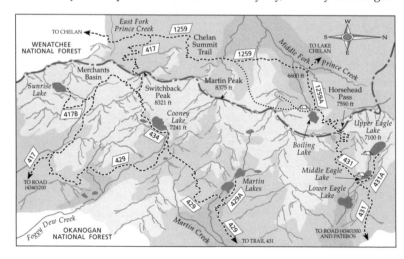

Drive to Eagle Lakes trail No. 431 (Hike 58), elevation 4700 feet.

The description here is counter-clockwise; clockwise is just as good. Either way, start on the Eagle Lakes trail, at 2 miles passing the Martin Creek trail (Hike 60), the final leg of the loop return. At 7 miles, 7110 feet, on a short spur from the main trail, is Upper Eagle Lake, with camps for the first night.

The second day's 6 miles, mostly above timberline, could keep a party of explorers happy for a week. Cross 7590-foot Horsehead Pass to Boiling Lake (Hike 58). (The Forest Service plans to reopen, for hikers only, an old sheep drive from Boiling Lake

Cooney Lake

south over a 7500-foot pass to join the Chelan Summit Trail, avoiding several miles of ORVs.) If not so signed, continue from Boiling Lake a mile down into open forest. At 9½ miles from the road is a junction with the Chelan Summit Trail (Hike 54), 6600 feet. Turn left on it, climbing back to meadows, passing nice campsites, to a 7100-foot saddle.

Contour from the saddle about ½ mile into the broad headwaters basin of East Fork Prince Creek and an unmarked junction of Switchback Peak trail No. 417. The one and only real difficulty is finding the exact spot where the way goes from lush sidehill onto a vast boulder field on the slopes of "Switchback Peak" (called this locally for generations). Look for tread, cairns, and/or horse manure heading off to the left and slanting up the meadows. Maintenance has been next to nothing in the century since sheepherders completed the engineering feat; a few boulders have fallen onto the tread.

The switchbacks lead to an 8000-foot high point on the shoulder of the 8321-foot peak, tremendously scenic. The way sidehills above Merchants Basin to the ridge above Cooney Lake. At a junction the right fork descends to Merchants Basin; take the left fork, on switchbacks that drop (steep snow here may force the unequipped to turn around or die) to a campsite bench near the upper end of Cooney Lake (Hike 57), at 7241 feet.

The third day is mostly downhill. From Cooney Lake, follow the outlet stream a few hundred feet to a junction with the Martin Creek trail. The right fork descends to the Foggy Dew trail; take the left, switchbacking down into forest and a junction with the sidetrail to Martin Lakes (Hike 60). Stay with the Martin Creek trail down to the crossing of Eagle Creek and up the 500 feet to the Eagle Lakes trail, reached at a point just 2 miles from the trailhead.

62 | LIBBY LAKE

Round trip: 11 miles
Hiking time: 6 hours
High point: 7618 feet
Elevation gain: 3200 feet
Trip length: One day or backpack
Hikable: July through September
Maps: Green Trails No. 83 Buttermilk Butte, No. 115 Prince Creek

Information: Forest Service Visitors Center, open mid-May to end of September, phone (509) 996-4000, or Methow Valley Ranger Station, phone (509) 997-2131. Ask about trail No. 415.

Massive rockslides dramatically ring the lake on three sides. On the fourth are giant larch trees that turn golden in fall. Solitude almost guaranteed, the lake seems ideal for skinny-dipping—until the water is tested with a toe and the year-round snowbank noticed at the far end. A connoisseur might judge the scene not quite as beautiful as the nearby Oval Lakes, but these typically entertain up to half a hundred horses a weekend, while your car may be the only one at the Libby Lake trailhead, the reason being that the trail has difficult spots too dangerous for horses.

Drive Highway 153 from either the Columbia River or Twisp, and just 1.2 miles east of Carlton between mileposts 21 and 22 turn uphill on the county road signed "Black Pine Lake." At 2.5 miles go left on road No. 43, again signed "Black Pine Lake." At 7.7 miles from the highway go left on road No. 4340, signed "North Fork Gold Creek." In another 1.2 miles go right on road No. (4340)700, signed "Libby Lake," then left on (4340)750, signed "Libby Creek," and drive a final 1.6 miles to the road-end and trailhead, elevation 4400 feet.

Logging has messed up the start of Libby Lake trail No. 415, but in the year 2000 the trail will be rebuilt, bypassing the clearcut and at the ridge top joining the old tread, which contours the ridge slopes and then, with some ups and downs (more ups than downs), levels off and enters the Lake Chelan–Sawtooth Wilderness. In about 2½ miles the trail crosses North Fork Libby Creek to a pleasant camp. It then climbs into a forest of pine and larch and glacier-polished slabs, at

5 miles passing remnants of a falling-down cabin. Several rocky stretches (where the horses cry "Neigh") lie along the way to the shores of the lake, 7618 feet, 5½ miles from the road.

The shore has very little flat ground. At the outlet is a rock-filled dam, evidently built by ranchers long ago and also forgotten long ago. (Golly knows what they had in mind. Irrigation?) A few hundred feet before the lake are some decent campsites.

Libby Lake

63 | OVAL LAKES

Round trip: To West Oval Lake, 16 miles
Hiking time: Allow 3 to 5 days
High point: 7000 feet
Elevation gain: 4000 feet

Round trip: To Middle Oval Lake, 21 miles
Hiking time: Allow 3 to 5 days
High point: 7700 feet
Elevation gain: 4700 feet in, 1000 feet out

Hikable: Mid-July through October
Map: Green Trails No. 83 Buttermilk Butte

Information: Forest Service Visitors Center, open mid-May to end of September, phone (509) 996-4000, or Methow Valley Ranger Station, phone (509) 997-2131. Ask about trails No. 410 and 410A.

Three mountain lakes, each in its own pocket scooped in the side of Sawtooth Ridge. Not quite as pretty as those in the Gold Creek area, but blessedly free from motorcycles, Oval Lakes are the most popular destination in the Twisp Ranger District. The use is equally divided between hikers and horse-riders. During a dry summer the horses pound the trail to inches-deep powder; better go early while the ground is still damp. However, don't go too early because during snowmelt season the crossing of Eagle Creek is extremely difficult. If the parking lot is jammed up by a dozen or two dozen horse trailers, each built for eight or more beasts, go elsewhere.

From the center of Twisp, drive the Twisp River road 14.7 miles, go left 0.3 mile on road No. 4430, signed "War Creek trail, Eagle Creek trail," then left 0.8 mile on road No. 4420, signed "Eagle Creek Trail," then turn sharply

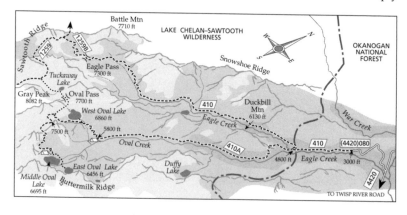

right and go 1.5 miles on road No. (4420)080 to the road-end and trail No. 410, elevation 3000 feet.

The first 1½ miles gain 1800 feet to a junction and the wilderness boundary. The right fork follows Eagle Creek to the crest of the Sawtooth Range, the recommended route for a loop. For a round trip to Oval Lakes, take the left fork (straight ahead). In ¼ mile cross Eagle Creek, which in early season is formidable for hikers; scout upstream and down for a safe crossing.

From Eagle Creek the trail gains 800 feet in a long ¾ mile and moderates, gaining 1200 feet in the next 3½ miles to a nice streamside campsite in a large meadow, 5800 feet. The next 1½ miles climb 1100 feet to a junction. Go right ¼ mile to West Oval Lake, 6860 feet.

The few nice campsites at West Oval Lake are so fragile that the Forest Service asks people to camp at Middle Oval Lake, too far for a day hike. If Middle Oval is the destination, plan to hike 5¾ miles to a first-night camp at the 5800-foot meadow.

For Middle Oval Lake go left at the junction, steeply at times, first in forest, then meadowland, and finally up barren slopes to a 7500-foot shoulder of Gray Peak. Drop 1000 feet to Middle Oval, 6695 feet. A way trail leads to East Oval Lake.

The Eagle Creek–Oval Lake loop is not recommended for novices. The trail, though not dangerous, often is so invisible that experienced highland roamers, fully map-equipped, are surprised when they find traces of tread. To do it, follow Eagle Creek 6 miles from the Oval Lake junction to 7300-foot Eagle Pass and drop 800 feet to Summit Trail No. 1259. Climb back to 7000 feet, and at a four-way junction go left on a sketchy trail to Tuckaway Lake, over 7700-foot Oval Pass to join the Middle Oval Lake trail. The loop totals 21 miles, elevation gain 5500 feet.

Oval Lakes trail between West and Middle Oval Lakes

64 | SCATTER LAKE

Round trip: 9 miles
Hiking time: 8 hours
High point: 7047 feet
Elevation gain: 3900 feet
Trip length: One day or backpack
Hikable: Mid-July through October
Map: Green Trails No. 82 Stehekin

Information: Forest Service Visitors Center, open mid-May to end of September, phone (509) 996-4000, or Methow Valley Ranger Station, phone (509) 997-2131. Ask about trail No. 427.

For a definition of "grueling," try this. Don't be tricked by the mere 4½ miles to the lake. They gain 3900 feet. Only mad dogs and Englishmen go out in this midday sun. Why do it, then? You'll know when you get there. From the cirque walls in the side of 8321-foot Abernathy Peak, the sterile brown talus, streaked with mineralized yellow and red, slopes to the shore of a stunning blue gem ringed by larches, their delicate green a striking contrast to vivid colors of the rock.

Drive the Methow Valley Highway to Twisp. Turn west on the Twisp River road, signed "Twisp River Rec. Area," and drive 22 miles (pavement ends at 14 miles). After crossing Scatter Creek go off right on a sideroad 500 feet, passing a corral, to the start of Scatter Creek trail No. 427, elevation 3147 feet.

The route begins on a cat track dating from selective logging (all the big pines were selected). In ¼ mile the way becomes a regular footpath and for several feet joins the Twisp River horse trail before climbing in earnest. The first mile makes long, gentle switchbacks above the Twisp valley.

Partridgefoot

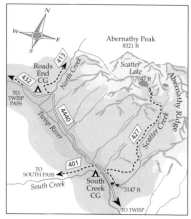

The second mile traverses and switchbacks high above Scatter Creek. At 2½ miles the creek is close.

At this point whoever built the trail apparently got tired of switchbacks; from now on when the hill is steep, so is the path. At 3½ miles cross the Scatter Lake fork of Scatter Creek and follow the right side of the stream. At 4 miles is a delightful camp in sound of a waterfall. The trail climbs above the falls, levels out, passes a tiny tarn, and reaches the shore of Scatter Lake, 7047 feet. It was worth it. Numerous pleasant camps but not much wood.

The highest point of the cirque wall is Abernathy. The summit is to the left of the point with a red cap.

Scatter Lake

65 | LOUIS LAKE

Round trip: 10½ miles
Hiking time: 5½ hours
High point: 5351 feet
Elevation gain: 2600 feet
Trip length: One day or backpack
Hikable: Mid-July through October
Map: Green Trails No. 82 Stehekin

Information: Forest Service Visitors Center, open mid-May to end of September, phone (509) 996-4000, or Methow Valley Ranger Station, phone (509) 997-2131. Ask about trails No. 401 and 428.

Beneath one of the most serrate stretches of Sawtooth Ridge is Louis Lake, large for this part of the Cascades, lying under terrific cliffs of 7742-foot Rennie Peak on the left and a nameless 8142-foot peak on the right. So narrow is the gash of a valley that even in midsummer the sun touches the floor only a few hours a day.

Drive the Methow Valley Highway to Twisp, turn west on the Twisp River road and go 22.5 miles, and just beyond South Creek Campground find the start of South Creek trail No. 401, elevation 3200 feet.

Cross the Twisp River on a bridge, cross the Twisp River horse trail, and ascend in sound of South Creek cascading down a slot canyon. At 2 miles, 3800 feet, is a junction. The main trail continues up South Creek another 5½ miles to the national park and a junction with the Rainbow Creek trail. Go left on Louis Lake trail No. 428, dropping a bit to camps and a bridge over South Creek. South Creek Butte can be recognized by its red crest.

At about 3½ miles the path enters Louis Creek valley; a hiker has the dark suspicion of entering a trap, a cul-de-sac with no escape through

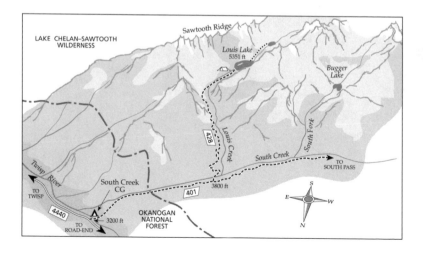

Louis Lake

precipices. The trail contours high above Louis Creek with many ups and a few downs. At 4 miles, where the way parallels the stream, an opening appears in the otherwise unbroken expanse of high walls and the route proceeds through it to the lake, 5351 feet.

The setting is spectacular. Near the far shore is a small, tree-covered island. The lake surface is largely choked with enormous masses of driftwood from gigantic winter avalanches. Camping at the lake is very limited and best not done at all; instead, use the sites several hundred feet before reaching the shore.

A second lake, tiny, is 1 mile away and 500 feet higher, which sounds like an easy amble, but it ain't, the access mostly over broad bad fields of big boulders. If determined to get there anyhow, find a trail of sorts that goes around a thicket of slide alder, then parallels the shore.

66 | Twisp Pass—Stiletto Vista

Round trip: To Twisp Pass, 9 miles
Hiking time: 6 to 8 hours
High point: 6064 feet
Elevation gain: 2400 feet
Trip length: One day or backpack
Hikable: Late June through October

Map: Green Trails No. 82 Stehekin
Information: Forest Service Visitors Center, open mid-May to end of September, phone (509) 996-4000, or Methow Valley Ranger Station, phone (509) 997-2131. Ask about trail No. 432.

Park Service backcountry use permit required for camping at Dagger Lake

Climb from Eastern Washington forest to Cascade Crest gardens, gla-cier-smoothed boulders, dramatic rock peaks, and views down to Bridge Creek and across to Goode and Logan. Then wander onward amid a glory of larch-dotted grass and flowers to an old lookout site with horizons so rich one wonders how the fire-spotter could ever have noticed smoke. For a special treat do the walk in autumn when the air is cool and the alpine country is blazing with color.

Drive the Methow Valley Highway to Twisp, turn west on the Twisp River road, signed "Twisp River Rec. Area," and drive 25 miles to a large trailhead parking area, elevation 3650 feet. (The road goes another 0.6 mile to the small Roads End Campground; no room to park there.)

The first ½ mile parallels the road before ascending moderately through woods, with occasional upvalley glimpses of pyramid-shaped Lincoln Butte. At 2 miles are a junction with Copper Pass trail No. 426 and the last well-watered campsite for a long, hot way. Cross the North Fork Twisp River on a footlog and continue fairly steeply on soft-cushioned tread to 3 miles; stop for a rest on ice-polished buttresses, in views down to valley-bottom forest and up to the ragged ridge of Hock Mountain, above the glaciated basin of the South Fork headwaters.

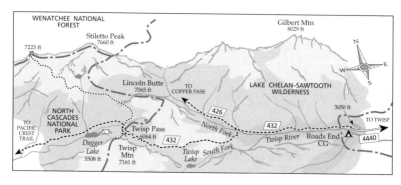

Dagger Lake from Twisp Pass

The trail emerges from trees to traverse a rocky sidehill, the rough tread sometimes blasted from cliffs. At about 4 miles the route enters heather and flowers. A final ¼ mile climbs to Twisp Pass, 6064 feet, 4½ miles, on the boundary of the North Cascades National Park. The pass is so fragile the Park Service prohibits camping on its side and the Forest Service wishes you wouldn't but doesn't bother to ban it because there isn't any water to speak of anyway.

The trail drops 450 steep feet in 1 mile to Dagger Lake camps at 5508 feet and 4 more miles to Bridge Creek and a junction with the Pacific Crest Trail.

For wider views ascend meadows north from the pass and look down to Dagger Lake and Bridge Creek and across to Logan, Goode, Black, Frisco, and much more. Don't go away without rambling the crest south from the pass about ¼ mile to the foot of Twisp Mountain and a magical surprise—a little pond hidden in alpine forest, surrounded by grass and blossoms.

The open slopes north of the pass demand extended exploration. And here is another surprise. Hikers heading in the logical direction toward Stiletto Peak will stumble onto sketchy tread of an ancient trail, fairly obvious the first mile, then less so. Follow the route up and down highlands, by sparkling creeks, to a green shelf under cliffs of 7660-foot Stiletto Peak, a fairy place of meandering streams and groves of wispy larch. Then comes a field of photogenic boulders, a rocky ridge, and the 7223-foot site of the old fire-lookout cabin. Look north over Copper Creek to Liberty Bell and Early Winter Spires; northwest to Tower, Cutthroat, Whistler, Arriva, and Black; southwest to McGregor, Glacier, and Bonanza; and south to Hock and Twisp—and these are merely a few of the peaks seen, not to mention the splendid valley. This vista is only 2 miles from Twisp Pass, an easy afternoon's round trip.

67 | COPPER PASS

Round trip: To pass, 10 miles
Hiking time: 6 hours
High point: 6760 feet
Elevation gain: 3100 feet
Trip length: One day

Loop trip: 21 miles
Hiking time: Allow 3 days
High point: 6760 feet
Elevation gain: 5500 feet

Hikable: July through mid-October
Map: Green Trails No. 82 Stehekin

Information: Forest Service Visitors Center, open mid-May to end of September, phone (509) 996-4000, or Methow Valley Ranger Station, phone (509) 997-2131. Ask about trails No. 426 and 432.

The climb to the heathery pass is steep, but the color is worth it. Try the trip in July when glacier lilies and yellowbells are blooming, or in August for asters and cow parsnip and paintbrush and gentians hurrying to set seed before the pollinators head south for the winter, or in late September when larch trees turn to gold.

The prospectors' trail of olden days connected the Twisp River to the Stehekin via Copper Pass and Bridge Creek. Unused for decades, in 1981 and 1982 it was reopened to the pass by volunteers from the Sierra Club and Outward Bound. The trail down to Bridge Creek has not been brushed but can be found and used for a 3-day loop trip, returning via Twisp Pass (Hike 66). This alternative requires a backcountry permit for the North Cascades National Park, obtainable at the Twisp Ranger Station.

Drive the Twisp River road to the end, elevation 3700 feet (Hike 66).

Hike Twisp River trail No. 432 for 2 miles to a junction just before crossing North Fork Twisp River (dwindled to a creek); go straight on trail No. 426, signed "Copper Pass." With more ups than downs the way follows the

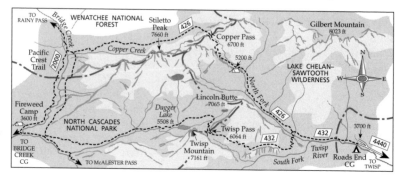

North Fork, mostly in woods. At 3½ miles cross the stream to a nice campsite, 5200 feet.

There's nothing now but up. In ¼ mile is a view of a double waterfall, and a bit farther, ruins of an old cabin. Scarcely deigning to switchback, the trail aims at the sky, partly in trees and partly in meadows.

At 6700 feet, 5 miles, is the sky—which is to say, Copper Pass, where herbaceous meadows yield to heather meadows. Day-hikers may gaze down Copper Creek, across to the rocky ridge of Early Winters Spire, out to faraway, ice-clad Goode Mountain, eat lunch, and go home satisfied.

Loopers can readily spot the trail dropping steeply to green meadows at the head of Copper Creek. A bit of searching at the far edge of the boggy meadow may be needed to find the resumption of tread in forest. In about 4 miles from the pass the path intersects the Pacific Crest Trail. Follow it down Bridge Creek 1 mile to enter North Cascades National Park, then 1 more mile to Fireweed Camp, 3600 feet. From Fireweed, 4 long, steep miles climb to Twisp Pass, 6064 feet, and 4 shorter miles drop to the trailhead, completing a loop of 21 miles.

Copper Pass

68 | WOLF CREEK

Round trip: To end of trail, 20 miles
Hiking time: Allow 2 to 3 days
High point: 5700 feet
Elevation gain: 3400 feet
Hikable: Mid-June through October
Maps: Green Trails No. 51 Mazama,
No. 83 Buttermilk Butte

Information: Forest Service Visitors
Center, open mid-May to end of
September, phone (509) 996-
4000, or Methow Valley Ranger
Station, phone (509) 997-2131.
Ask about trail No. 527; if
exploring, also ask about trail
No. 527A.

For the hiker who wants to be alone, really alone, try Wolf Creek (but
not in hunting season). It's a long walk up a long valley to meadows, old
mines, and abandoned sidetrails to golly knows where. Adventure! Get
lost—or at least bemused.

From the center of Winthrop drive Highway 20 east across the Methow
River bridge and go straight ahead, on the Twin Lakes road, signed "Sun
Mountain Lodge." At 1.3 miles turn right on the Wolf Creek road 4.3 miles,
then left on a road signed "L. Fork Wolf Creek." At 4.7 miles from Highway 20 turn right on road No. 5005, signed "Wolf Creek Trail," and at 8.4
miles go straight ahead, dropping to the large, road-end parking area and
trail No. 527, elevation 2400 feet, 9 miles from Highway 20 in Winthrop.

In the first easy ½ mile the trail enters the Lake Chelan–Sawtooth Wilderness. At about 3 miles is a campsite at the crossing of North Fork Wolf
Creek. In another ¼ mile is the unsigned and abandoned North Fork trail
No. 528 (if it can be found), which goes 5 miles to the 6000-foot divide between McKinney Mountain and Storey Peak. Somewhere along this trail
an old stock driveway takes off east past Milton Mountain to Gardner
Meadows; Milton Mountain is a former lookout site, so it must have a trail.

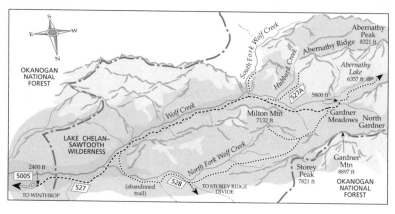

On the main Wolf Creek trail at 4 miles from the road-end, a short spur goes left to campsites near an old patrol cabin. The trail becomes more rugged with a few steep pitches and (in 1998) a washout gully 6 feet deep. At 7 miles is the abandoned South Fork Wolf Creek trail, dead-ending in 2 miles. At 7½ miles the abandoned Hubbard Creek trail No. 527A goes off left to climb high to a cirque on Abernathy Ridge.

By 8 miles, 5700 feet, the Gardner Meadows have shaped up nicely, giving a good look at Abernathy Ridge. The maintained trail ends at about 10 miles, 5800 feet. An abandoned trail, lost in vegetation, continues another 2 miles to a long-ago prospect in 7400-foot meadows below the bare cliffs of Abernathy Ridge. A cross-country explorer could visit Abernathy Lake, 6357 feet.

Gardner Meadow and Abernathy Ridge

69 | DRIVEWAY BUTTE

Round trip: 8 miles
Hiking time: 6 hours
High point: 6982 feet
Elevation gain: 3000 feet
  Trip length: One day
Hikable: Late May through
  September

Map: Green Trails No. 50 Washing-
  ton Pass
Information: Forest Service Visitors
  Center, open mid-May to end
  of September, phone (509) 996-
  4000, or Methow Valley Ranger
  Station, phone (509) 997-2131.
  Ask about trail No. 481.

The former lookout site has views down the Methow Valley to ranches and towns and across to the Pasayten Wilderness, south to Gardner Mountain and the glaciers on Silver Star Mountain, and west to peaks of the Cascade Crest. There's a price to pay—sweat, much sweat. Be advised—don't try those 3000 feet in the heat of day; most are out in the full glare of the cruel sun. Snow melts early on the south-facing slopes, making the hike possible in late May or early June when fields of sunflowers (balsamroot) are in full bloom. However, snow lingers in the high timber until middle or late June, halting a party not prepared to cope. Except during hunting season the trail is almost deserted.

Of the three routes to Driveway Butte, two haven't been maintained for 20 years: trail No. 450, from Early Winters Campground; and trail No. 481, from Rattlesnake Campground, which begins with a difficult ford of the

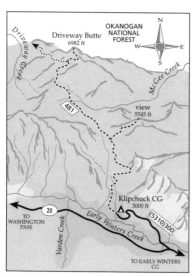

Methow River. The way described here is from Klipchuck Campground.

Drive Highway 20 east 12.6 miles from Washington Pass or 2.6 miles west from the Forest Service's Early Winters Campground. Between mileposts 175 and 176, turn onto road No. (5310)300, signed "Klipchuck Campground," and drive 1 mile to the campground entrance; park here. A few feet back from the entrance find a gated service road. Walk it about 150 feet to the start of Driveway Butte trail No. 481, elevation 3000 feet.

The trail sets out in a selective-logging area. (See the big stumps of the pines worthy of being selected.)

Site of the Driveway Butte Lookout

The grade is moderate at first but soon slants steeply up fields of bright yellow balsamroot, shade trees only too occasional.

After climbing 2100 feet in approximately 1¾ miles (that seem like 3), the path levels a bit, enters a dense forest, and comes to a junction. The campsites here have no water after the snow melts in middle or late June. If snow covers the main trail, which forks left, take the right fork steeply to the top of a 5545-foot nameless butte. A window in the trees gives a spectacular view of Silver Star Mountain.

From the junction the angle of the main trail moderates but the tread grows rougher, at times is obscured by brush, and at about 3½ miles disappears. A few rock cairns lead across open slopes of Driveway Butte. Take careful note of the point where the tread vanishes; you'll want to find this point on your way home. Should you lose the trail on the way up, simply zig and zag to the summit. Marvel how completely the old horse trail has vanished on the slopes, only to reappear 100 feet from the top.

The history of fire-watching from Driveway Butte began long, long ago with a platform in a tree. This was replaced in 1934 by a building on a 30-foot tower. In 1953 it was torn down and burned. Bits of glass and a scattering of rusty nails remain. So does the view.

70 | ABERNATHY PASS

Round trip: 18 miles
Hiking time: Allow 2 days
High point: 6400 feet
Elevation gain: 3400 feet
Hikable: July through October
Maps: Green Trails No. 50 Washington Pass, No. 51 Mazama

Information: Forest Service Visitors Center, open mid-May to end of September, phone (509) 996-4000, or Methow Valley Ranger Station, phone (509) 997-2131. Ask about trail No. 476.

Finding the trails along the North Gollydang Highway too peopled for your solitudinous tastes? Try Cedar Creek. Climb splendid forests, first in a narrow V valley and then in a broad U trough between Silver Star and Gardner Mountains, which do not expose themselves in full-frontal nudity but do fill the eyes through many peeping-Tom windows. Proceed to Abernathy Pass for the big picture. Or strike off through the open woods and get really lonesome and very high on slopes of the Big Kangaroo.

Drive Highway 20 west 2.3 miles from Early Winters Campground or east 13 miles from Washington Pass. Between mileposts 175 and 176 turn onto road No. 200, signed "Cedar Creek Trail." At 0.4 mile pass a large opening and reach the road-end at 0.9 mile, in a gravel pit. Cedar Creek trailhead No. 476 is atop the bank to the left, elevation 3000 feet.

Though the trail starts 400 vertical feet higher than the creek, to stay

Cedar Creek Falls

above the wild torrent it gains 500 feet in a scant 2 miles to Cedar Falls, a spectacular twin cataract, the destination of most hikers, many of whom stay at the camp here overnight despite the danger to their hearing.

The way continues to climb steeply to keep dry. At about 3 miles is a peephole view of the craggy summit of North Gardner Mountain. At 4 miles the post-glacial notch is left below and the U-shaped glacial trough entered, with a consequent flattening of the grade. The path crosses occasional aspen-dotted meadows that give looks at the impressive shoulders of Silver Star right and Gardner left, and far up the valley to a wall of mountains, part of the Abernathy Peak massif.

The pleasant forest walk is enlivened by creeks that may or may not be log-bridged and in snowmelt time may or may not be easy to cross. Campsites are scattered along the way, including one at West Fork Cedar Creek and another, the best and the last, a scant mile farther at Middle Fork, 7 miles, 5000 feet. (The old mile markers predate the Sandy Butte road, so subtract a mile.)

The valley head appears to be a cul-de-sac, no possible route through the solid wall of granite peaks. The 2 miles and countless switchbacks that climb 1400 feet to Abernathy Pass, 6400 feet, therefore seem a magic trick. The summit of the pass is a narrow cleft and the trail immediately drops to North Creek and the Twisp River. For views, scramble the granite knobs west from the pass, on architecturally handsome ledges and slabs and buttresses, in picturesque pines and larches. The climax knob is ¾ mile, 7002 feet. Look north to Snagtooth Ridge and Silver Star Mountain and south across North Creek to Gilbert Mountain and pyramid-shaped Reynolds Peak, and back down the long valley whence you came.

The greatest hiking hereabouts is on paths beaten out by climbers. In open forests aromatic with Labrador tea and white rhododendron ("skunkbush"), and boggy glades dotted with insect-eating butterwort, then on steep heather meadows and rockslides, follow Middle Fork Cedar Creek to the south end of Kangaroo Ridge, or West Fork to the north end. Since this country has some of the most famous granodiorite in the Cascades, that of the Golden Horn batholith, watch out for Yellow Helmets chalking their fingers and snapping their carabiners.

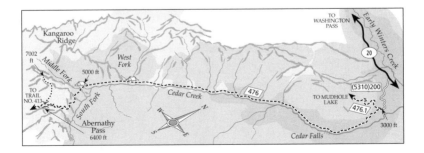

71 | CUTTHROAT PASS

Round trip: From Cutthroat Creek road-end to Cutthroat Pass, 12 miles
Hiking time: 6 to 8 hours
High point: 6800 feet
Elevation gain: 2300 feet
Trip length: One day or backpack

Hikable: July through mid-October
Map: Green Trails No. 50 Washington Pass

One-way trip: From Rainy Pass to Cutthroat road-end, 10½ miles
Hiking time: 6 to 7 hours
High point: 6800 feet
Elevation gain: 2000 feet
Trip length: One day

Information: Forest Service Visitors Center, open mid-May to end of September, phone (509) 996-4000, or Methow Valley Ranger Station, phone (509) 997-2131. Ask about trails No. 483 and 2000.

A high ridge with impressive views, among the most scenic sections of the Pacific Crest Trail. If transportation can be arranged, a hike can start at Rainy Pass and end at Cutthroat Creek, saving 400 feet of elevation gain. However, because a short sidetrip to sparkling Cutthroat Lake makes a refreshing rest stop, the trail is described starting at Cutthroat Creek.

Drive Highway 20 east from the Skagit Valley over Rainy and Washington Passes, or west from the Methow Valley. At milepost 167, near the

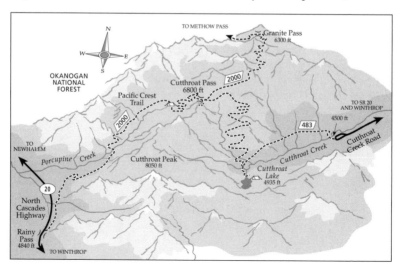

Cutthroat Creek bridge, turn up the Cutthroat Creek road and go 1 mile to the road-end and trailhead, elevation 4500 feet. The upper regions are dry, so have a full canteen.

The trail quickly crosses Cutthroat Creek and begins a gentle 1¾-mile ascent amid sparse rainshadow forest to a junction with the Cutthroat Lake trail. The 4935-foot lake is ¼ mile away, well worth a look; here, too, are the last practical all-summer campsites.

The next 2½ miles climb through big trees and little trees to meadows and a campsite (no water in late summer). A final scant 2 miles lead upward to 6800-foot Cutthroat Pass, about 6 miles from the road-end.

It is absolutely essential to stroll to the knoll south of the pass for a better look at the country. Cutthroat Peak, 8050 feet, stands high and close. Eastward are the barren west slopes of Silver Star. Mighty Liberty Bell sticks its head above a nearby ridge. Far southwest over Porcupine Creek is glacier-clad Dome Peak.

If time and energy permit, sidetrip 1 mile north on the Pacific Crest Trail to a knoll above Granite Pass and striking views down to Swamp Creek headwaters and across to 8444-foot Tower Mountain, 8366-foot Golden Horn, and Azurite, Black, and countless more peaks in the distance. This portion of the Crest Trail may be blocked by snow until mid-August.

From Cutthroat Pass the Crest Trail descends Porcupine Creek, passing several campsites, a pleasant 5 miles to Rainy Pass, the first 2 miles in meadows and the rest of the way in cool forest by numerous creeks. The trail ends a few hundred feet west of the summit of 4840-foot Rainy Pass.

Mountain goats at Cutthroat Pass

72 | MAPLE PASS

Round trip: To pass, 6½ miles
Hiking time: 4½ hours
High point: 6600 feet
Elevation gain: 1800 feet

Loop trip: 7 miles
Hiking time: 5 hours
High point: 6850 feet
Elevation gain: 1950 feet

Trip length: One day
Hikable: Mid-July through mid-October
Maps: Green Trails No. 49 Mt. Logan, No. 50 Washington Pass, No. 81 McGregor Mtn., No. 82 Stehekin

Information: Forest Service Visitors Center, open mid-May to end of September, phone (509) 996-4000, or Methow Valley Ranger Station, phone (509) 997-2131. Ask about trail No. 740.

Lakes, little flower fields, small meadows, a loop, and big views pretty well sum it up. The Forest Service built the trail to the pass (over the objection of the Park Service), intending it to be a segment of the Pacific Crest Trail, only to discover what had been obvious to the Park Service—that the impact on fragile meadows by hundreds of hikers, and especially by horses, brought by construction of the trail would be disastrous.

Drive Highway 20 east some 38 miles from Newhalem or west 35 miles from Winthrop to Rainy Pass and park at the south-side rest area. Find trail No. 740, signed "Lake Ann—Maple Pass." Elevation, 4855 feet.

Within a few feet the trail splits; the left fork is the return route. Altitude is gained at the obnoxiously easy grade typical of the freeway. At 1½ miles, 5400 feet, is a spur to the left, to Lake Ann, destination of most hikers. The ½-mile path goes along the outlet valley, nearly level, by two shallow

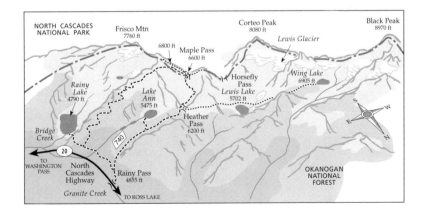

Lake Ann and Black Mountain

lakelets, around marshes, to the shore. Due to the dense population, camping is prohibited within ¼ mile of the lake.

The main trail ascends across a large rockslide well above Lake Ann. At 2¼ miles is 6200-foot Heather Pass; from a switchback, look northwest to Black Peak, Lewis Peak, and the cirque of Wing Lake, out of sight under the peak. A meager way trail tortuously traverses steep hillsides of heather, snow, and boulders to Lewis Lake and Wing Lake.

The main trail continues from Heather Pass, contouring over the top of cliffs 1000 feet above Lake Ann to Maple Pass at 3⅓ miles, 6600 feet.

For the loop and more views, a primitive trail follows the ridge crest eastward to a 6850-foot shoulder of Frisco Mountain and then descends, steeply at times, the ridge between the two spectacular cirques that hold Lake Ann and Rainy Lake. The trail joins the Rainy Lake trail ½ mile from the loop's start.

73 | STILETTO PEAK LOOKOUT SITE

Round trip: 14 miles
Hiking time: 10 hours
High point: 7223 feet
Elevation gain: 3200 feet in, 500 feet out

Trip length: One day or backpack
Hikable: July through October
Map: Green Trails No. 82 Stehekin
Information: Marblemount Ranger Station, phone (360) 873-4500

So you were totally enthralled by the Maple Pass loop (Hike 72)? But you did wish your raptures had not been so frequently disrupted by the ecstasies of other lovers? Sometimes a person wants solitude to pick his nose. The High Lonesome. Well, try a trailhead just a mile away from "The Lakes" sign. For chaps in no mood to talk, Stiletto, that's the walk.

Drive Highway 20 to between mileposts 158 and 159 and spot the Bridge Creek trailhead, located at the lowest point between Rainy Pass and Washington Pass, elevation 4500 feet.

Set out down the Bridge Creek valley on the Pacific Crest Trail. In a scant 1 mile go left on the Copper Pass–Stiletto Peak trail to a campsite near the Copper Creek trail. Cross Copper Creek. Proceed downvalley a scant ¼ mile to a junction. The straight-ahead ends in a few hundred feet at an abandoned mining camp; the real trail makes an abrupt left turn, climbs a bit, then drops some more. Cross a braided stream as best you can. About 2½ miles from the highway, having lost some 500 feet, enter the North Cascades National Park. In several hundred feet turn left on the Stiletto Peak trail, 4000 feet, the trail sign obscured by vegetation.

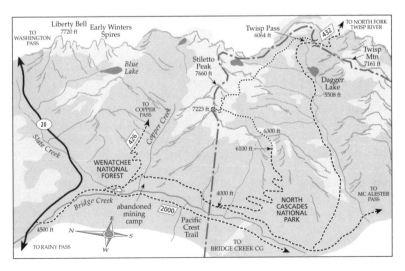

The trail, mostly in good shape, gets down to the business of climbing 2100 feet in 3 miles. Halfway, views begin to open wide, excuses to pause and let the sweat cool. At 3 miles, 6100 feet, at the edge of a large rock-strewn meadow, tread of the horse trail built in 1931 to service the Stiletto Lookout vanishes in a mishmash of animal trails. A sometimes sketchy and intermittent path continues to a 6300-foot saddle in a spur ridge. The main trail to Twisp Pass (Hike 66) contoured beneath Stiletto Peak. The sidetrail to the lookout site turns left uphill. Just follow your nose along the spur to the top. Actually, the lookout was at the dead end of a spur trail from the main trail, which continued—and can still be found here and there—to Twisp Pass (Hike 66). The final scant mile or so of the route to the lookout is not difficult to find. Just trust your nose, avoiding all cliffs. The lookout is exactly where it should have been, at 7223 feet on the tip of the ridge west from the 7660-foot summit of Stiletto Peak. Little evidence of its existence remains except the usual litter of rusty nails, shards of glass, charred timber from the cabin-burning ceremony of the 1950s.

Get out the map to see what you can see. Box the compass the full circle of 360 degrees. Peaks: Early Winter Spires, Liberty Bell, Cutthroat, Whistler, Black, Corteo, Frisco, Goode, Formidable, Dome, McGregor, Glacier, Bonanza, Hock, and Stiletto. Deep valleys: Copper Creek, State Creek, Rainy Pass between Granite Creek and Bridge Creek, Stehekin River. Glaciers: The Sandalee on McGregor particularly catches the eye.

Time to put away the map and camera and run for home. That bright light just touching the western horizon of crags and ice, that's the setting sun.

Meadow at the end of Stiletto Peak trail

74 | GOLDEN HORN

Round trip: 23 miles
Hiking time: Allow 2 days
High point: 6900 feet
Elevation gain: 2700 feet in, 600 feet out
Hikable: August through September
Map: Green Trails No. 50 Washington Pass

Information: Forest Service Visitors Center, open mid-May to end of September, phone (509) 996-4000, or Methow Valley Ranger Station, phone (509) 997-2131. Ask about trail No. 2000.

Several explanations are in order. First, three drainages are traversed on this spectacular section of the Pacific Crest Trail; the area designation as "Early Winters" is arbitrary. Second, the hike is not to the summit of Golden Horn (Mountain), but to the Snowy Lakes, in a subalpine basin between Golden Horn and Tower Mountain. Third, the scene is not in a national park or wilderness because—danged if we know. When the North Cascades National Park was being considered, no trail penetrated the area, thus few hikers could from personal experience speak for its inclusion in the park. State and federal officials deigned to do a fast flyover and—from 10,000 feet—pompously declared the area to be "not of national park caliber." Now there is a trail. So go take a hike. Then open your mouth and yell at Congresspersons and any other ears within reach.

Why do we call the trip "Golden Horn"? The rugged peaks and green

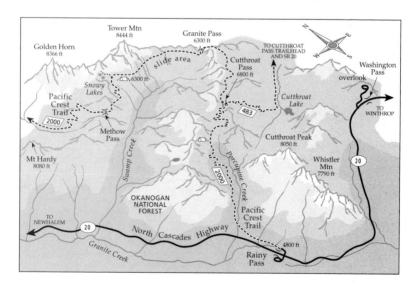

Tower Mountain (center) and Golden Horn (left) from Granite Pass

meadows and groves of larch that turn gold in fall are not unique in the North Cascades. But the rock is. The haunting hue of pinkish-goldish feldspar gives the peak its name; geologists adopted the name "Golden Horn Granodiorite" for the batholith. In our mind the rock alone establishes national park caliber.

Upper Snowy Lake

Drive Highway 20 some 35 miles from Winthrop or 37.6 miles from Newhalem to Rainy Pass and park in the north-side trailhead area, elevation 4800 feet.

At a grade that refuses to exceed a horsey 10 percent, the two-horses-wide Crest Trail ascends through forest to big and bigger meadows. At 4 miles pass a campsite; at 5½ miles reach Cutthroat Pass, 6800 feet (Hike 71). The way continues up meadows and rockslides to a 6900-foot high point with a view of needlelike Tower Mountain and the golden horn of Golden Horn, then drops 600 feet to Granite Pass; snow may linger on the tread until August in this vicinity, at a steepness that will force hikers lacking ice axes to turn around.

From the pass the freeway-wide trail has been dynamited in cliffs and gouged out of steep unstable slopes for a long 2 miles across Swamp Creek headwaters. Due to slides this section is often impassable to horses and timorous hikers. At about 2 miles from Cutthroat Pass the trail reaches a small stream, 6300 feet, in a meadow flat not yet recovered from the devastating impact of the construction crew that camped here just a single summer in the 1960s. See if you can find their horseshoe pits. Nevertheless, this is the place to camp. If you reach a switchback you have gone too far.

An unmarked way trail climbs steeply ½ mile to Lower Snowy Lake, 6735 feet, and a bit more to Upper Snowy Lake, 6839 feet, miraculously located precisely in the summit of Snowy Lakes Pass. Thoughtless hikers and horse-riders have contributed their share of damage to the acres of fragile meadows. Cowboys and cowgirls, leave your horses beside the Crest Trail and walk; don't take them to dig post holes with their hooves in the soft turf. Pedestrians, spread your sleeping bags by the Crest Trail, not on the heather or fragile meadows near the lakes. No fires, please!

The view from Snowy Lakes Pass is straight up Golden Horn and Tower Mountain and out across Methow Pass to the spires of Mt. Hardy, above headwaters of the West Fork Methow River. The determined hiker can scramble higher on slopes of Golden Horn Mountain for marginally larger views; but the feldspar crystals are just as stunning throughout the batholith.

75 | GOAT PEAK

Round trip: 5 miles
Hiking time: 6 hours
High point: 7001 feet
Elevation gain: 1400 feet
Trip length: One day
Hikable: June through October
Map: Green Trails No. 51 Mazama

Information: Forest Service Visitors Center, open mid-May to end of September, phone (509) 996-4000, or Methow Valley Ranger Station, phone (509) 997-2131. Ask about trail No. 457.

A commanding view of the Methow Valley and the north face of Silver Star Mountain, the most spectacular peak in the area. Most of the way is on a south slope, and all the way is hot and bone-dry, so start early and carry buckets of water.

Drive Highway 20 west 12 miles from Winthrop. Just before crossing the Methow River, go right on county road No. 1163 toward Mazama. At 6.2 miles turn right on road No. 52, go 2.8 miles from this intersection, turn left on road No. 5225, signed "Goat Mountain trail 9 miles." At 8.3 miles from the Mazama road, go right on road No. (5225)200, and at 12.2 miles reach a saddle and trailhead, elevation 5600 feet.

Goat Peak trail No. 457 takes off south, sometimes tree-shaded, sometimes in open, sparse meadows, sometimes on rocky ridges with great views. If often steep and rough, the tread is quite decently walkable as it switchbacks to the lookout building atop Goat Peak, 7001 feet.

Though 9 miles distant, 8901-foot Silver Star easily dominates the scene. North Gardner Mountain, 8956 feet, highest in the region, is a little to the

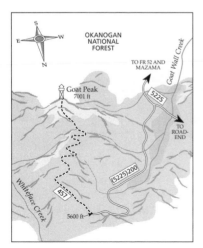

Goat Peak Lookout

Methow Valley and Silver Star Mountain from Goat Peak

south. Farther away are the precipitous Washington Pass peaks. Northward rise the rolling, high ridges of the Pasayten Wilderness; this view of their south slopes makes them seem barren and unimpressive, very unlike the reality experienced by hikers.

76 | LOST RIVER

Round trip: 8 miles
Hiking time: 4 hours
High point: 2700 feet
Elevation gain: 600 feet in, 300 feet out
Trip length: One day or backpack
Hikable: Mid-May through October

Maps: Green Trails No. 50 Washington Pass, No. 51 Mazama
Information: Forest Service Visitors Center, open mid-May to end of September, phone (509) 996-4000, or Methow Valley Ranger Station, phone (509) 997-2131. Ask about trail No. 484.

A trail ambles by a loud river through forest and across rockslides to pleasant camps at the mouth of the legendary Lost River Gorge, a part of the Pasayten Wilderness that is as wild as it was a century ago and likely to be so a century from now. Look all you want, and maybe even touch, if you dare.

From Winthrop, drive Highway 20 west to the hamlet (post office, gas station, grocery) of Mazama. Coming from the west on Highway 20, at 1.5 miles past Early Winters Campground turn left, cross the Methow River, and go 0.4 mile to Mazama. From the hamlet, drive upvalley on Harts Pass road No. 54, which becomes No. 5400 at the Lost River. Cross the Lost River and at 7.1 miles from Mazama turn right on road No. (5400)040, signed "Monument Creek trail No. 484." Drive 0.3 mile to the trailhead, signed "Eureka Trail," elevation 2400 feet.

Call the trail what you want, the wide and soft tread, next thing to flat, pokes along in forest 2 miles to the high point of 2700 feet. The next 2 miles are generally rough, in an alternation of trees and rocks. At about 3¼ miles (omitting miles of wild valley) is the boundary of the Pasayten Wilderness. At 4 miles is the dramatic confluence of two gorges, Eureka Creek from the left, Lost River from the right. A sturdy bridge crosses

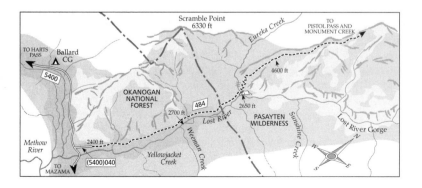

Lost River near Eureka Creek

Eureka Creek to choice campsites located a bit upstream beside the Lost River at 2650 feet.

The usual plan is to loiter here for lunch or overnight, then loiter on back to the car. The trail does something perfectly awful—climbs 4600 feet up the hogback between the two canyons to 7300-foot Pistol Pass, and nary a drop to drink, then drops 2800 feet into Monument Creek. Ascending the brutal path to hot-as-a-Pistol Pass is as recommendable as a Fourth of July picnic in Death Valley. However, it's worth huffing up ½ mile to a great view downriver toward Gardner Mountain.

At no point can a trail-walker see more than the awesome exit of the Lost River Gorge, a chasm where the hand of trail-constructing man never has set foot. The few doughty explorers who venture into its mysteries usually do so in late summer, when the river is low. They mostly wade, silently praying that no cloudbursts occur while they are in the trap. Forest Service rangers refer to it as "the wilderness Wilderness."

77 | ROBINSON PASS

Round trip: To pass, 18 miles
Hiking time: Allow 2 days
High point: 6200 feet
Elevation gain: 3600 feet
Hikable: Late May through October

Loop trip: 43 miles
Hiking time: Allow 5 to 7 days
High point: 7500 feet
Elevation gain: 10,100 feet
Hikable: Mid-July to October

Maps: Green Trails No. 50 Washington Pass; for loop add No. 18 Pasayten, No. 51 Mazama, No. 19 Billy Goat

Information: Forest Service Visitors Center, open mid-May to end of September, phone (509) 996-4000, or Methow Valley Ranger Station, phone (509) 997-2131. Ask about trails No. 478, 474, and 484.

The geography here is not of the big glacier–monster crag sort characteristic of the North Cascades National Park, but spectacular it surely is— high, massive, shaggy ridges, naked and cliffy, reminding of Montana, and enormous U-shaped glacial troughs gouged by Pleistocene ice from Canada, and boggling swaths of climax avalanches that periodically sweep thousands of feet down from the ridge to valley bottoms and hundreds of feet up the far sides. Also, lovely streams rush through parkland forests. And among the greatest appeals, trips in the "wilderness Wilderness" are like taking a ride in a time machine back to the 1930s. Solitude! Though Robinson Creek is a main thoroughfare into the heart of the Pasayten Wilderness, and a favorite with horsefolk, most come in the fall hunting season. Summer is lonesome even on the main trail and on byways one can roam a hundred miles and maybe never see another soul.

Drive the Harts Pass road upvalley from Mazama (Hike 76, Lost River). At 7 miles pavement ends. At 8.3 miles cross Robinson

Robinson Creek trail

Creek and at 8.5 miles turn right into a small trailhead camp area, elevation 2600 feet.

The trail follows the creek ¼ mile, then switchbacks a couple hundred feet above the water. At 1 mile cross a bridge over Robinson Creek and shortly enter the Pasayten Wilderness. Partly in rocky-brushy opens, partly in forest of big ponderosa pines, then smaller firs, the way climbs steadily, moderately, at just short of 3 miles crossing a steel bridge over Beauty Creek, which waterfalls down from Beauty Peak. At 4 miles recross Robinson Creek on a bridge. The avalanche country has been entered, wide aisles cut in the forest, huge jackstraws piled up; from here on the way is a constant garden.

At 6 miles are a log crossing of Robinson Creek, now much smaller, and Porcupine Camp, in the woods and unappealing except in a storm. To here, avalanche meadows have here and there interrupted the continuous forest. From now on strips of forest here and there interrupt the ridge-to-creek meadows. A nice camp is located in the first broad meadow above Porcupine; an even better one in the second, at 6½ miles, 4900 feet, by the creek in a grove of large spruce trees; and a third just before Robinson Pass, in the trees 300 feet below the trail.

The trail sidehills through flower fields, rock gardens, and avalanche gardens, to Robinson Pass at 9 miles, 6200 feet, a great broad gap through which the continental glacier flowed. Long-ago forest fires cleared the big timber and now the wildflowers blaze.

The pass is a trip in itself, but also is the takeoff for longer journeys. To begin, the open slopes above the pass invite easy roaming—to the left, up to big views from Peak 6935 and onward to Slate Pass, just 2 miles from Robinson Pass, and another mile to Slate Peak, or the other way on the long, lonesome heights of Gold Ridge, and maybe along the ridge a mile to Devils Peak, or (climbers only) 2 miles more to 8726-foot Robinson Mountain, the neighborhood giant.

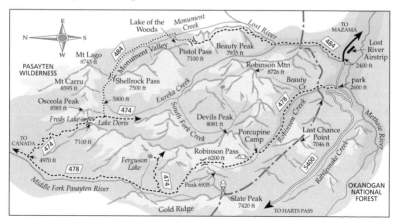

Robinson Creek trail near Robinson Pass

If trail-walking is preferred, descend Middle Fork Pasayten River, through gaspers of avalanches from Gold Ridge, the most impressive series of swaths in the Cascades; 15 miles from the pass is Soda Creek, and in another 8 miles, Canada. The classic long loop of the region is as follows: Descend the Middle Fork 6½ miles, go up by Freds Lake to a 7100-foot pass, and down by Lake Doris to the end of maintained trail. From here the old tread may be hard to follow around the headwaters of Eureka Creek, under Osceola, Carru, and Lago, three peaks between 8587 and 8745 feet, and up to Shellrock Pass, 7500 feet, 8 miles from the Middle Fork trail. Proceed 8½ miles down forests of Monument Creek and up by Lake of the Woods to Pistol Pass, 7100 feet. Finish with 10¾ infamous miles down, down, and down, hot and thirsty, to the Lost River and out to the Methow road, reached at a point 2 miles from Robinson Creek. Total loop, 43 miles, elevation gain about 10,000 feet. Allow a week.

78 | WEST FORK METHOW RIVER

Round trip: 12 miles
Hiking time: 6 hours
High point: 3600 feet
Elevation gain: 900 feet, plus ups and downs
Trip length: One day or backpack
Hikable: Late May through mid-October

Map: Green Trails No. 50 Washington Pass
Information: Forest Service Visitors Center, open mid-May to end of September, phone (509) 996-4000, or Methow Valley Ranger Station, phone (509) 997-2131. Ask about trail No. 480.

Early in the season, when the highlands are of no use to anyone but skiers, is the happy time to walk this trail, sometimes beside the West Fork Methow River, always in sound of the roar, with look-ups through the trees to the country where the flowers will not appear for months. But they're already blossoming here.

Drive to Mazama (Hike 76, Lost River) and proceed upvalley on the Harts Pass road 9 miles to a junction. Keep left on road No. (5400)060, signed "River Bend Campground," 0.8 mile to the road-end informal campground. The trailhead is located at the upper campsite, elevation 2700 feet.

The trail crosses Rattlesnake Creek (yes, keep an eye out) and ambles up and down in forest and around and across giant rockslides. At about 2 miles it crosses Trout Creek on a log bridge and passes a campsite. At about 3 miles a delightful camp is located beside the river. At 4 miles the way ascends above the water and doesn't come back down for a mile. At 6 miles, 3600 feet, it leaves the river for good; time to go home.

The West Fork trail goes on, of course. At 8⅓ miles, 4100 feet, it intersects the Pacific Crest Trail. Turning right (north) isn't recommended; Grasshopper Pass is better reached from Harts Pass. Turning left might be considered, because in that direction lie Methow Pass, Snowy Lakes Pass, and Golden Horn (Hike 74).

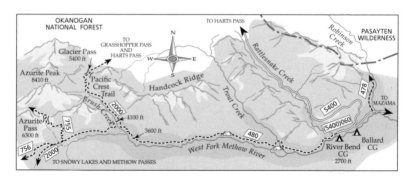

West Fork Methow River

79 | TROUT CREEK

Round trip: 6 miles
Hiking time: 4 hours
High point: 5425 feet
Elevation gain: 100 feet in, 800 feet out
Trip length: One day or backpack
Hikable: July through September

Map: Green Trails No. 50 Washington Pass (trail not shown)
Information: Forest Service Visitors Center, open mid-May to end of September, phone (509) 996-4000, or Methow Valley Ranger Station, phone (509) 997-2131. Ask about trail No. 479.

When the meadows of the Harts Pass (very) highlands are engulfed in clouds, why fight the mists? Settle for a lower level, the (still quite) highlands, the vast meadows of South Fork Trout Creek. The trail doesn't get much maintenance, so it's rough and brushy in spots. In the meadows where the grass and flowers grow to a hiker's hips it can scarcely be seen or even found by probing feet. On a wet day this is an ideal place to test the claims of the manufacturers of those hoity-toity-pricey rain pants.

Drive to Mazama (Hike 76, Lost River) and proceed upvalley on the Harts Pass road. From the valley floor abruptly ascend the Big Hill, past the one-car-wide (a small one) cliffhanger of Dead Horse Point to meadowland and subalpine forest. At 16.7 miles from Mazama (just 2.3 miles short of Harts Pass) find Trout Creek trail No. 479 in a meadow with a small flat space to park, elevation 5425 feet. (In 1998 the sign was missing.)

The trail wanders up and down, seemingly without aim, the first ¼ mile. In the next ¼ mile it drops 250 feet from a rocky knoll. The next ¼ mile

Columbine

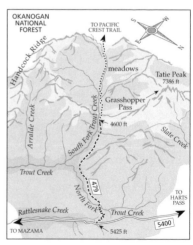

Flower field in the headwaters of Trout Creek

descends more moderately to a crossing of North Fork Trout Creek. The way continues down in woods, over several large boulder fields. At 2½ miles is the low point, 4600 feet, at the edge of meadowland.

The path now tilts slightly up, following the South Fork. In early July the tread might be findable another mile but by the end of the month, forget it. On the far side of the meadow are possible campsites.

80 | GRASSHOPPER PASS

Round trip: 11 miles
Hiking time: 6 hours
High point: 7000 feet
Elevation gain: 1000 feet in, 1000 feet out
Trip length: One day or backpack
Hikable: July through October

Map: Green Trails No. 50 Washington Pass
Information: Forest Service Visitors Center, open mid-May to end of September, phone (509) 996-4000, or Methow Valley Ranger Station, phone (509) 997-2131. Ask about trail No. 2000.

Wide-open, big-sky meadow ridges, grand views of giant peaks and forested valleys. The entire hike is above timberline, contouring hillsides, traversing gardens, and sometimes following the exact Cascade Crest.

Drive to Mazama (Hike 76, Lost River). Continue 19 miles upvalley to 6198-foot Harts Pass. From the pass turn left on the Meadows Campground road. At 1.5 miles keep right at a fork, to the road-end at 2 miles and the trailhead, elevation 6400 feet.

Azurite Peak and Grasshopper Pass

The Pacific Crest Trail immediately leaves the trees, going along an open slope below diggings of the Brown Bear Mine and above a pretty meadow. The first mile is a gentle ascent to the 6600-foot east shoulder of a 7400-foot peak. The way swings around the south slopes of this peak to a saddle, 7000 feet, overlooking Ninetynine Basin at the head of Slate Creek, then contours 7386-foot Tatie Peak to another saddle, 6900 feet, and a magnificent picture of Mt. Ballard.

A moderate descent, with a stretch of switchbacks, leads around a 7500-foot peak. In a bouldery basin at 4 miles, 6600 feet, is the only dependable water on the trip, a cold little creek flowing from mossy rocks through a flower-and-heather meadow ringed by groves of larch. Splendid camps.

The trail climbs gradually a final mile to the broad swale of 6700-foot Grasshopper Pass. (Fine camps in early summer when snowmelt water is available.) But don't stop here—go ¼ mile more and a few feet higher on the ridge to a knob just before the trail starts down and down to Glacier Pass. The views are dramatic across Slate Creek forests to 8440-foot Azurite Peak and 8301-foot Mt. Ballard. Eastward are meadows and trees of Trout Creek, flowing to the Methow.

Each of the peaks contoured by the trail invites a sidetrip of easy but steep scrambling to the summit, and the wanderings are endless amid larches and pines and spruces, flowers blossoming from scree and buttress, and the rocks—colorful shales, slates, conglomerates, and sandstones, and an occasional igneous intrusion.

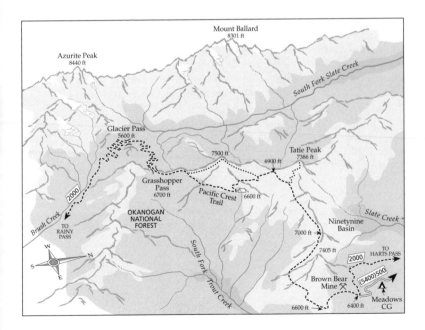

81 | WINDY PASS

Round trip: 7 miles
Hiking time: 5 hours
High point: 6900 feet
Elevation gain: 500 feet in, 1000 feet out
Trip length: One day or backpack
Hikable: Early July through October

Maps: Green Trails No. 18 Pasayten Peak, No. 50 Washington Pass
Information: Forest Service Visitors Center, open mid-May to end of September, phone (509) 996-4000, or Methow Valley Ranger Station, phone (509) 997-2131. Ask about trail No. 2000.

In all the hundreds of miles of the Pacific Crest Trail in Washington, this ranks among the easiest and most scenic segments. The hike starts in meadows and stays high the entire way, contouring gardens thousands of feet above the trees of Slate Creek, magnificent views at every step.

Drive to Harts Pass (Hike 80, Grasshopper Pass), turn right on the Slate Peak road, and drive about 1.5 miles to the first switchback and a small parking area at the trailhead, elevation 6800 feet.

If the trip is being done in early July, don't be discouraged if the road beyond Harts Pass is blocked by snow and the trail beginning is blinding-white; snow lingers here later than on any other portion of the hike, and mostly clear trail can be expected after a frosty start.

The Pacific Crest Trail gently climbs a meadow shelf the first ½ mile, contours steep slopes of Slate Peak, and drops into lovely little Benson Basin, a creek and nice camps a few hundred feet below the tread. The way swings up and out to a spur ridge, contours to Buffalo Pass and another spur, and then descends above the gorgeous greenery of Barron Basin to 6257-foot Windy Pass and delightful camps in flowers and larch trees.

Sad to say, the wreckers have been here. Barron Basin is one of the most magnificent family-accessible glorylands in the Cascades, but it is mainly

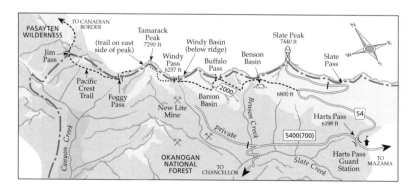

Pacific Crest Trail in Benson Basin

"private property" and the "owners" have raised havoc, gouging delicate meadows with bulldozers, dumping garbage at will. This hike is bound to convert any casual walker into a fierce enemy of the ultra-permissive federal mining laws, which make it next to impossible for the Forest Service to protect the land. Some of the desecration is very new but much is a century old—note how long Nature needs to restore ravaged meadows.

Sidetrips from the pass will make a person want the basin to be reclaimed for the public domain and placed within the Pasayten Wilderness; the boundary presently follows the divide, excluding the miner-mangled slopes to the west and the entire route thus far of the Pacific Crest Trail. Wander meadows north to the panoramas from 7290-foot Tamarack Peak, or walk the Crest Trail a short mile into Windy Basin, offering the best (and most heavily used) camps.

Views on the way? They start with Gardner Mountain, the Needles, Silver Star, Golden Horn, Tower Mountain, and especially the near bulks of Ballard and Azurite. Westerly, Jack and Crater dominate, but part of Baker can also be seen, and many more peaks. Easterly is the Pasayten country, high and remote.

Before or after the hike, take a sidetrip to the fire lookout on the 7440-foot summit of Slate Peak, formerly the highest point in Washington State attainable by automobiles; the road (built early in the Cold War to ward off Soviet bombers) is now gated ¼ mile from the summit, and that's a good start; moving the gate back another mile would help more—that last stretch of road is uncomfortably dizzy for flatland drivers.

82 | ELBOW BASIN —THREE FOOLS LOOP

One-way trip: From Castle Pass to Ross Lake, 23 miles
Hiking time: Allow 3 to 5 days
High point: 6687 feet
Elevation gain: About 9000 feet

One-way trip: From Harts Pass to Ross Lake, 51 miles
Hiking time: Allow 7 to 9 days

One-way trip: From near Allison Pass (Canada) to Ross Lake, 35 miles
Hiking time: Allow 5 to 7 days

Hikable: Mid-July through September
Maps: Green Trails Nos. 18 Pasayten Peak; 50 Washington Pass; 17 Jack Mtn.; 16 Ross Lake
Information: Forest Service Visitors Center, open mid-May to end of September, phone (509) 996-4000, or Methow Valley Ranger Station, phone (509) 997-2131. Ask about trails No. 2000 and 749.

A classic highland wander from the Cascade Crest to Ross Lake (reservoir), up and down a lonesome trail through some of the wildest valleys, ridges, and meadows in the range. A one-way trip is recommended, starting either at Harts Pass or near Manning Park headquarters in Canada and ending at the reservoir. (See note on border crossings in Hike 100, Pacific Crest National Scenic Trail.) Special transportation arrangements are required: a drop-off at Harts Pass (or near Manning Park headquarters—see Hike 84, Cascade Loop Trail and Monument 83); and a pickup by boat from Ross Lake Resort (Hike 44, Desolation Peak), though a party can, if desired, exit via the East Bank Trail (Hike 42).

Drive to Harts Pass (Hike 81, Windy Pass) and go right on the Slate Peak road about 1½ miles to the first switchback and trailhead.

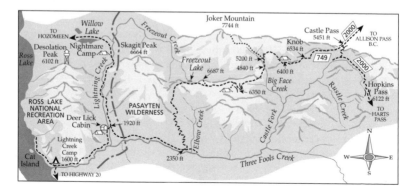

Woody Pass Peak from the side of Three Fools Peak (Harvey Manning photo)

Hike the Pacific Crest Trail (Hike 100) 27 miles from Harts Pass (or 11 miles from near Manning Park headquarters) to Castle Pass, elevation 5451 feet. Turn west on Elbow Basin trail No. 749, climbing steeply in forest, then meadows. At 1½ miles, 5800 feet, enter a little basin with a welcome creeklet, the first dependable water since before Castle Pass, and the last for several more miles. Tread ascends from the basin, swings around a spur, descends meadows to a saddle, and climbs the crest to a 6534-foot knob that ranks among the most magnificent viewpoints of the region. Look north across the headwaters of Castle Creek to Castle Peak, Frosty Mountain in Canada, and Mt. Winthrop; look south across forests of Three Fools Creek to peaks along and west of the Cascade Crest; look in every direction and look for hours and never see all there is to see. The way drops from the knob and climbs ridge-top heather and parklands to 5 miles, 6200 feet, and a grandly scenic camp—but the only water, if any, is from snowmelt.

The trail angles down across a broad, steep flower garden. At 5½ miles is a tumbling creek; below the trail here is a campsite on a tiny, wooded shelf. The way then switchbacks down forest to Big Face Creek, beneath the impressive wall of Joker Mountain, 7 miles, 5000 feet, reaching the valley bottom. For a mandatory sidetrip, fight through a bit of brush and climb the open basin of the creek to a high saddle with views out to Hozomeen and the Chilliwacks and below to a snowy cirque lake draining to Freeze-out Creek.

The trail goes gently downstream in trees to a crossing of Big Face Creek at 7 miles, 4840 feet, then turns right in a gravel wash to the ford. A possible camp here on gravel bars.

A long climb begins up forest to avalanche greenery; when tread vanishes in the grass go directly uphill, watching for sawn logs. The ascent continues in trees, opens to meadows, and at 9 miles, 6350 feet, tops out in the wide green broad-view pass between Big Face and Elbow Creeks. A sidetrail drops ¼ mile to a campsite and meandering stream in the glorious park of Elbow Basin. The main trail—tread missing for long stretches—contours and climbs north around the basin to a grassy swale (and a scenic camp, if snowmelt is available) near the ridge crest at 10½ miles. Be sure to walk to the 6687-foot plateau summit of the ridge and views: east to the Cascade Crest; south to Jack Mountain; west to the Pickets, Chilliwacks, Desolation, and especially the nearby towers of Hozomeen; north into Canada.

The trail descends near and along the crest, giving a look down to the tempting cirque of Freezeout Lake (accessible via a steep scramble), passing through a spectacular silver forest. A stern drop commences down and down hot and dry burn meadows and young trees. The mouth grows parched, the knees floppy. At 14 miles, 2350 feet, the trail at last touches Three Fools Creek and a possible camp; stop for an orgy of drinking and foot-soaking and an understanding of why this trip is not recommended to begin at Ross Lake (reservoir).

Hopes of an easy downhill water-grade hike are quickly dashed by a 1000-foot climb. The trail then goes down, goes up, and down and up, and finally on a forest bench to Lightning Creek at 19 miles, 1920 feet. Just before the crossing is a junction with the trail north to Nightmare Camp and Hozomeen (Hike 42, East Bank Trail). Just beyond the ford is Deer Lick Cabin (locked) and a campsite.

Again the trail climbs 1000 feet and goes down and up, high on the side of the Lightning Creek gorge, coming at last to a superb overlook of Ross Lake (reservoir) a thousand feet below. The conclusion is a switchbacking descent to the shore and Lightning Creek Camp, 1600 feet, 23 miles from Castle Pass.

Weathered snag

83 | SILVER LAKE

Round trip: 10 miles
Hiking time: 7 hours
High point: 6900 feet
Elevation gain: 1200 feet in, 2000 feet out
Trip length: One day or backpack
Hikable: Mid-July through September

Maps: Green Trails No. 18 Pasayten Peak, No. 50 Washington Pass
Information: Forest Service Visitors Center, open mid-May to end of September, phone (509) 996-4000, or Methow Valley Ranger Station, phone (509) 997-2131. Ask about trail No. 498.

Fields of alpine flowers dotted with trees, crying out for Christmas baubles and tinsel, leading to a shallow cirque lake. Half the way is a romp on a wide, smooth trail. The other half is a different story. Some parts are rough and some are downright mean. Do the trip in late July when the meadows are green or in late September when the larch trees have turned to gold.

From Mazama drive 20 miles to Harts Pass. Go right on Slate Peak road No. (5400)600 (Hike 82). At the second switchback, 1.7 miles from Harts Pass, find Buckskin Ridge–Silver Lake trail No. 498, elevation 6900 feet.

Silver Lake trail

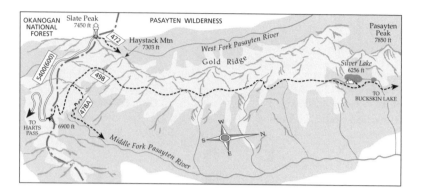

A short steep climb to a saddle is followed by a long switchback 400 feet down to meadows high above the Middle Fork Pasayten River, the beginning of miles of parkland. The color is not in overpowering masses of flowers as at Mt. Rainier, but in sprinkles of pretty in the green.

In a long ½ mile is a junction. The right fork drops to the Middle Fork Pasayten trail. Stay high on Gold Ridge for 2 mostly parkland miles. Three times the trail climbs a rib to 6800 feet, and three times it loses 200 to 300 feet into a valley. At 4½ miles it drops steeply 400 feet to an unmarked junction. Go left an almost level ⅕ mile to Silver Lake, 6256 feet. Camping there and several places along the way.

Silver Lake

84 | CASCADE LOOP TRAIL AND MONUMENT 83

Loop trip: 32 miles
Hiking time: Allow 2 to 3 days
High point: 6550 feet
Elevation gain: 4900 feet

Round trip: To lookout, 20 miles
Hiking time: 12 hours
High point: 6500 feet
Elevation gain: 2800 feet
Trip length: One day

Hikable: Late June through October
Map: Green Trails No. 18 Pasayten Peak (U.S. only)

Information: Forest Service Visitors Center, open mid-May to end of September, phone (509) 996-4000, or Methow Valley Ranger Station, phone (509) 997-2131. Ask about trails No. 533 and 2000.

When built in the 1920s the fire lookout at Monument 83 probably was the most remote in the Cascades. It still is if approached from the United States via Slate Peak, West Fork Pasayten River, the pass near Dead Lake, and the Boundary Trail—a wilderness walk of nearly 30 miles that is well worth the doing, especially as part of a loop that returns down the Pacific Crest Trail. However, since construction of Trans-Canada Highway 3 across

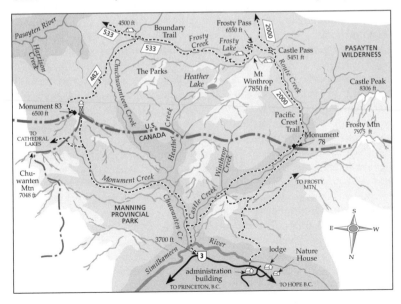

Old and new lookouts on Monument 83

Manning Provincial Park in Canada, Monument 83 is only 10 miles from a road and lies on the very popular Cascade Loop Trail, featuring miles of splendid forest, climaxes of alpine meadows, and the thrill of (technically illegal) international travel.

Drive Highway 3 from Hope, British Columbia, across Allison Pass to Manning Provincial Park administration office, lodge, and visitors center (Nature House), where U.S. Forest Service wilderness permits (no longer needed) used to be available for camping in the Pasayten Wilderness. Drive 1.8 miles farther to the Monument 83 parking lot on the right side of the road, elevation 3700 feet.

The "trail" to Monument 83 is a rough, seldom-used service road, closed to public vehicles. In ¼ mile the way crosses the Similkameen River, then ascends gradually in forest along Chuwanten Creek and Monument Creek. At about 9 miles pass a sidetrail signed "Cathedral Lakes" and continue on the service road to the flowery little meadow of Monument 83, 10 miles, 6500 feet.

In the 1920s the U.S. Forest Service built the small log cabin on the highest point, which happens to lie in Canada. In 1953 the tower, tall enough to see over the foreign hill, was erected in the United States. The grave marker memorializes a pack mule that broke its leg and had to be shot.

From the lookout the now-true trail goes ¾ mile to join trail No. 533, which descends 4½ miles along Chuchuwanteen (the American spelling of "Chuwanten") Creek to a campsite at the Frosty Creek crossing and a junction with trail No. 533, 4500 feet, 15 miles from Highway 3. Go right, upstream, on Frosty Creek trail No. 533, to a camp ¼ mile past tiny Frosty Lake at 5345 feet. The trail steepens and switchbacks to meadows of 6550-foot Frosty Pass, 21 miles, then drops 1½ miles to Castle Pass, 5451 feet, and a junction with the Pacific Crest Trail. Head north, passing water and a campsite in ½ mile. The Crest Trail descends gently above Route Creek, then Castle Creek, 3 miles to the border at Monument 78. Go right, leaving the Crest Trail and descend the 7½ miles along Castle Creek to the starting point.

85 | COPPER GLANCE LAKE

Round trip: 6 miles
Hiking time: 6 hours
High point: 6400 feet
Elevation gain: 2600 feet in, 300 feet out
Trip length: One day or backpack
Hikable: June through October

Maps: Green Trails No. 19 Billy Goat Mtn., No. 51 Mazama
Information: Forest Service Visitors Center, open mid-May to end of September, phone (509) 996-4000, or Methow Valley Ranger Station, phone (509) 997-2131. Ask about trail No. 519.

Beneath the cliffs of Isabella Ridge and 8204-foot Sherman Peak, ringed by fields of boulders and clumps of larch trees, sits Copper Glance Lake, a drop of snowmelt that by itself might scarcely be considered worth the walk. The walk is short. Not to say that it's quick. The trail gains 2500 feet in 3 miles (oh, dear!). Some stretches are quite flat. All the worse, as any student of mountain mathematics understands—when so much is to be climbed, and there are flat stretches, other stretches are going to have to make up the difference. Oh, cruel! But the scenery is worth the sweat. So are the meadows.

Drive Highway 20 to Winthrop. Chewuch trailheads can be reached two ways. From the center of town the shortest way is to follow the East Chewuch River road, signed "Pearrygin Lake." Pass the sideroad to Pearrygin Lake State Park and in 6.6 miles cross the Chewuch River to a junction with the West Chewuch River road. If coming from the west or wishing to stop at the Winthrop Forest Service Visitors Center for maps and information, the best choice is the West Chewuch River road, which starts at the west side of town opposite the city park and Forest Service Visitors Center. At 7 miles reach the aforementioned junction with the East Chewuch River road. In a short distance the road enters the national forest and becomes road No. 51. At 2.5 miles from the junction go left on Eightmile road No. 5130 for 12.5 miles and find Copper Glance trail No. 519 at a gate on the lefthand side, elevation 3800 feet.

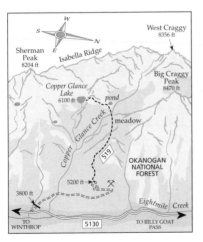

The trail starts on a steep four-wheel-drive mining road (gated).

At about 1 mile, just after the second switchback, are remains of a log cabin. At 1½ miles is a mine shaft, 5200 feet, and the end of the mining road. True trail climbs on, at about 2 miles entering large, lush meadows dotted in season with lupine, aster, paintbrush, columbine, and valerian. The way returns to the woods, at 2¾ miles passing a small pond. That stretch of flatness has to be made up, and it is, by a supersteep ascent of a rockslide, topping out at 6400 feet. To loosen up the knees, the way descends 300 feet to the shore of the lake, 6100 feet.

Copper Glance trail

86 | PARSON SMITH TREE—HIDDEN LAKES

Round trip: To Big Hidden Lake, 35 miles
Hiking time: Allow 3 days
High point: 5800 feet
Elevation gain: 2200 feet in, 2700 feet out
Hikable: Late June through September

Map: Green Trails No. 19 Billy Goat Mtn.
Information: Forest Service Visitors Center, open mid-May to end of September, phone (509) 996-4000, or Methow Valley Ranger Station, phone (509) 997-2131. Ask about trail No. 477.

> *I've roamed in many foreign parts my boys*
> *And many lands have seen.*
> *But Columbia is my idol yet*
> *Of all lands she is queen.*
> — *Parson Smith, June 8, 1886*

From the middle of the nineteenth century, miners passed through the Pasayten on their way to Canadian goldfields. A few stopped to poke around. After all this time there is virtually no evidence of their passage except for Allen L. Smith, known as Parson Smith, prospector, sometime

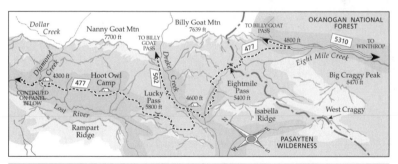

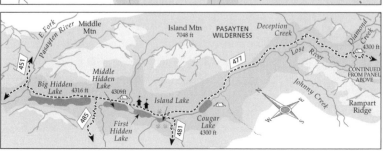

trapper, artist, and poet, who on a return trip from Canada camped for a few days on the Pasayten River. There, on a pine tree just 12 feet from the U.S.–Canada border, he carved his poem.

Parson Smith's poem was first reported in 1903 by men of the International Boundary Survey crew clearing a 10-foot swath on each side of the boundary line. It was rediscovered in 1913 by rangers Frank Burge and George Wright, and in 1926 by ranger Bill Lester. In 1965 the tree was dead and a shelter was built over the stump. In 1971 the stump was placed on the National Register of Historic Places. However, the shelter wasn't saving the wood from rot and the last straw was when a bear chewed up the stump. In 1980 it was moved to the Winthrop Forest Service Visitors Center, where it is on display.

Today's hikers can see for themselves the pioneering route taken by Parson Smith. From Winthrop drive (Hike 85, Copper Glance Lake) to the

Middle Hidden Lake

union of the East and West Chewuch River roads (which become road No. 51). Drive another 2.5 miles and go left on Eightmile Creek road No. 5130 for 16.7 miles to the end at the hikers' parking area, elevation 4800 feet.

The trail starts on a mine road; walk around the gate. In ¼ mile, at the second switchback, go left on Hidden Lakes trail No. 477. At 1¼ miles is a good view of Eightmile Pass and the steep gully Parson Smith may have descended. At 1½ miles cross the 5400-foot pass and drop to a campsite and bridge over Drake Creek, 4 miles from the road, 4600 feet. This is the last campsite with reliable water for the next 6 miles.

Passing the Drake Creek trail, hikers have a choice of how to climb 1200 feet to Lucky Pass, 5800 feet. The pass can be gained in one long switchback on a 5-percent grade, or a quick but steep 15- to 20-percent trail. At 8 miles pass Hoot Owl Camp (doubtful water supply) and at 10 miles reach a campground at the

Parson Smith Tree

crossing of Diamond Creek, 4300 feet, lowest point of the trip.

Beyond Diamond Creek the trail climbs 300 feet, with ups and downs to dodge cliffs. Pass Deception Creek (underground most of the summer). At about 13 miles the trail finally nears Lost River and enters a fine old-growth forest that was spared by the great fire of around 1920. At 14 miles, 4300 feet, is lovely Cougar Lake and campsites. At 15½ miles is usually dried-up Island Lake, and at 16 miles First Hidden Lake. Beyond are two Forest Service patrol cabins and separate campsites for horses and hikers. Next is Middle Hidden Lake, then a slight rise and the crossing-over to Pasayten drainage. The trail soon reaches 1½–mile-long Big Hidden Lake, 4300 feet, 17½ miles from the road.

Most hikers are content to turn around here, but in 1½ miles, at the far end of Big Hidden Lake, wonders are to be seen: a large shelter and a rusted grader. A final 7½ miles lead to the Canadian border, where Parson Smith carved his tree; however, don't look for it there; go instead to the Winthrop Forest Service Visitors Center.

87 | BILLY GOAT PASS—BURCH MOUNTAIN

Round trip: 10 miles
Hiking time: 5 hours
High point: 7782 feet
Elevation gain: 3000 feet
Trip length: One day
Hikable: Late June through October
Map: Green Trails No. 19 Billy Goat Mtn.

Information: Forest Service Visitors Center, open mid-May to end of September, phone (509) 996-4000, or Methow Valley Ranger Station, phone (509) 997-2131. Ask about trails No. 502A and 538.

Hike to the edge of the Pasayten Wilderness, climb toward an old lookout site, and see miles and miles of broad valleys and open ridges. Carry plenty of water and start before the sun gets into high gear. This is big-scale country, often with long stretches between points of scenic interest. For hikers, therefore, early summer is the best season, when flowers and snowfields supply entertainment.

From the Chewuch River road, drive Eightmile Creek road No. 5130 (Hike 85, Copper Glance Lake) 16.7 miles to the parking area at the end, elevation 4800 feet.

Skinny around the gate and walk the mining road up Eightmile Creek, staying right at the first junction (unmarked). At the second switchback in about ¼ mile the trail splits. The left goes to Eightmile Pass (Hike 86, Parson Smith Tree—Hidden Lakes); go right and zigzag steeply up 1800 feet in a scant 3 miles through open forest to Billy Goat Pass, 6600 feet, on the border of the Pasayten Wilderness.

Hike a few hundred feet over the pass and just before the switchback,

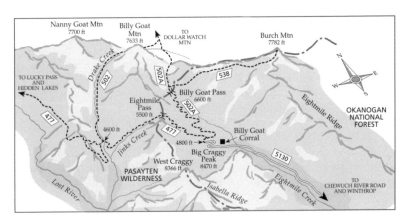

Big Craggy Peak from Burch Mountain

find Burch Mountain trail No. 538 angling upward on the east (right-hand) side. This well-constructed trail was once used by horse packers to supply a lookout on top of Burch Mountain. At first the tread is lost in meadows, but as the hillside steepens the trail becomes distinct and, except for dodging an occasional tree growing in the path, following it is no problem. The ascent is abrupt, quickly emerging to views southeast to Isabella Ridge and beyond to a horizon of 8000-foot peaks, the most dramatic being Big Craggy. Gaining some 600 feet in ¾ mile, the trail nearly reaches the ridge top, then contours around a high, rocky knoll to a broad saddle at 7200 feet. From there it switchbacks up to the 7782-foot summit of Burch Mountain, 5 miles from the road-end. The lookout cabin has been gone many years but the views are as good as ever.

Want more? From Billy Goat Pass, continue on trail No. 502A, dropping to Drake Creek and following it down to campsites near Jinks Creek at 4600, the lowest point, then return over Eightmile Pass to the starting point, adding 6½ miles to the hike and 800 feet to the elevation gain.

88 | DOLLAR WATCH MOUNTAIN

Round trip: 28 miles
Hiking time: Allow 3 to 4 days
High point: 7679 feet
Elevation gain: 4000 feet in, 1100 feet out
Hikable: Mid-July through mid-September
Map: Green Trails No. 19 Billy Goat Mtn.

Information: Forest Service Visitors Center, open mid-May to end of September, phone (509) 996-4000, or Methow Valley Ranger Station, phone (509) 997-2131. Ask about trails No. 502A, 502, 451, and 462.

Fanciful names, fanciful views—altogether fanciful country—and trails to take you wherever you fancy. Dollar Watch Mountain sits smack in the middle, ideal as a destination in itself or as a sidetrip on a many-day loop. Campsites are plentiful; some even have water all summer.

Drive to the end of Eightmile Creek road No. 5130 (Hike 85, Copper Glance Lake) and the hikers' parking area, elevation 4800 feet.

Climb 3 miles to Billy Goat Pass, 6600 feet (Hike 87), and enter the Pasayten Wilderness. In a hundred feet pass the Burch Mountain trail and pause to enjoy the long view out to rolling hills of the Methow Valley. Plunge on down to Drake Creek, 5500 feet. Good camps here—with water, very tasty. At 5 miles cross Two Bit Creek and join the Drake Creek trail. The united way ascends an old burn to the broad gap (scoured out by the continental glacier) of Three Fools Pass, 6000 feet, and casually drops through woods and meadow toward Diamond Creek. At 6½ miles, about ½ mile below the pass, pass a well-used campsite and, at 7 miles, Diamond Point trail No. 514. Stay left on trail No. 502, cross the creek, 5500 feet, and begin a long sidehill, keeping nearly constant elevation into the valley of Larch Creek.

At 8½ miles a shortcut trail (perhaps unsigned) to the left can save ½

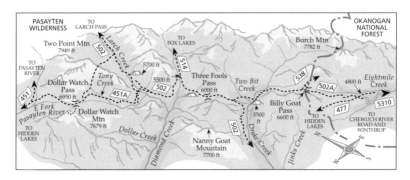

Marshy area on Drake Creek trail

mile. However, it is easier to stay on the main trail another ½ mile to a campsite at Larch Creek, 5700 feet, and then go left on trail No. 451A, climbing to Dollar Watch Mountain.

The Dollar Watch trail climbs steadily with occasional views south to Three Fools Pass and Nanny Goat Mountain. At 2 miles above Larch Creek it passes through the upper basin of Tony Creek, the last reliable water supply before Dollar Watch Pass and Mountain. At 3 miles above Larch Creek, 12 miles from the road, a faint abandoned trail branches right (east), crossing Two Point Mountain to reach Larch Pass, the first of several loop possibilities. Shortly beyond here the main trail crosses Dollar Watch Pass, 6950 feet, and drops to a campsite bench, 6870 feet. From there it descends to McCalls Gulch at 6000 feet, and a junction with East Fork Pasayten River trail No. 451.

The old lookout trail up Dollar Watch is lost in the bench meadows, so contour the upper slopes, find tread again, and climb to a saddle at 7063 feet. The trail branches; keep right, switchbacking to the lookout site atop Dollar Watch Mountain, 7679 feet, 14 miles from the road. Presumably the watch was an Ingersoll pocket turnip. (Mickey Mouse watches came later.)

89 | FORGOTTEN TRAILS OF THE METHOW VALLEY RANGER DISTRICT

Map: Not on any Green Trails map
Information: Forest Service Visitors Center, open mid-May to end of September, phone (509) 996-4000, or Methow Valley Ranger Station, phone (509) 997-2131.

In the 1930s fire lookouts were located on high points throughout the forest. The views were fantastic. That's what they were there for. When, in the 1950s, airplanes took over the looking, most of the posts and trails that served them were abandoned. Nowadays, so many trails of the Golden Age have been lost to logging roads, so many surviving trails have become plagued by "multiple-use" wheels, and the pedestrian population has so mushroomed, that hikers are elbow to elbow, boot to boot, and desperately need room to stretch their legs without tripping over somebody's tent. Many of the abandonments have survived neglect and lie handy to the feet. Since trail-builders of old obeyed the obvious logic of topography, hikers able to read can discover intact remnants that, except for a few step-over logs, are in quite decent shape—though the lower reaches of some, such as to Doe Mountain and Setting Sun Mountain, have been so obliterated by logging that finding the start of tread can be a brainteaser.

Washington Pass Trail, elevation 5600 feet

Round trip: ½ mile
Map: 1963 edition USGS Washington Pass

Most of the way from the Methow Valley the old trail followed Early Winters Creek, but where today's highway veers off to desecrate the basal cliffs of Liberty Bell Mountain, the trail proceeded in short switchbacks directly up to Washington Pass and crossed over to flowery meadows, campsites at their edge, on the west side. The tread on the north side of the meadow is still there, unloved, unmarked, blued in late summer by acres of gentians.

Doe Mountain, elevation 7154 feet

Round trip: 6 to 8 miles
Elevation gain: 2600 feet
Map: Old 15-minute USGS Doe Mountain

Views overlooking the Chewuch River valley, the rocky summits of Ike Mountain and Farewell Peak, Winthrop farms, Mt. Gardner, Silver Star, and into the North Cascades.

Driving directions keep changing as new logging roads are built and old ones put to bed. Finding the right road may be as big a challenge as finding the trail. Locate Doe Creek on the USGS Doe Mountain quadrangle. Then go to the large-scale Forest Service map of the Winthrop District and spot the road attaining the highest elevation close to the creek.

For openers, drive the Chewuch River road (Hike 85, Copper Glance Lake) past Eightmile Creek road No. 5130, past Falls Creek Campground, and go left uphill on road No. 5140 for 4.3 miles. So much for the easy part. Now keep the map handy. Unless there have been changes since the Forest Service issued its map (look sharp!), go left on No. (5140)145 to the highest drivable point, near Doe Creek.

The old trail, which at this point ran beside Doe Creek, is lost in the

Silver Star Mountain from Setting Sun Lookout site

brushed-over clearcut, so follow put-to-bed spur roads to the forest edge, eyes peeled for tread. Where the slope steepens, the trail crossed Doe Creek and contoured upward to the left to the summit ridge. Mentally mark this spot because the tread here is faint—missing the turn on the descent could mean ending up miles away on the wrong road. Once on the ridge, go right on the crest to the top.

Setting Sun Mountain, elevation 7253 feet

Round trip: 4 to 6 miles
Elevation gain: 2500 feet

Map: Trail not shown on any map printed after 1950, but see USGS McLeod Mountain

Dramatic views into the Lost River gorge, to peaks in the Pasayten Wilderness, and across the Methow Valley to Silver Star.

The first time we hiked this trail it started from an old (even then) cabin (but still there in 1998) on the Lost River, went several miles up Yellowjacket Creek, and then headed up a draw to the lookout. A rude trail servicing a telephone line ran eastward along the ridge crest to golly knows where.

From near Mazama, drive Goat Creek road No. 52 and then road No. 5225 (Hike 75, Goat Peak). Pass the sideroad to the Goat Peak trail and approximately 11 miles from road No. 52 park at a pass, 5000 feet.

You could try to find the old trail in the brush of a 1970s clearcut in the Yellowjacket Creek valley to the west. The easier alternative is to scramble up the very steep spur ridge to the north, on the crest of the high ridge intersect the telephone line trail, and follow it west about ¾ mile to the summit.

90 | BLACK LAKE

Round trip: 8½ miles
Hiking time: 4 hours
High point: 3982 feet
Elevation gain: 800 feet
Trip length: One day or backpack
Hikable: Mid-May through October
Map: Green Trails No. 20 Coleman
Peak

Information: Forest Service Visitors
Center, open mid-May to end of
September, phone (509) 996-
4000, or Methow Valley Ranger
Station, phone (509) 997-2131.
Ask about trail No. 500.

A mile-long lake in forest beneath 7000-foot peaks. The quick and easy walk makes it perhaps the most popular spot in the whole Pasayten Wilderness.

Drive Highway 20 to Winthrop and choose either the East Chewuch River road or the West Chewuch River road (Hike 85, Copper Glance Lake). In a short distance from the junction of the two roads enter the national forest; here the road becomes No. 51. At 2.5 miles from the junction pass the Eight Mile road to Copper Glance Lake and Billy Goat Pass. At 15.5 miles from the junction turn left on Lakes Creek road No. (5160)100 and drive 2.4 miles to the road-end and trail No. 500, elevation 3162 feet.

Behind the horse ramp find the trail climbing above noisy rapids. In ½ mile enter the Pasayten Wilderness. With only minor ups and downs, the trail follows close by Lake Creek in delightful forest; come in early August to feast on blueberries and raspberries, usually ripe by then. At about 1½ miles note a boulder, 10 by 20 feet, that rumbled down the ridge in the winter of 1984–85, crashed and smashed through the trees, and came to rest wedged among four trees a few feet from the trail.

At 4½ miles the trail reaches the shore of Black Lake, 3982 feet. Both ends of the lake have campsites; those at the far end may be horsier. The crowds stop at the lake. For solitude continue a mile along the shore path and 7 more miles to tiny Fawn Lake, and then just keep on tramping deeper and deeper into the heart of wildness.

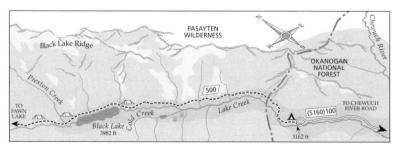

Black Lake

91 | ANDREWS CREEK—CATHEDRAL LAKES

Round trip: 42 miles
Hiking time: Allow 5 to 7 days
High point: 7400 feet
Elevation gain: 4900 feet in, 400 feet out
Hikable: July through September
Map: Green Trails No. 20 Coleman Peak

Information: Forest Service Visitors Center, open mid-May to end of September, phone (509) 996-4000, or Methow Valley Ranger Station, phone (509) 997-2131. Ask about trails No. 504 and 533

The most-photographed scene in the eastern Pasayten Wilderness is Upper Cathedral Lake, sitting in a rock bowl amid ice-polished slabs, beneath the leaping cliffs of 8601-foot Cathedral Peak and 8358-foot Amphitheater Mountain. Cameras infest the place in fall, when the larch trees are bright gold, but also in summer, carried on hands and knees over the miles of lush herbaceous meadows and stony tundra that demand the close-up lens. For all the beauty and the fame, though, crowds are thin, held down by 21 miles of trail.

Drive Chewuch River road No. 5160 (Hike 90, Black Lake) some 17 miles to Andrews Creek trail No. 504, elevation 3050 feet.

The trail has a fit of steepness at the start but, after crossing Little

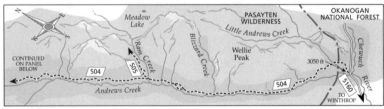

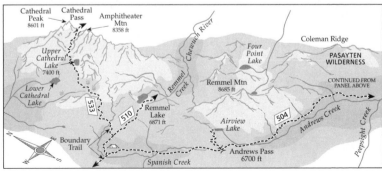

Andrews Creek and a little divide, settles down, at about ½ mile dropping a bit into Andrews Creek valley. Alternating between long valley-bottom flats and short, abrupt steps, it proceeds patiently toward its remote destination. At about 1 mile begins the 2-mile swath of a 1984 forest fire. At 3⅓ miles, near Blizzard Creek, pass two small buildings and the cable car of a stream-gauging station. At about 4 miles the path divides. The main trail goes right, above a bluff, gaining and losing 200 feet. Straight ahead is a narrow "hikers-only" water-level path that is a delight, if the creek hasn't washed part of it away.

At 5½ miles pass the Meadow Lake trail. At about 8 miles begins an earnest climb to Andrews Pass, 6700 feet, 13 miles from the road. On one side rises the west face of Remmel Mountain, on the other the rounded dome of Andrews Peak.

The way now loses 400 feet into Spanish Creek valley, at 15 miles passing the Spanish Creek trail. The ever-expanding meadows submerge memories of the long, sweaty, fly-bitten miles. Choose a spot for a basecamp near the junction with the Boundary Trail, close by the tread or off in a secluded nook. But camp—the sites at Cathedral Lakes are few and small and probably full and those at Remmel Lake are very horsey.

Boundary Trail No. 533 goes right, passing Chewuch River trail No. 510, to Upper Cathedral Lake, 7400 feet, 21 miles from the road. You definitely will want to walk the roller-skate-smooth slabs and examine the gouges made by the glaciers; this area has experienced both local alpine glaciation, from such cirques as that of the Cathedral Lakes, and continental glaciation from the accumulation centers in Canada, which sent out ice sheets that rode over and rounded the tops of all the peaks in the eastern Pasayten except a very few, including Cathedral.

You also may wish to descend on a sidetrail to Lower Cathedral Lake. Nor should you forget that the Boundary Trail goes west, ascending to just under the summit of Bald Mountain; spend a night on top and see who comes to the dance. A very large proportion of the Cascades terrain that satisfies the technical definition of "tundra" is located hereabouts; wander it this way and that, to the summit ridge of Amphitheater, should it please you. Sit amid the high-alpine blossoms and the lichen-covered stones and gaze to the Arctic Ocean.

Cathedral Lake

92 | CHEWUCH RIVER—REMMEL LAKE

Round trip: 34 miles
Hiking time: Allow 3 to 5 days
High point: 6871 feet
Elevation gain: 3400 feet
Hikable: July through September
Map: Green Trails No. 20 Coleman
   Peak

Information: Forest Service Visitors
   Center, open mid-May to end of
   September, phone (509) 996-
   4000, or Methow Valley Ranger
   Station, phone (509) 997-2131.
   Ask about trail No. 510.

Much of what has been said about Cathedral Lakes (Hike 91) also can
be said about Remmel Lake—and indeed, they are near enough together
that visiting back and forth is easy and quick. There are meadows around
the shore, covered in season with blue lupine and deep red paintbrush and
yellow "sunflowers." There are higher and drier meadows—true tundra,
as in the Arctic, spongy and wet early in the season, buckled into small
ridges and mounds by frost heaves, and peppered with innumerable holes
of Columbian ground squirrels—"rockchucks," which behave in a most
marmotlike manner, diving into their homes to escape the ever-patrolling
raptors, as well as the fun-loving humans who carry .22 pistols for the ami-
able all-seasons (illegal) sport of "plinking."

Drive from Winthrop 30 miles on the Chewuch River road (Hike 90,
Black Lake) to its end at Thirtymile Camp and the start of Chewuch River
trail No. 510, elevation 3500 feet.

Heavily stomped and tramped by horses, hikers, and cattle (the route is
still listed as a stock driveway), the trail starts wide and dusty and pretty

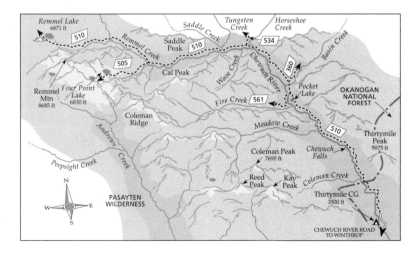

Remmel Lake and Remmel Mountain

much stays that way, except when it's wide and muddy. In 1 mile it enters the Pasayten Wilderness. Just 300 feet are gained in the scant 3 miles to Chewuch Falls. The way passes swampy Pocket Lake to the junction with the Fire Creek–Coleman Ridge trail (Hike 93) at about 5 miles, and at 8 miles the Tungsten Creek trail, having gained thus far only 1100 feet. At 12 miles is the junction with the Four Point Lake–Coleman Ridge trail (Hike 93). The tread now grows tired, worn, and rocky but the angle inclines upward only a little as forest thins to parkland. The rugged north face of Remmel Mountain appears and the path flattens to the shore of Remmel Lake, 6871 feet, 14 miles from the road.

If there were a market for horse apples, this would be a good field to harvest. The lake is ringed with campsites but unless one has grown up in a barnyard and likes that smell, finding a spot to eat supper is a problem. One would think that the Forest Service would keep horses at least 500 feet from camps and lakeshores or designate some of the campsites for hikers. For clean camps continue above the lake to a small creek. But watch out for sheep, too. They also have the right-of-way over hikers.

93 | FOUR POINT LAKE—COLEMAN RIDGE LOOP

Loop trip: 41 miles
Hiking time: Allow 3 to 5 days
High point: 7300 feet
Elevation gain: 4000 feet
Hikable: Late June through
September
Map: Green Trails No. 20 Coleman
Peak

Information: Forest Service Visitors
Center, open mid-May to end of
September, phone (509) 996-
4000, or Methow Valley Ranger
Station, phone (509) 997-2131.
Ask about trails No. 510, 561,
and 505.

If Four Point Lake alone is the goal—as it may well be, rimmed by white granite, pines and larch, and a silver forest, in views to the cliffs of 8685-foot Remmel Peak—the easiest approach is to hike the Chewuch River trail (Hike 92) 12 miles and turn left to go 3 miles on the Four Point Lake trail. However, long and rugged though the loop is, there are compensations.

Drive from Winthrop 30 miles on Chewuch River road No. 51 (Hike 90, Black Lake) to its end at Thirtymile Camp and the start of Chewuch River trail No. 510, elevation 3500 feet.

Hike the Chewuch River trail (Hike 92) 5¼ miles and turn left on Fire Creek trail No. 561. Ford the river (no cinch in early summer), 4400 feet, and strike off up the steep trail, torn to shreds by cows (they graze here in alternate years), gaining 800 feet in switchbacks, then moderating. The way traverses a succession of wet meadows where tread is lost in a maze of cow

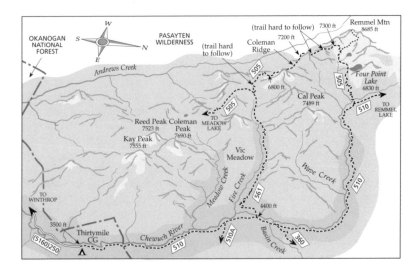

tracks and pies (when thoroughly dry, these latter make as excellent a fire as buffalo chips). In one of the cow-mushed meadow-marshes, watch for a hiking boot half-buried in muck. What became of the hiker? Somewhere in the muck is an unmarked junction. Go right and search for Coleman Ridge trail No. 505.

At about 6 miles from the Chewuch River the Coleman Ridge trail tops the divide, 6800 feet, between Fire Creek and Andrews Creek, and proceeds steeply up the meadows of Coleman Ridge to 7200 feet. When the tread vanishes, watch for cairns. At the ridge-end the trail plummets some 300 feet, then climbs more meadows to a 7300-foot saddle between Andrews Creek and Four Point Creek. Here is a view to Four Point Lake, followed by a descent over a rockslide of gleaming white granite. At 11 miles from the Chewuch River (16 miles from the road) a little detour leads to the shore of Four Point Lake, 6830 feet.

A horse trail once continued to the top of 8685-foot Remmel Mountain to service the fire lookout located there from 1932 to 1956. The trail was abandoned and expunged from government maps, but hikers report the tread survived the official "disappearing." From the spur to Four Point Lake go back about ½ mile to a series of switchbacks, follow a stream up a few feet, and scout on the hillside for evidence of human and equine presence in the form of a well-preserved trail.

To complete the loop, descend steeply 3 miles (the sign says 2) from Four Point Lake to a ford of the Chewuch River, an easy step when the water is low, and proceed down and out 12 miles to the car.

Coleman Ridge trail

94

HONEYMOON CREEK—NORTH TWENTYMILE PEAK LOOKOUT

Round trip: 13 miles
Hiking time: 7 hours
High point: 7437 feet
Elevation gain: 4200 feet
Trip length: One day or backpack
Hikable: June through October
Map: Green Trails No. 52 Doe Mountain

Information: Forest Service Visitors Center, open mid-May to end of September, phone (509) 996-4000, or Methow Valley Ranger Station, phone (509) 997-2131. Ask about trail No. 560.

Behold an infinity of forested ridges extending from Silver Star Mountain in the west to Canada north, Tiffany Mountain east, and beyond the Methow Valley south. In all the wild scene only a single road can be seen, along the Chewuch River a vertical mile below. Ah, but the hand of man, if hidden, is everywhere busy, sawing and chopping. To be sure, clearcuts give him away but most of the logging here is selective, meaning he is selecting all the beautiful, big, old ponderosa pine and Douglas fir, leaving the small trees, which never will be allowed to grow old, big, and beautiful unless placed in protected wilderness. Fill the canteens before starting—for this is the eastern North Cascades, where the sun shines bright all day, except during thunderstorms. The trail is closed to motorcycles; hopefully, any fat-tire bikers you encounter will not be going 55 miles per hour training for the world championship downhiller at Metabief, France (similar to the World Cup downhill ski races).

Drive either the East or West Chewuch River roads to their junction, where they become road No. 51 (Hike 85, Copper Glance Lake). At 11.3 miles from the junction turn right on road No. 5010, cross the Chewuch

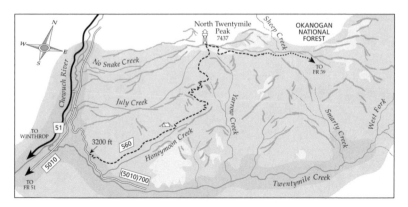

Old and new lookouts on North Twentymile Peak

River, pass road No. (5010)800, and in 0.6 mile go left a final 1.7 miles on road No. (5010)700 to the trailhead, elevation 3200 feet.

Walk an abandoned road 0.3 mile to the beginning of true trail No. 560, whose good tread gains 500 to 800 feet a mile. At 2 miles is the first and last water, at a campsite beside Honeymoon Creek. At about 5 miles the way attains the ridge crest and views that grow steadily in the last 1½ miles to the summit, 7437 feet.

The ground-level lookout cabin was built in 1923 and may be the state's last surviving example of the cupola design; it is on the National Historic Register. The 30-foot tower was built in 1948 and was staffed until the 1980s.

An abandoned trail goes east 10 miles to Thirtymile Meadows and road No. 39. If the proposed Twentymile–Thirtymile Wilderness fails to be established (as it was not by the 1984 Washington Wilderness Act), this trail likely will be reopened for motorcycles. Barring that catastrophe, the first mile along the ridge from the summit is a marvelous meadow stroll. One would love to camp here if one could find (or carry) water. But one would not love to be here when the lightning bolts endemic to the eastern North Cascades are zapping prominently upright organisms.

95 | TIFFANY MOUNTAIN

Round trip: From Freezeout Pass to the summit, 6 miles
Hiking time: 4 hours
High point: 8242 feet
Elevation gain: 1700 feet

One-way trip: Via Tiffany Lake, 8 miles
Hiking time: 5 hours
High point: 7100 feet
Elevation gain: 800 feet

Trip length: One day
Hikable: July through September
Map: Green Trails No. 53 Tiffany Mountain

Information: Tonasket Ranger Station, phone (509) 486-2186. Ask about trails No. 345 and 373.

A superb ridge walk to an 8242-foot summit, views west to distant peaks of the North Cascades, north into the Pasayten Wilderness, and east to farmlands of the Okanogan. The hike can be done as a round trip or—by use of two cars or a nonhiking companion to move the car—as a one-way trip.

Drive north from Winthrop on the paved East Chewuch River road (Hike 85, Copper Glance Lake). At 6.6 miles, just before crossing the Chewuch River, turn right on road No. 37. In less than 2 miles the way turns uphill and follows Boulder Creek. In 18 miles go left on road No. 39 and continue 3 rough miles to Freezeout Pass and the trailhead, elevation 6500 feet.

From Freezeout Pass, Freezeout Ridge trail No. 345 climbs steadily 1½ miles through trees, then 1 mile above timberline, and begins a contour

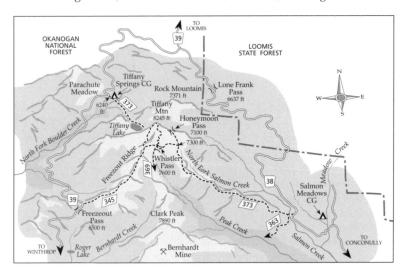

around the east side of the peak. Be sure to make the ½-mile (each way) sidetrip up grassy slopes (the old trail was obliterated by grazing) to the unlimited views from the top of Tiffany Mountain, once the site of a fire lookout, elevation 8245 feet.

For the one-way trip, the recommendation is to leave a car at Freezeout Pass and drive 4 more miles to Tiffany Springs and the Tiffany Lake trailhead, 6240 feet. Hike the scant mile to the head of Tiffany Lake, then go upstream, following faint traces of trail. At about 7100 feet the trail improves; go right to Whistler Pass. The trail again becomes faint but the route is easy to spot.

Tiffany Mountain from Tiffany Meadows

96

BERNHARDT TRAIL—NORTH SUMMIT TRAIL

Round trip: 11 miles
Hiking time: 6 hours
High point: 7500 feet
Elevation gain: 2300 feet in, 250 feet out
Trip length: One day

Hikable: June through September
Map: Green Trails No. 53 Tiffany Mountain
Information: Tonasket Ranger Station, phone (509) 486-2186. Ask about trail No. 369.

The North Summit trail is an old stock driveway, which might not sound much like fun, but the cows and sheep haven't been around these parts in years, ever since the cowboys and shepherds moved their enterprises to the lower country, where they were less likely to have their animals frozen to death in an August blizzard. So, it's a long and lonesome ridge of pines and meadows, the flora the more interesting because on sunny slopes there is sagebrush steppe, and on wetter slopes, rock gardens of lupine, paintbrush, buckwheat, and stonecrop. The views, too, are distinctive, combining long looks out to rolling highlands of Eastern Washington and long looks west to distant peaks of the North Cascades. Closer up are the green meadows of Clark Peak and Tiffany Mountain. In view of all this, it's amazing the trail is so lonesome. Bring full canteens; there's no water.

The trip has two starting points, the North Summit trail and the Bernhardt trail. By use of two cars, either or both can be combined with the hike to Tiffany Mountain (Hike 95).

Tiffany Mountain from North Summit trail

Drive from Winthrop on the East Chewuch River road 6.6 miles. Just before the Chewuch River bridge go right on road No. 37, following the river a short way, then climbing into Boulder Creek valley (Hike 95, Tiffany Mountain). In another 11.4 miles (sign says "Winthrop 19 miles") is a junction. For the Bernhardt trail, go straight ahead on road No. 39 for 1.2 miles to Bernhardt trail No. 367, elevation 5750 feet. For the North Summit trail, at the junction go right, staying on road No. 37 for another 2.6 miles to a gravel pit (just east of milepost 18) and North Summit trail No. 369, elevation 5850 feet. Park on the shoulder.

A faint boot-beaten path starts up the right side of the gravel pit, crosses over the top, and enters forest. In ½ mile the route, marked by large cairns, skirts the top of a large sagebrush–steppe meadow, then returns to trees. At about 1¼ miles is another sagebrush meadow, the cairns fewer and smaller; if you lose the route, contour and climb, searching for cairns; find tread in the trees on the far side. Woods and meadows alternating, the trail climbs to a 7220-foot saddle and crosses the ridge to a great spot, 2½ miles from the road, to view the world and call it a day.

From the viewspot follow the ups and down, first on the east side, then the west side of North Ridge for 1 long mile, then steeply drop 250 feet to a low point. The way swings around the east slopes of the next high point of the crest to the next low point, at 3½ miles, and here meets the Clark Ridge trail. The North Summit trail now contours the west side of Clark Peak, passing the Bernhardt trail, an alternate return, at 4½ miles, and at 5½ miles ending at Whistler Pass, 7600 feet. At the pass is a four-way intersection offering a choice of climbing Tiffany Mountain, descending the Freezeout Ridge trail, or turning around to go back the way you came.

The Bernhardt trail is an equally superb alternative. In a scant ½ mile the trail crosses Bernhardt Creek and then a tributary—twice. In about 1 mile it skirts a boggy meadow and around 1½ miles starts up, seldom bothering with switchbacks. At about 2¼ miles the path goes left of a sturdy log cabin with a leaky roof (attention, Bernhardt family) to an unmarked junction. The right dead ends in ½ mile at some diggings, presumably Bernhardt's; go left, in the some-times-steeply gear, taking care not to stray off on the many animal paths. At 3 miles, 7400 feet, reach North Summit trail No. 369 and its miles of views.

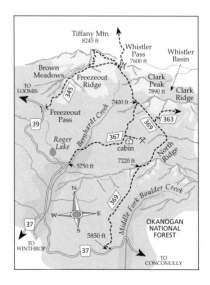

97 | HORSESHOE BASIN (PASAYTEN)

Round trip: To Sunny Pass, 9 miles
Hiking time: 6 hours
High point: 7200 feet
Elevation gain: 1200 feet
Trip length: One day or backpack
Hikable: Late June through mid-October

Round trip: To Horseshoe Basin, 19 miles
Hiking time: Allow 2 days
High point: 7200 feet
Elevation gain: 1300 feet in, 200 feet out
Hikable: July through mid-October

Map: Green Trails No. 21 Horseshoe Basin

Information: Tonasket Ranger Station, phone (509) 486-2186. Ask about trail No. 533.

At the northeast extremity of the Cascades is a tundra country so unlike the main range a visitor wonders if he/she hasn't somehow missed a turn and ended up in the Arctic. Meadows for miles and miles, rolling from broad basins to rounded summits of peaks above 8000 feet, in views south over forests to Tiffany Mountain, east to Chopaka Mountain and the Okanogan Highlands, north far into Canada, and west across the Pasayten Wilderness to glaciated, dream-hazy giants of the Cascade Crest.

Drive from Tonasket to Loomis and turn north. In 1.5 miles turn left at a sign for Toats Coulee, cross the valley of Sinlahekin Creek, and start a long, steep climb up Toats Coulee on road No. 39. At 11 miles from Loomis is North Fork Campground. In another 5 miles, next to milepost 36, is a junction signed "Iron Gate." Go right on narrow dirt road No. (3900)500. Drive 7 rough and steep (in 1999 the nicest word was atrocious) miles to the road-end and beginning of Boundary Trail No. 533, elevation 6100 feet, at Iron

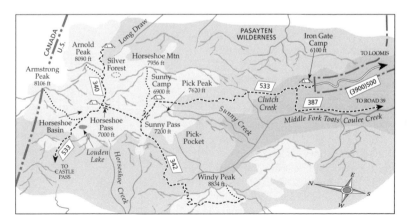

Louden Lake in Horseshoe Basin

Gate Camp (no water) on the edge of the Pasayten Wilderness. (One might prefer to stay on the paved road another 3 miles and hike the Middle Fork Toats Coulee trail No. 387, adding 3-plus miles each way to the hike.)

The first ½ mile is downhill along the abandoned road to the pre-wilderness Iron Gate Camp (no water). The trail from here begins in small lodgepole pine (most of this region was burned off by a series of huge fires in the 1920s) on the old road to Tungsten Mine, which peddled stock to the gullible as recently as the early 1950s. The grade is nearly flat for ½ mile to cool waters of a branch of Clutch Creek and then starts a moderate, steady ascent. At 3¼ miles the route opens out into patches of grass and flowers. After a brief steep bit, at 4 miles the way abruptly emerges from trees to the flowery, stream-bubbling nook of Sunny Basin and splendid Sunny Camp, 6900 feet.

The trail climbs ½ mile to 7200-foot Sunny Pass; be prepared to gasp and rave. All around spreads the enormous meadowland of Horseshoe Basin, demanding days of exploration. From the pass the Tungsten road-that-was drops left and the "pure" trail goes right, contouring gentle slopes of Horseshoe Mountain to grand basecamps in and near the wide flat of Horseshoe Pass, 7000 feet, 5¾ miles, and then contouring more glory to tiny Louden Lake, 6¼ miles (this lake dries up in late summer), and then on and on as described in Hike 98, Boundary Trail.

The roamings are everywhere. All the summits are easy flower walks—7620-foot Pick Peak, 7956-foot Horseshoe Mountain, and 8090-foot Arnold Peak. The ridge north from 8106-foot Armstrong Peak has the added interest of monuments to mark the U.S.–Canadian boundary. A more ambitious sidetrip is south from Sunny Pass 6 miles on the down-and-up trail to 8334-foot Windy Peak, highest in the area and once the site of a fire lookout. Don't omit a short walk east through Horseshoe Pass to the immense silver forest at the head of Long Draw.

98 | BOUNDARY TRAIL

One-way trip: (Main route) from Iron Gate via Castle Pass to Harts Pass, 94 miles
Hiking time: Allow 10 or more days
High point: 7600 feet
Elevation gain: 13,000 feet
Hikable: July through September
Maps: Green Trails No. 16 Ross Lake, No. 17 Jack Mountain, No. 18 Pasayten Peak, No. 19 Billy Goat Mtn., No. 21 Horseshoe Basin, No. 50 Washington Pass

Information: Forest Service Visitors Center, open mid-May to end of September, phone (509) 996-4000, or Methow Valley Ranger Station, phone (509) 997-2131, or Tonasket Ranger Station, phone (509) 486-8186. Ask about trail No. 533.

As the golden eagle flies, it's 40 miles from the east edge of the Pasayten Wilderness to the Cascade Crest; as the backpacker walks it's twice that far, and some distance still remaining to reach civilization. Though the Pasayten country lacks the glaciers of more famous mountains west, and with few exceptions the peaks are rounded, unchallenging to a climber, there is a magnificent vastness of high ridges, snowfields, flower gardens, parklands, cold lakes, green forests, loud rivers. The weather is better and summer arrives earlier than in windward ranges. The trails are high much of the distance, often above 7000 feet, but are mostly snowfree in early July, an ideal time for the trip.

Length of the route precludes a detailed description in these pages. In any event the journey is for experienced wilderness travelers who have the routefinding skills needed

Boundary Trail and Remmel Mountain

to plan and find their own way. The notes below aim merely to stimulate the imagination.

Begin at the Iron Gate road-end (Hike 97, Horseshoe Basin) and walk to Horseshoe Basin and Louden Lake (6¾ miles). With ups and downs, always in highlands, the trail goes along Bauerman Ridge to Scheelite Pass (13¾ miles), to the old buildings and garbage of Tungsten Mine (17¾ miles), and over Cathedral Pass to Cathedral Lakes (22 miles). The route this far makes a superb 4- to 7-day round trip from Iron Gate.

Continue west to campsites at the junction of the Andrews Creek trail (26 miles), to Bald Mountain, and the first descent to low elevation, at the Ashnola River (31½ miles). Climb high again, passing Sheep Mountain (34½ miles), Quartz Mountain (38 miles), and Bunker Hill (43 miles), then dropping to low forests of the Pasayten River (50½ miles).

Follow the Pasayten River upstream past abandoned and impassable Harrison Creek trail and turn up Soda Creek to Dead Lake (60 miles), 5100 feet. Ascend Frosty Creek past Frosty Lake to Frosty Pass (66 miles) and on to Castle Pass (67 miles). From here, take the Pacific Crest Trail 27 miles south (Hike 100) to Harts Pass, ending a trip of some 94 miles. (For a shorter alternate, hike up the Pasayten River to Three Forks and ascend the West Fork Pasayten to Harts Pass. Trails branch west from this valley route to reach the Cascade Crest at Woody Pass and Holman Pass.)

For the complete Boundary Trail, go west from Castle Pass on the Elbow Basin Trail (Hike 82), hike south to Ross Dam and cross Ross Lake (reservoir) to the Little Beaver, and traverse the North Cascades National Park via Whatcom and Hannegan Passes (Hike 14), concluding at the Ruth Creek road.

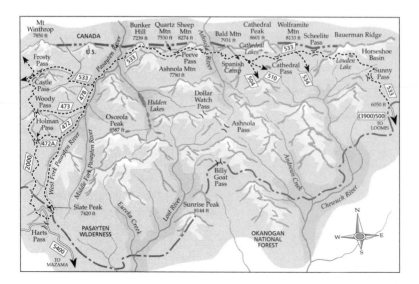

99 | MOUNT BONAPARTE

Round trip: 9 miles
Hiking time: 6 hours
High point: 7257 feet
Elevation gain: 2752 feet
Trip length: One day

Hikable: Mid-June through October
Map: USGS Mt. Bonaparte
Information: Tonasket Ranger
Station, phone (509) 486-2186.
Ask about trail No. 306.

No, campers, we're not in the North Cascades proper here, but well to the east across the Okanogan Valley, in highlands that may be considered a suburb of the Selkirk Range. Two unique features of the mountain are the highest fire lookout in Eastern Washington, and the original lookout building, constructed in 1914 of hand-hewn logs (see the ax marks) and now on the National Register of Historic Buildings.

Among the 20 miles of trail in the roadless area (proposed for wilderness status, but left out of the 1984 Washington Wilderness Act, leaving the job still to be done) around Mt. Bonaparte are three routes to the top, each with its own attractions. The South Side trail, 5½ miles long, starts at 4500 feet on road No. (3300)100 and gives views of Bonaparte Lake. The Antoine trail, 6 miles, is a favorite with horse riders. The Myers Creek trail described here is the shortest and starts highest; be advised the way is waterless and has no views until the summit.

Drive east from the north end of Tonasket on county road No. 9467, signed "Havillah." In 16 miles, just short of Havillah Church, turn right on a road signed "Lost Lake." Pavement ends in 0.9 mile; turn right on road No. 33. At 4.2 miles from the county road turn right on road No. (3300)300 (abbreviated on the sign to 300). Follow it 1.2 miles to the Mt. Bonaparte trailhead sign, elevation 4640 feet. Park here.

Walk the road about 100 feet to Mt. Bonaparte trail No. 306, in a replanted clearcut. Dodge several motorcycle runways; follow horse- and

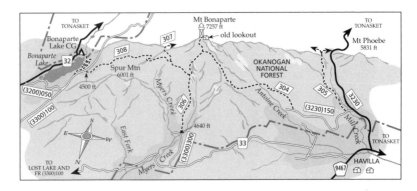

footprints straight ahead. At 1¼ miles is the end of logging and the start of virgin forest of lodgepole pine. The trail steepens to a junction at 2½ miles with the South Side trail. At 3¾ miles is a junction with the Antoine trail. Lodgepole pines yield to subalpine fir, which at 4½ miles yields to open meadows and all-around-the-compass views over forested hills to valley ranches. The summit of the Okanogan Highlands has been attained, 7257 feet.

Below the modern lookout tower is the 1914 lookout building, slightly bent out of shape by the weight of winter snow. The tower atop the cabin had to be removed years ago. In early days the lookout communicated by heliograph, an instrument that aimed a beam of sunlight and by means of a shutter transmitted Morse code to a receiver as far away as 30 miles. On cloudy days and at night the lookout did not communicate, not until telephone lines were installed in the 1930s. When the lines were broken by falling trees or limbs the lookout did not communicate, not until the 1960s and the proliferation of radios.

Historic lookout building on Mount Bonaparte

100 PACIFIC CREST NATIONAL SCENIC TRAIL

One-way trip: Allison Pass to Stehekin River, 87 miles
Hiking time: Allow 10 to 12 days
Elevation gain: 12,400 feet
Hikable: August through September

Maps: Green Trails No. 82 Stehekin, No. 50 Early Winters, No. 18 Pasayten Peak, No. 17 Jack Mtn.
Information: Methow Valley Ranger Station, phone (509) 997-2131. Ask about trail No. 2000.

For rugged mountain scenery, the portion of the Pacific Crest National Scenic Trail between the Canadian border and Stevens Pass is the most spectacular walking route of such length in the nation. Undependable weather, late-melting snow, and many ups and downs make it also one of the most strenuous.

Few hikers have time to complete the trip in one season; most spread their efforts over a period of years, doing the trail in sections. Those taking the whole trip at once generally prefer to start from the north, since pickup transportation at journey's end is easier to arrange at the south terminus.

Pacific Crest Trail contouring around Slate Peak

Though higher, the northern part of the trail lies in the rainshadow of great peaks to the west and thus gets less snow than the southern part; the north country and south country therefore open to travel simultaneously.

There is no legal way for a hiker to cross the U.S.–Canada border on the Pacific Crest Trail. However, U.S. Forest Service wilderness permits for hiking in the Pasayten Wilderness on the U.S. side of the border were available until 1985, when they were no longer needed, at the visitors center in Manning Provincial Park, Canada.

Hikers must draw their own conclusion and decide whether or not to join the hundreds of folks who cross the border on this and the Monument 83 Trail (Hike 84).

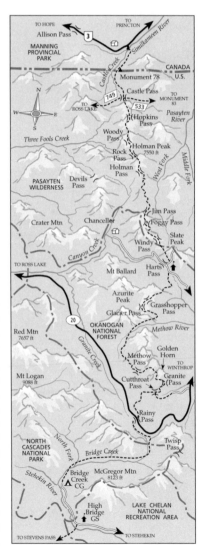

Drive Trans-Canada Highway 3 to Manning Provincial Park and find the trailhead on an unmarked sideroad 0.5 mile east of the hotel-motel complex at Allison Pass.

Allison Pass to Harts Pass

One-way trip: 40 miles
Elevation gain: About 8000 feet
Hiking time: Allow 4 days

Hike 7½ miles up Castle Creek to the international boundary at Monument 78. Look east and west from the monument along the swath regularly clearcut through the forest, for what reason nobody knows, but they keep on doing it, apparently just because they have been doing it for nigh onto a century and a half and nobody has ever told them to quit—though we incessantly ask them to. Ascend Route Creek to Castle Pass, from which point south to Harts Pass the trail is almost continuously in meadowland, touching Hopkins Pass, climbing to Lakeview Ridge, crossing Woody Pass into Conie Basin and Rock Pass into Goat Lakes Basin, dropping to Holman Pass, swinging around Jim Peak to Jim Pass, Foggy Pass, and Oregon Basin,

Pacific Crest Trail below Snowy Lakes

crossing a shoulder of Tamarack Peak into Windy Basin, and from there continuing to Harts Pass as described in Hike 81 (Windy Pass).

Harts Pass to Rainy Pass

One-way trip: 31 miles　　　　**Elevation gain:** About 4400 feet
Hiking time: Allow 4 days

From Harts Pass the next road junction is at Rainy Pass. The trail contours around Tatie Peak to Grasshopper Pass (Hike 80), drops to Glacier Pass, drops more into the West Fork Methow River, climbs over Methow Pass, and contours high around Tower Mountain to Granite Pass and on to Cutthroat Pass and down to Rainy Pass (Hikes 71 and 73).

Rainy Pass to High Bridge

One-way trip: 16 miles　　　　**Elevation gain:** None
Hiking time: Allow 2 days

The next segment is all downhill. Walk east a bit on Highway 20 to the Bridge Creek trail and descend forest to the Stehekin River road at Bridge Creek Campground (Hike 51, Park Creek Pass). Hike 5 miles down the Stehekin River road to High Bridge Campground. To continue south, see *100 Hikes in Washington's North Cascades: Glacier Peak Region* (I. Spring and H. Manning).

APPENDIX

The Green Trails maps listed in the information block for each trail are all most hikers need. For the benefit of those who love poring over maps, 7.5-minute USGS maps are listed below for each trail.

1 Heliotrope Ridge: USGS Goat Mountain, Mt. Baker (trail not shown on map)
2 Skyline Divide: USGS Mt. Baker, Bearpaw Mountain
3 Canyon Ridge—Point 5658: USGS Glacier, Bearpaw Mountain
4 Excelsior Mountain—High Divide: USGS Bearpaw Mountain
5 Bearpaw Mountain Lake: USGS Bearpaw Mountain
6 Church Mountain: USGS Bearpaw Mountain
7 Cougar Divide: USGS Bearpaw Mountain, Mount Baker
8 Welcome Pass—Excelsior Ridge: USGS Mt. Larrabee
9 Yellow Aster Butte: USGS Mt. Larrabee
10 Gold Run Pass—Tomyhoi Lake: USGS Mt. Larrabee
11 Twin Lakes—Winchester Mountain: USGS Mt. Larrabee
12 Nooksack Cirque: USGS Mt. Larrabee, Mt. Sefrit, Mt. Shuksan
13 Goat Mountain Meadows and Lookout Site: USGS Mt. Larrabee
14 Hannegan Pass and Peak: USGS Mt. Sefrit
15 Copper Mountain: USGS Mt. Sefrit, Copper Mountain
16 Easy Ridge: USGS Mt. Sefrit, Copper Mountain, Mt. Blum
17 Whatcom Pass: USGS Mt. Sefrit, Copper Mountain, Mt. Redoubt
18 Lake Ann: USGS Shuksan Arm
19 Chain Lakes Loop: USGS Shuksan Arm
20 Ptarmigan Ridge: USGS Shuksan Arm
21 Elbow Lake: USGS Twin Sisters Mountain
22 Cathedral Pass: USGS Twin Sisters Mountain, Baker Pass
23 Park Butte—Railroad Grade: USGS Baker Pass
24 Scott Paul Trail: USGS Baker Pass
25 Noisy-Diobsud Hikes: USGS Bacon Peak
26 Boulder Ridge: USGS Mt. Baker, Shuksan Arm, Baker Pass (not shown on map)
27 Rainbow Ridge: USGS Shuksan Arm (trail not shown on map)
28 Rainbow Creek: USGS Shuksan Arm
29 Shannon Ridge: USGS Mt. Shuksan
30 Baker River: USGS Lake Shannon, Mt. Shuksan
31 Cow Heaven: USGS Marblemount (trail not shown on map)
32 Lookout Mountain—Monogram Lake: USGS Big Devil Peak
33 Hidden Lake Peaks: USGS Eldorado Peak, Sonny Boy Lakes
34 Boston Basin: USGS Cascade Pass
35 Cascade Pass—Sahale Arm: USGS Cascade Pass

36 Thornton Lakes—Trappers Peak: USGS Mt. Triumph
37 Sourdough Mountain: USGS Diablo Dam and Ross Dam
38 Pyramid Lake: USGS Diablo Dam and Ross Dam
39 Thunder Creek: USGS Ross Dam, Forbidden Peak, Mt. Logan, Goode Mountain
40 Beaver Loop: USGS Hozomeen Mountain, Mt. Spickard, Mt. Challenger, Mt. Prophet, Pumpkin Mountain
41 Panther Creek—Fourth of July Pass: USGS Crater Mountain, Ross Dam
42 East Bank Trail: USGS Ross Dam, Pumpkin Mountain, Skagit Peak, Hozomeen Mountain
43 Little Jack Mountain: USGS Ross Dam, Crater Mountain
44 Desolation Peak: USGS Hozomeen Mountain
45 Crater Lake—Jackita Ridge—Devils Loop: USGS Crater Mountain, Azurite Peak, Shull Mountain, Jack Mountain, Pumpkin Mountain
46 Canyon Creek—Chancellor Trail: USGS Azurite Peak, Crater Mountain
47 Easy Pass—Fisher Creek: USGS Mt. Arriva, Mt. Logan
48 Chelan Lakeshore Trail: USGS Lucerne, Prince Creek, Sun Mountain, Stehekin
49 Rainbow Loop: USGS Stehekin
50 North Fork Bridge Creek: USGS McGregor Mountain, Mt. Logan
51 Park Creek Pass: USGS Goode Mountain
52 Horseshoe Basin (Stehekin): USGS Cascade Pass
53 Lake Chelan to Cascade River: USGS Goode Mountain, Cascade Pass
54 Chelan Summit Trail: USGS South Navarre, Martin Peak, Prince Creek, Oval Peak, Sun Mountain, Stehekin
55 Summer Blossom Trail: USGS South Navarre Peak, Martin Peak
56 Foggy Dew Creek: USGS Martin Peak
57 Cooney Lake: USGS Martin Peak
58 Eagle Lakes—Boiling Lake: USGS Martin Peak
59 Crater Lakes: USGS Martin Peak
60 Martin Lakes: USGS Martin Peak
61 Golden Lakes Loop: USGS Martin Peak
62 Libby Lake: USGS Hoodoo Peak, Martin Peak
63 Oval Lakes: USGS Oval Peak
64 Scatter Lake: USGS Gilbert
65 Louis Lake: USGS Gilbert
66 Twisp Pass—Stiletto Vista: USGS Gilbert and McAlester Mountain
67 Copper Pass: USGS Gilbert and McAlester
68 Wolf Creek: USGS Midnight Mtn., Thompson Ridge, Gilbert, Mazama
69 Driveway Butte: USGS Silver Star and Robinson Mountain
70 Abernathy Pass: USGS Mazama and Silver Star Mountain
71 Cutthroat Pass: USGS Washington Pass
72 Maple Pass: USGS Mt. Arriva, McGregor Mountain, Washington Pass, McAlester Mountain
73 Stiletto Peak Lookout Site: USGS McAlester Mountain

74 Golden Horn: USGS Washington Pass
75 Goat Peak: USGS Mazama
76 Lost River: USGS McLeod Mountain, Robinson Mountain
77 Robinson Pass: USGS Slate Peak, Robinson Mountain, Pasayten Peak, Mt. Lago, Mazama, Lost Peak
78 West Fork Methow River: USGS Robinson Mountain, Azurite Peak, Slate Peak
79 Trout Creek: USGS Slate Peak
80 Grasshopper Pass: USGS Slate Peak
81 Windy Pass: USGS Slate Peak, Pasayten Peak
82 Elbow Basin—Three Fools Loop: USGS Slate Peak, Pasayten Peak, Shull Mountain, Castle Peak, Skagit Peak, Hozomeen Mountain
83 Silver Lake: USGS Slate Peak, Pasayten Peak (trail not shown on maps)
84 Cascade Loop Trail and Monument 83: USGS Frosty Creek, Castle Peak
85 Copper Glance Lake: USGS Sweetgrass Butte, Billy Goat Mountain
86 Parson Smith Tree—Hidden Lakes: USGS Billy Goat Mountain, Lost Peak, Ashnola Mountain, Tatoosh Bttes
87 Billy Goat Pass—Burch Mountain: USGS Billy Goat Mountain (trail not shown on map)
88 Dollar Watch Mountain: USGS Billy Goat Mountain, Lost Peak, Ashnola Mountain
89 Forgotten Trails of the Methow Valley Ranger District: Doe Mountain: USGS Doe Mountain; Setting Sun Mountain: USGS McLeod Mountain (trails not shown on maps)
90 Black Lake: USGS Mt. Barney
91 Andrews Creek—Cathedral Lakes: USGS Remmel Mountain, Mt. Barney, Coleman Peak
92 Chewuch River—Remmel Lake: USGS Remmel Mountain, Coleman Peak, Bauerman Ridge
93 Four Point Lake—Coleman Ridge Loop: USGS Remmel Mountain, Bauerman Ridge, Coleman Peak
94 Honeymoon Creek—North Twentymile Peak Lookout: USGS Doe Mountain, Coleman Peak
95 Tiffany Mountain: USGS Tiffany Mountain; Bernhardt Trail: USGS Tiffany Mountain
96 Bernhardt Trail—North Summit Trail: USGS Tiffany Mountain, Old Baldy (trail not shown ony map)
97 Horseshoe Basin (Pasayten): USGS Horseshoe Basin
98 Boundary Trail: USGS Horseshoe Basin, Bauerman Ridge, Remmel Mountain, Ashnola Pass, Ashnola Mountain, Tatoosh Buttes, Frosty Creek, Castle Peak
99 Mount Bonaparte: USGS Mt. Bonaparte
100 Pacific Crest National Scenic Trail: USGS McGregor, McAlester, Washington Pass (not shown), Mt. Arriva (not shown), Slate Peak, Pasayten Peak, Shull Mtn., Castle Peak

HIKING SEASON AND TRAIL DIFFICULTY

The recommended time of year for hiking a particular trail is when the trail is generally free of snow. From year to year this varies by a week or more; for a few weeks after the recommended time, snowpatches can be expected on the trail. Above 5000 feet snowstorms occur quite frequently until mid-July and after late August and occasionally in between. However, midsummer snow usually melts in a few hours or a day

HIKE NUMBER	TRAIL OR SECTION OF TRAIL	MARCH–NOV	MAY	JUNE	EARLY JULY	MID-JULY	AUGUST	EASY	MODERATE	STRENUOUS	CAMPSITE
1	Heliotrope Ridge						•		•		•
2	Skyline Divide						•		•		
3	Canyon Ridge—Point 5658					•			•		
4	Excelsior Mountain—High Divide					•			•		
5	Bearpaw Mountain Lake					•			•		•
6	Church Mountain						•			•	
7	Cougar Divide					•			•		
8	Welcome Pass—Excelsior Ridge				•				•		
9	Yellow Aster Butte					•			•		•
10	Gold Run Pass				•				•		•
10	Tomyhoi Lake				•					•	•
11	Twin Lakes					•			•		•
11	Winchester Mountain						•		•		
12	Nooksack Cirque						•			•	•
13	Goat Mountain Meadows			•						•	•
13	Goat Mountain Lookout Site			•					•		
14	Hannegan Pass					•			•		•
14	Hannegan Peak					•				•	
15	Copper Mountain					•				•	•
16	Easy Ridge					•				•	•
17	Whatcom Pass					•				•	•
18	Lake Ann						•		•		•

HIKE NUMBER	TRAIL OR SECTION OF TRAIL	MARCH–NOV	MAY	JUNE	EARLY ULY	MID-JULY	AUGUST	EASY	MODERATE	STRENUOUS	CAMPSITE
19	Chain Lakes Loop						•		•		•
20	Ptarmigan Ridge						•		•		•
21	Elbow Lake, South Approach				•			•			•
21	Elbow Lake, North Approach				•				•		•
22	Cathedral Pass					•				•	•
23	Park Butte—Railroad Grade					•			•		•
24	Scott Paul Trail					•				•	
25	Anderson Butte					•			•		
25	Watson Lakes					•			•		•
25	Lower Anderson Lake					•			•		•
26	Boulder Ridge				•				•		•
27	Rainbow Ridge						•		•		
28	Swift Creek		•					•			
29	Shannon Ridge				•				•		
30	Baker River		•					•			•
31	Cow Heaven				•				•		
32	Lookout Mountain				•					•	
32	Monogram Lake				•					•	•
33	Hidden Lake Peaks						•		•		•
34	Boston Basin				•				•		•
35	Cascade Pass					•			•		
35	Sahale Arm					•				•	•
36	Thornton Lakes—Trappers Peak					•				•	•
37	Sourdough Mountain				•					•	•
38	Pyramid Lake		•						•		
39	McAllister Creek		•						•		•
39	Park Creek Pass				•					•	•
40	Beaver Pass				•					•	•
40	Beaver Loop				•					•	•
41	Panther Creek—Fourth of July Pass				•					•	•
42	East Bank Trail to Hozomeen		•							•	•
42	East Bank Trail to Rainbow Camp		•							•	•
43	Little Jack Mountain				•					•	•
44	Desolation Peak				•					•	
45	Crater—Jackita Ridge—Devils Loop					•				•	•

HIKE NUMBER	TRAIL OR SECTION OF TRAIL	MARCH–NOV	MAY	JUNE	EARLY JLY	MID-JULY	AUGUST	EASY	MODERATE	STRENUOUS	CAMPSITE
46	Canyon Creek—Chancellor Trail to Boulder Creek			•				•			•
46	Canyon Creek—Chancellor Trail to Mill Creek			•					•		•
47	Easy Pass—Fisher Creek					•				•	
48	Chelan Shore Trail from Prince Creek	•							•		•
48	Chelan Shore Trail from Moore Point	•							•		•
49	Rainbow Loop	•							•		•
50	North Fork Bridge Creek					•				•	•
51	Park Creek Pass					•				•	•
52	Horseshoe Basin (Stehekin)					•				•	•
53	Lake Chelan to Cascade River					•				•	
54	Chelan Summit Trail				•					•	•
55	Summer Blossom Trail				•				•		
56	Foggy Dew Falls			•				•			
56	Sunrise Lake				•					•	•
57	Cooney Lake				•					•	•
58	Eagle Lakes—Boiling Lake				•				•		•
59	Crater Lakes				•				•		•
60	Martin Lakes				•					•	•
61	Golden Lakes Loop				•				•		•
62	Libby Lake				•					•	•
63	Oval Lakes				•					•	•
64	Scatter Lake				•					•	•
65	Louis Lake				•				•		•
66	Twisp Pass—Stiletto Vista				•				•		•
67	Copper Pass				•					•	
68	Wolf Creek			•						•	•
69	Driveway Butte		•						•		
70	Abernathy Pass				•					•	•
70	Cedar Falls		•					•			
71	Cutthroat Pass				•				•		
72	Maple Pass					•			•		
73	Stiletto Peak Lookout Site				•					•	•
74	Golden Horn						•			•	•

HIKE NUMBER	TRAIL OR SECTION OF TRAIL	MARCH–NOV	MAY	JUNE	EARLY ULY	MID-JULY	AUGUST	EASY	MODERATE	STRENUOUS	CAMPSITE
75	Goat Peak			•						•	
76	Lost River	•							•		•
77	Robinson Pass	•							•		•
78	West Fork Methow River	•							•		•
79	Trout Creek				•				•		•
80	Grasshopper Pass				•				•		•
81	Windy Pass				•				•		•
82	Elbow Basin—Three Fools Loop					•				•	•
83	Silver Lake					•				•	•
84	Cascade Loop Trail and Monument 83			•						•	•
85	Copper Glance Lake			•						•	•
86	Parson Smith Tree—Hidden Lakes			•						•	•
87	Billy Goat Pass—Burch Mountain			•						•	•
88	Dollar Watch Mountain					•				•	•
89	Doe Mountain				•				•		
89	Setting Sun Mountain					•			•		
90	Black Lake		•					•			•
91	Andrews Creek—Cathedral Lakes				•					•	•
92	Chewuch River—Remmel Lake				•					•	•
93	Four Point Lake—Coleman Ridge Loop				•					•	•
94	Honeymoon Creek—North Twentymile Peak Lookout			•						•	•
95	Tiffany Mountain				•				•		
96	Bernhardt Trail—North Summit Trail				•				•		
97	Sunny Pass			•					•		•
97	Horseshoe Basin (Pasayten)				•					•	
98	Boundary Trail				•					•	•
99	Mount Bonaparte			•						•	
100	Pacific Crest National Scenic Trail						•			•	•

INDEX

ABOUT THE AUTHORS

A well-known outdoor photographer, Ira Spring devotes much of his time to organizations advocating trail and wildlife preservation. He is a co-founder of the Washington Trails Association and was one of twenty-four Americans to receive the Theodore Roosevelt Conservation Award in 1992. Harvey Manning is one of the Pacific Northwest's most influential and outspoken advocates of wilderness preservation. The founder of the Issaquah Alps Trail Club, Manning was instrumental in the fight to preserve the Alpine Lakes area to establish North Cascades National Park. Both Spring and Manning played key roles in the passage of the 1984 Washington Wilderness Act.

Over the past thirty years, their guidebooks have introduced legions of hikers, and future environmentalists, to the Northwest wilderness. Spring and Manning have collaborated on over twenty books, including the award-winning *Cool, Clear Water*; *Wildlife Encounters*; the four-volume *Footsore* series; *Hiking the Great Northwest*; *Hiking the Mountains to Sound Greenway*; *50 Hikes in Mount Rainier National Park*; *55 Hikes in Central Washington*; and four titles in the *100 Hikes in*™ series.

OTHER TITLES YOU MAY ENJOY FROM THE MOUNTAINEERS BOOKS:

100 HIKES IN™ WASHINGTON'S ALPINE LAKES, 3d Edition, *Ira Spring, Vicky Spring, & Harvey Manning*

100 HIKES IN™ THE INLAND NORTHWEST, *Rich Landers & Ida Rowe Dolphin*

100 HIKES IN™ WASHINGTON'S SOUTH CASCADES & OLYMPICS, 3d Edition, *Ira Spring & Harvey Manning*

100 CLASSIC HIKES IN™ WASHINGTON, *Ira Spring & Harvey Manning*
A full-color guide to Washington's finest trails by the respected authors of more than thirty Washington guides, written with a conservation ethic and a sense of humor, and featuring the best hikes in the state.

EXPLORING WASHINGTON'S WILD AREAS: A Guide for Hikers, Backpackers, Climbers, X-C Skiers & Paddlers, *Marge & Ted Mueller*
A guide to the undisturbed trails of Washington's federally preserved backcountry, featuring 55 wilderness and roadless areas and over 1000 mapped trails.

BACKPACKER'S EVERYDAY WISDOM: 1001 Expert Tips for Hikers, *Karen Berger*
Expert tips and tricks for hikers and backpackers selected from one of the most popular *Backpacker* magazine columns. Problem-solving techniques and brilliant improvisations show hikers how to make their way, and make do in the backcountry.

BACKPACKER'S WILDERNESS 911: A Step-by-Step Guide for Medical Emergencies and Improvised Care in the Backcountry, *Eric A. Weiss, M.D.*
Written by a *Backpacker* medical editor and emergency room veteran, this guide covers the injuries and incidents most likely to happen in the backcountry. Instructions for self-care are kept simple and easy to follow.

GPS MADE EASY: Using Global Positioning Systems in the Outdoors, 2d Edition, *Lawrence Letham*
Up-to-date version of the handbook for understanding how GPS works. A practical guide for those who ski, climb, or hike above treeline, and also helpful for sea kayakers and those who work in remote, featureless areas.

CONDITIONING FOR OUTDOOR FITNESS: A Comprehensive Training Guide, *David Musnick, M.D. & Mark Pierce, A.T.C.*
The most comprehensive guide to conditioning, fitness, and training for all outdoor activities, written by a team of sports fitness experts. Offers "whole body" training programs for hiking, biking, skiing, climbing, paddling, and more.